Mortgage on America

Mortgage on America

Leonard Downie, Jr.

PRAEGER PUBLISHERS
New York · Washington

Published in the United States of America in 1974
by Praeger Publishers, Inc.
111 Fourth Avenue, New York, N.Y. 10003

Second printing, 1974

333.33
D7508

Library of Congress Cataloging in Publication Data

Downie, Leonard.
  Mortage on America.

  Bibliography: p. 233.
  1. Real estate business—United States. I. Title.
HD255.D68   333.3′3   73-18751
ISBN 0-275-51230-6 .

Printed in the United States of America

For David and Scott

Contents

Acknowledgments

This book would not have been possible without the extensive research assistance and editing of Geraldine Rebach; the manuscript editing of Joan Tapper and editorial direction of Lois Decker O'Neill of Praeger Publishers; a year's travel and research fellowship from the Alicia Patterson Foundation under the guiding hand of Richard H. Nolte; and invaluable experience gained at the *Washington Post* in the investigation of urban problems.

Mortgage on America

Prologue

Profitopolis

Uninhabitable slums, exploited suburbs, chewed-up countryside, poisoned air and water, high taxes and declining public services, inflated land and housing prices, economic and racial segregation— these symptoms of the spreading cancer in urban America are recognized by almost everyone. Yet there are those who look at the sprawl and decay of our cities and see in them golden opportunity: the opportunity to make big money, often very quickly, and to protect from taxation the money they already have.

These people are land speculators, developers, builders, realtors, landlords, bankers, and other real estate investors of all kinds, from millionaires and giant corporations to many millions of ordinary homeowners. To all of them the foreboding megalopolis of the urban critic's nightmare is really *profitopolis:* a promised land of windfall profits, capital gains, mortgage interest, and tax benefits.

Too often, when these people gain, others stand to lose. Blockbusters make their quick profits frightening some families out of their homes, buying the houses, and reselling them at inflated prices to others, who are desperate for a place to live but often unable to maintain either their high mortgage payments or their homes. Slum landlords, operating mostly on bank credit, take over deteriorating houses and apartments and collect excessive rents as long as they can, spending nothing on maintenance until the buildings fall into irreversible decay and are eventually abandoned. Big developers, often with government backing, bite large chunks out of still healthy neighborhoods, level the housing there, and throw up

3

giant office buildings, displacing working people from their homes and killing city social life. Speculators double and triple their money buying up farmland and subdividing it for the rapid development of cheaply built houses and apartments, denuding and paving over the soil, channeling overflowing sewage into nearby streams and rivers, and bringing in more cars to fill the air with exhaust fumes. Promoters grab land along seashores, around lakes, on mountains, and in forests to parcel out as vacation homesites and commercial resorts, despoiling the nation's most precious natural areas. Many homebuyers themselves, by insisting on bigger houses on more ground in increasingly exclusive neighborhoods because these homes bring bigger resale profits, encourage the waste of land, reinforce patterns of segregation, and help push home prices beyond the reach of a growing number of the less affluent.

Nothing is more genuinely American than owning your own home, your own plot of ground, your own share of the great, big country. It is part and parcel of the American Dream, the legacy of our agrarian past. "Land is part of God's estate in the Globe," Henry Ward Beecher once wrote, "and when a parcel of ground is deeded to you and you walk over it, and call it your own, it seems as if you had come into partnership with the original proprietor of the earth."

And nothing has proved to be more dependably profitable than investing in the steadily increasing dollar value of this land and most buildings on it. "Of all the things you can buy with money today, land is one of your best values," visitors to a California land dealer's office are advised by a large wall poster quoting from *House Beautiful* magazine. "In a time of inflation, when cash is worth less each year, land you own has a solid value. It is real and is not called real estate for nothing." Every homeowner counts on appreciation of "property values" to enable him, in effect, to live rent-free and still come out money ahead in the end; Richard Nixon, with his California and Florida estates, is perhaps the extreme example. Every investor in commercial real estate envisions himself as the hero of one of the many true-life Horatio Alger stories of sudden fortunes made in the buying and selling of land and buildings. "Ninety per cent of all millionaires become so through owning real estate," Andrew Carnegie said. "More money has been made in real estate than in all industrial investments combined."

Not to mention the tax benefits. Homeowners can deduct from their taxable incomes the interest they pay on their home mortgages, along with their real estate taxes. Bigger tax breaks are available to people with large incomes if they invest in commercial real estate, such as an apartment or office building. To compensate for the building's supposed depreciation in value, each investor can deduct from his taxable income a sizable amount annually. In fact, rather than tax theory, however, the building—and especially the land under it—is more likely to be increasing in salable value all the time. The use of depreciation deductions to offset large amounts of taxable income makes the property a "tax shelter" for a doctor, lawyer, or other high-income person. The right kind of tax shelter can be as profitable to the taxpayer using it as the oil depletion allowance is for the oil millionaire. Moreover, any profits eventually realized from the sale of the real estate are taxed at capital-gains rates, which are usually lower than the personal-income rates for wealthier people.

It is not necessary to invest much of one's own money to realize big real estate profits or build lucrative tax shelters. Smart investors borrow most of the money they need to buy land and buildings. Banks, savings and loan associations, insurance companies, mortgage companies, and individual financiers are willing to lend 90 per cent or more of the purchase price, provided they receive as security a mortgage on the real estate involved. And the interest the borrower must pay on a mortgage loan is tax-deductible.

Interest on mortgage loans is an important source of income for banks and insurance companies—and it is the mainstay of savings and loan associations, which originally were founded as cooperative savings societies to make home loans to their members. Many savings and loans, however, have long since been taken over by real estate men who line their own pockets by making loans instead to big developers, land speculators, and slum landlords. Even the biggest and most respected banks have been unable to resist doing business with speculators and blockbusters, who have frequently been steady borrowers willing to pay higher-than-market interest rates. It is the mortgage loan income that matters to the bankers, not the way in which it is earned.

Time after time, the quality of housing, community life, and environment suffer—not because that is the only way a profit can be made but because the housing, communities, and environmental conditions produced are no more than neglected by-products of the monopoly-like manipulation of land and buildings for maximum gain. The real business of the multimillion-dollar real estate industry—of its brokers, land speculators, builders, landlords, homeowners, and their financial backers, the banks, savings and loan associations, insurance companies, and individual investors—is what the professionals call "creation of value." As land is bought, sold, rezoned, built on, and traded many times over, its paper value steadily increases because every day there are more and more Americans to live on and use the fixed amount of land in the country. This created value is over and above the actual construction or replacement cost of the building on the land. Although physically intangible, created value is quite real financially—in the form of land and building price appreciation, interest paid on real estate mortgage loans, and tax benefits for real estate owners.

Any house is thus less important financially as shelter or as part of a community than as a vehicle for creating new paper value for the land under it. It need only be sufficiently habitable to somehow be sold or rented. A poorly kept up slum building, as long as it is occupied by tenants paying some rent, can be just as valuable—through sale, mortgage, or tax depreciation of the building—as much more substantial, safe, and sanitary housing. The real estate industry builds profits, not necessarily decent housing, workable communities, or a livable environment.

Every day rules are stretched, laws broken, and the public good ignored in the headlong race for real estate profits. Realtors and financial institutions discriminate widely in the sale and financing of homes. Blockbusters exacerbate racial tensions and engage in pernicious sales practices. Landlords flout housing codes and landlord and tenant laws. Land speculators push farmers off their land and employ deceit and bribery to rezone and subdivide it. Developers knowingly throw up shoddy housing. Bank and savings and loan officials ignore conflict-of-interest regulations and make "insider" mortgage loans to themselves, relatives, and friends.

Government agencies and programs to improve housing and community life also have been corrupted by the real estate industry. The Federal Housing Administration (FHA) and its predecessors, created to help more families acquire better housing with guarantees of mortgage loans, turned its back on black Americans and the central city to underwrite the mass movement of the white middle class to the suburbs, where speculators, developers, and their financial backers found what had been relatively low-priced land so profitable to develop. When the FHA was pressured in recent years to do more for low-income families, blacks, and the cities, the agency responded by approving and guaranteeing loans for the deals of blockbusters and sharp operators in inner-city real estate who actually cheated the families the FHA was supposed to help. The Federal Home Loan Bank Board, set up to provide government backing and supervision for savings and loan associations and to encourage the making of home mortgage loans, has done little to stop savings and loan officials from diverting mortgage loan money from individual homebuyers to speculators and insiders or from using the savings of inner-city residents to finance development activities only in the suburbs and beyond. Local planning and zoning officials, charged with controlling new development to improve community life and protect the environment, have too often capitulated to developers instead, frequently because these officials are also real estate investors themselves or have been compromised or immobilized in other ways.

These basics of urban real estate activity are generally overlooked by leading urban critics. In their diagnoses of city problems and their prescriptions for improvement, they dwell on land-use planning, zoning, building design, urban sociology—factors largely irrelevant to the way the real estate industry works.

One prominent school of thought on what is wrong with urban America is headed by Lewis Mumford, who sees our cities as inherently inhuman in scale, overly congested, hopelessly disorganized, and too cut off from nature because, in his view, their growth has been uncontrolled. Mumford writes about the real estate industry as only one of several interests that have benefited from conditions as they are. He sees its profiteering as a consequence, rather than a root cause, of our urban dilemma. Mumford and his disciples, who have come to dominate urban planning circles, have advocated greater governmental control of urban growth through strict planning and have urged carefully plotted development of model neighborhoods and small new cities in the countryside, patterned on the "garden cities" pioneered in England. Developers, pressured by planners but characteristically paying only lip service to the plans, have responded by building what they call "planned neighborhoods" and "new towns." Despite curving streets and other surface changes, however, these projects differ little in substance from present big-city suburbs and suffer from many of the same problems.

An anti-Mumford revolution was started by architectural critic Jane Jacobs, who accuses Mumford of basically disliking city life. For her part, Jacobs celebrates the concentration, variety, bustle, and interrelationships of urban living as exemplified by European cities. In the United States, she argues, these elements of city life have been endangered by the meddling of Mumford-inspired planners. She points to the gutting of still-lively inner-city neighborhoods like Boston's West End, the difficulties placed in the path of residents trying to preserve neighborhoods like New York's Greenwich Village, the building of lifeless urban renewal projects like that in Washington, D.C.'s southwest quarter, and the proliferation of sterile Levittown-like suburbs and new town projects. Jacobs believes the cities themselves are going through a natural, not altogether unhealthy, evolutionary stage and that they could still come out all right if only the planners would let them alone. She urges government to support residents now working on their own to "unslum" such neighborhoods as Society Hill in Philadelphia, Bolton Hill in Baltimore, or Capitol Hill in Washington by restoring their homes and reviving street life. She fails to realize, however, that it is usually the real estate industry that determines whether destruction by "renewal" or revival through "unslumming" will take place, depending on which it finds more profitable. Unslumming creates higher property values, and sooner or later real estate profiteers usually manage to cut themselves in on these, making neighborhood restoration an expensive business. This limits the usefulness of renovation to only a few small areas of any city where eventually only the well-to-do can afford to live, defeating the social goals of its ideological backers.

A third view of inner-city decay is held by much of the business community and the real estate industry itself. This view has been most frequently and forcefully espoused by George Sternlieb, a widely published university lecturer and writer on urban studies from the businessman's point of view, who argues that our central cities today are largely occupied by people who cannot and will not support profitable business investment. Today's inner-city dwellers, the poor and the minorities, have actually driven businessmen and real estate investors out of town, according to Sternlieb, by failing to buy sufficient goods and pay high enough rents, by defaulting on their debts, by failing to help keep property up, and by joining with local officials and do-gooders to place unprofitable restrictions, like repair codes for landlords, on the few businessmen and real estate owners who have stayed behind. As a result, Sternlieb concludes, the central cities are losing their economic value, and he warns that they are doomed unless the government can attract business and real estate investors back into them and make it profitable to stay. But Sternlieb says nothing about the real estate industry's own role in adding to the economic dilemma of our cities—driving up central-city property values to impossible heights and then draining off much of that money to invest in speculation and development of initially lower-priced land in the suburbs, while continuing to bleed city properties and residents of every possible dime. Only when government belatedly and timidly stepped in to try to stop that kind of profiteering, or when the well simply ran dry, did the real estate industry begin to complain that it could no longer invest in the inner city without heavy subsidies.

First our cities and now the increasingly scarce land for miles around them have been mortgaged heavily for maximum quick profit by the real estate industry. Whole inner-city neighborhoods are in ruins. Older suburbs, with their poorly built housing, congested traffic, pollution, and worsening social problems, are increasingly becoming slums themselves. And beyond the cities, more and more once open countryside is being destroyed by real estate exploitation. Only the very rich can insulate themselves from this process. Middle-class Americans, like a people whose country has been occupied by a powerful and ruthless invader, have found themselves adjusting to necessary sacrifices. They move often, buy or rent overpriced and unsatisfactory housing, waste hours commuting each day, depend on at least two cars per family, breathe foul air, drink dirty water, and race everyone else to spend more money on escapist vacation homes or investment real estate. Millions of less fortunate citizens endure life in the still spreading slums, trapped ever farther away from better housing, jobs that have been moved to distant suburbs, and open land that not long ago had been so abundant.

Look at Newark, New Jersey. There the blockbusters have helped to chase out the white middle class—and overcharged those who have been forced to stay—while the rest of the real estate industry has withdrawn its capital to invest elsewhere. With the money and the middle-class residents have gone other important resources and much of the social stability of the city. Left behind are 375,000 people—three-fourths of them black or Puerto Rican—with no first-run movie house, only half as many physicians as were there ten years ago, no jobs for 15 per cent of the able-bodied men and only part-time work for another 25 per cent, the nation's highest per capita crime and drug-addiction rates, the highest percentage of substandard housing, and the highest rates of venereal disease, new tuberculosis cases, and maternal mortality.

Look at Los Angeles, the city that won't stop growing, that classic of American real estate waste, where everything is so spread out that more people drive more cars farther each day than anywhere else, and everyone, rich and poor, in the city and out in its suburbs, must live with and adjust to the resulting smog. Sociologists like to say that the people there have discovered a new lifestyle. Real estate professionals freely admit, however, that the pattern of spread-out development was merely the easiest, fastest, most lucrative way to cash in on the motor-age California land rush: Buy a tract of vacant land, wait a short time for the population and roads to move toward it, subdivide it into lots for cheaply built single-family homes, and sell them to builders at prices that total several times the land's original cost—then take your profit and buy another, larger tract of land farther out to begin the process all over again. California's freeways were an accommodation to this sprawl, not the cause of it.

Today, from a vantage point in mountainous Griffith Park above the center of Los Angeles, the consequences can be seen only too well. From there, essayist Timothy Tyler found, the smog has a "topography all its own":

> Massive chocolate mountains of it below you to the east, a permanent black tumor over Hollywood and the downtown area seeping in channels through the passes out into the Valley and on into the Mojave Desert; to the west, over West L.A., Inglewood and Santa Monica, the smog is unexplainably green, and you realize that you

are surrounded by a rainbow of smog, all of it a part of the land, undeniable, permanent, so that soon you'll be able to say, "I live in the green part"—or the brown part, or the black part. Up there in Griffith Park you realize that the city does not have long to go.

Such is Profitopolis. What does it mean for our future? What are the terms of the mortgage we have permitted—indeed, in our pursuit of the dollar, encouraged and aided—real estate speculators to place on America? What is the cost to our cities, to our countryside, to ourselves and our children?

I

The Gold in Those Slums

The long blocks of empty brownstones and 4-story walk-up tenements in the Bedford-Stuyvesant neighborhood of Brooklyn resemble an evacuated war zone. The streets and sidewalks, eerily empty of people, are covered with trash and broken glass. In buildings not yet boarded up, only jagged edges remain of smashed windows. Doors teeter precariously on broken hinges. Plumbing and fixtures have been ripped out, and toilet bowls without covers have been stopped up with excrement and garbage. Rotting floors are covered with the debris of collapsed ceilings and crumbling walls.

New York City's housing shortage is so acute that thousands of families on relief have been crowded, one family to a room, into converted "welfare hotels," and uncounted squatters have occupied, without water or heat, condemned buildings scheduled for demolition. Yet at the same time thousands of houses and apartment buildings containing well over 100,000 dwelling units—housing for up to half a million people—stand empty in neighborhoods like Bedford-Stuyvesant, Brownsville, East New York, and other sections of Brooklyn, the Bronx, Queens, and Manhattan. They have been abandoned by both tenants and owners to squatters, vandals, drug addicts, rats, and roaches.

Abandonment also is spreading like a plague through other American cities. It has attacked the low brick row houses of central Philadelphia, Baltimore, and Washington, D.C.; the rambling old frame houses of the Hough and Glenville neighborhoods of Cleveland and the near east side of Detroit; the brick duplexes of the Lawndale section of Chicago and the north side of St. Louis; and the slab homes on streets dotted with palm trees in the Watts area of Los Angeles. Whole neighborhoods in otherwise teeming cities are becoming urban ghost towns.

Conventional wisdom can explain abandonment itself. Landlords, pressed for cash, let maintenance slide in declining neighborhoods. Increasingly poor and irresponsible tenants pay less and less rent. When winter comes, there is no heat. Pipes freeze and burst, and soon there is no water. As more and more tenants leave, no one comes to take their place except the wandering alcoholics and drug addicts who help drive out the building's stragglers. Then the vandals take over: first the "midnight plumbers" who rip out everything that can be sold, then the bored and bitter kids who mindlessly batter down the walls and ceilings with broken pipes from the disemboweled plumbing. The building's owner wants to sell, of course, but no one will buy. So he turns his back on the unusable shell, letting the mortgage and real estate taxes he owes fall into default. The mortgage holder or the federal government (which may have guaranteed the mortgage through the Federal Housing Administration or the Veterans Administration) or the city (which eventually takes possession when the property taxes are not paid) winds up with still another abandoned building on its hands.

Real estate professionals call the process "disinvestment" and blame it on rent controls in New York, rent strikes and tenant militancy elsewhere, and the pressures on slum landlords everywhere to do something about the obviously deplorable condition of inner-city housing. The slum landlord is depicted as the victim of brutal ghetto economics and pressures, his cash intake slowing to a trickle at the same time that tenants and the government are demanding that he spend much more money on upkeep. "Pretty soon the slum landlord has the feeling he is controlled like a public utility," laments one former slum housing owner, Murray Telenfeld, who turned to lecturing on real estate at the University of Pittsburgh. "So he just walks away from his properties and says to hell with it."

But few slum property traders or their financial backers really lose when abandonment occurs. They actually have risked little of their own money in their slum properties, and usually they have already reaped large returns on their investment. Abandonment is less a sudden misfortune for them than the predictable end result of their systematic exploitation of aging city neighborhoods.

Even as they are transforming those neighborhoods into uninhabitable ruins, the slum real estate manipulators realize surprisingly big profits. For a brief period before their final demise, the old buildings are gold mines. And most of the problems of social change that slum investors complain about—racial fears and property deterioration—turn out to be among their most important business assets.

The ruination of Bedford-Stuyvesant provides a particularly good example of how the slum exploitation process can drain an aging but healthy neighborhood of money and life. As recently as the early 1950s Bedford-Stuyvesant was a lively, stable, working-class community of Jewish, Italian, and Irish homeowners and renters— "a well kept, middle income white area," according to testimony before Congress in May 1972 by John P. Lomenzo, New York's secretary of state.

But the nineteenth-century brownstone row houses and early twentieth-century 4-story walk-up apartment buildings were too crowded and too frequently in need of repair for the neighborhood's younger generation, which began moving out in increasing numbers to new, roomier housing in the suburbs. As they left, black families trying to escape even more crowded and run-down neighborhoods elsewhere began moving in, and the heretofore hidden racial prejudices of the dwindling white majority surfaced. Not only were the whites personally displeased about living in close proximity to blacks, they also worried that when they tried to move out of the neighborhood they would lose much of the money they had invested in their homes. They were not eager to sell to blacks themselves, and they feared that other whites would no longer buy homes in the area.

It was then that blockbusting real estate dealers moved into Bedford-Stuyvesant. "The blockbuster tagged the area," Lomenzo explained, "because it was 10 to 15 per cent integrated," the point at which white families could probably be sufficiently stampeded to sell their houses to a dealer at below-market prices. With circulars and telephone and door-to-door solicitation, the blockbusters spread the word that if the whites did not sell to them soon, the price would drop even lower. Some dealers bought a few brownstones and apartment buildings to rent out themselves. They made certain the tenancy changed from white to black and then let maintenance slide so that white residents could see with their own eyes some deterioration of the neighborhood. "This is the evil in blockbusting," Lomenzo testified, "the main ingredient of which is panic."

The frightened white families did not know that the value of Bedford-Stuyvesant property would actually leap upwards for a time with the influx of eager black homebuyers and tenants. After buying at depressed prices from departing whites, blockbusting real estate dealers were able to sell the houses several thousands of dollars above their real market value to incoming blacks desperate for decent housing.

These black families had been denied an opportunity to buy inexpensive new suburban housing with the FHA-guaranteed, low-down-payment mortgage loans so plentiful for white homebuyers. Realtors and mortgage lenders openly discriminated against the blacks in suburban home sales, and the Federal Housing Administration did nothing to stop it. At the same time blacks were also denied FHA-backed mortgage loans for home purchases in "changing" inner-city neighborhoods like Bedford-Stuyvesant. FHA systematically "red-lined" huge sections of the city; the agency refused to guarantee home mortgage loans in these areas, even though many of them were far from slums at the time, claiming that the influx of blacks made the deals too risky. Without FHA backing, banks and savings and loan associations that were being so free with their mortgage money in the suburbs refused to make loans to homebuyers in red-lined areas of the city.

Black families thus were unable either to take advantage of new housing opportunities in the suburbs or purchase housing through conventional means in the only areas open to them in the city. And those white families in neighborhoods like Bedford-Stuyvesant who tried to sell their houses themselves to either white or black buyers found that no reputable real estate broker, bank, or savings and loan would touch the deal.

This vacuum, created by the legitimate real estate industry with the help of the government, was filled by the blockbusting real estate dealers. As it became clear that no more homes in Bedford-Stuyvesant could be sold by conventional means, white families in a hurry to leave were grateful for the blockbuster's bid of a lump sum in cash for their homes—even if the offer for a house worth $15,000 was usually only $10,000 to $12,000. The blockbuster then turned around and immediately sold the same house to a black family, without making any repairs or improvements, for $22,000 to $25,000, according to records cited by Lomenzo. Instead of serving as a broker for a fixed commission, the blockbusting real estate dealer acted as a speculator, buying at depressed prices and selling at much higher ones.

The black buyer accepted the inflated price because the dealer also provided the financing needed to pay for the house. A buyer agreeing, for instance, to pay $24,000 for a home really worth about $15,000 would pay a very small amount or nothing down and then sign three mortgages to the real estate dealer covering the purchase price. The amount of the first mortgage, about $10,000 to $12,000 in this instance, according to Lomenzo, would be reasonable for a house actually worth $15,000. The dealer could sell this mortgage to a bank, with no unusual risk for the bank because it was the first mortgage and for less than the market value of the home. Thus, if the payments were missed, the bank could always foreclose, take over the house, and sell it to satisfy the debt. Meanwhile, of course, the bank profits from the interest it collects and from the payments on principal over the years.

By selling the mortgage to a bank, the speculating dealer recovers the money he originally used to buy the house. His big profit, however, comes from the high-interest second and third mortgages that the homebuyers signed for the $10,000 to $14,000 balance of the $24,000 purchase price. The dealer could collect on these mortgages himself, increasing his profit in the long run by getting their full face value plus interest whenever possible. If the homebuyer defaulted in his payments, the dealer could take over the house himself, with the bank's first mortgage remaining in force, and resell it with new second and third mortgages to a new buyer, starting the cycle all over again. Lomenzo testified that recently when one real estate dealer "who operated exclusively in Bedford-Stuyvesant" for many years died, it was discovered that he still held $674,000 worth of notes owed by black residents there.

The real estate dealer could also sell the notes to people—often other real estate dealers or professional people with extra money to invest—who make a business of buying and collecting on them. These investors usually pay only 50 to 75 per cent of the face value of these mortgages, because if the homeowner stopped paying on them, these second and third mortgage holders could not collect from the proceeds of a foreclosure sale until after the bank got the

$10,000 to $12,000 owed it on the first mortgage. The block-buster's profit—even with a somewhat smaller cash gain from the quick sale of the second and third mortgages—in this case would still be about $6,000 to $8,000 on a house for which he paid only $10,000 to $12,000 in the first place.

Once he got his business rolling, a blockbuster never really needed to invest any more of his own money. The cash to buy the next house from a departing white family came from the sale to the bank of the first mortgage from the last deal. Thus, the same banks that refused to deal directly with black homebuyers, making it impossible for them to buy homes at reasonable prices with conventional financing, were more than willing to make loans for home purchases by these same buyers through the blockbusting real estate speculator who was able to skim exorbitant profits for serving as the middleman. The banks preferred to do business with the real estate dealer because he was such a large, regular customer, and they were able to charge him higher interest rates and extra fees, which he passed along to the black homebuyers. The banks also knew that if the homebuyers defaulted on their payments, the dealer himself would likely foreclose on a mortgage he held and resell the house, protecting the bank's investment and keeping the bank at arm's length from the slum exploitation it was financing.

The more profitable this system was for the real estate dealers and the banks and second mortgage buyers who financed them, the more destructive it was for Bedford-Stuyvesant. Many black families, who in their eagerness to escape slum conditions elsewhere snapped up the blockbuster's offer of low or no down payment, soon found themselves overwhelmingly burdened by the huge monthly payments they owed on those big mortgages. And the houses themselves did not prove to be what they seemed at first. It was time to make extensive repairs and improvements for which the overextended homebuyers had no money. The new owners also found that the high cost of their shelter was bleeding them of money needed for other expenses. In the end, both the mortgage payments and the houses themselves frequently became unbearable. Many families simply turned their backs on what little equity they had built up and left to find cheaper housing elsewhere.

After making cosmetic repairs in some cases, the dealers tried to resell the repossessed houses on the same all-credit terms to lower-income black and Puerto Rican families who were even more desperate for decent housing. The newcomers were even less able, however, to maintain the mortgage payments or upkeep of the houses; and they, too, eventually abandoned the homes.

As the houses fell into worse and worse disrepair and attracted few new buyers, the speculators sold the buildings to slum landlords or rented them out themselves. The houses were cut into small flats to bring in enough rent to cover the monthly payments on the still outstanding mortgages. Then the landlords usually pocketed what was left of the rent money, spending little or nothing on maintenance. The deterioration of the now overcrowded buildings accelerated.

By the time the original mortgages were nearly paid off, a span of less than two decades, the Bedford-Stuyvesant brownstones were no longer habitable. Even the poorest tenants, offered the lowest possible rents, would not live in them. And the real estate dealers and slumlords, who had bled every dime they could from the buildings, also abandoned them. In one generation of intense exploitation, Bedford-Stuyvesant, which had been mortgaged to the hilt, was destroyed.

Today, despite new laws designed to stop it, blockbusting still flourishes in outlying neighborhoods of Brooklyn, several other parts of New York, and some of the older suburbs. If anything, as Lomenzo told Congress, the machinery of the system has only been more finely tuned. Blockbusters spread the word a bit more subtly now, flooding a neighborhood with offers to buy homes for cash without saying anything about obvious racial changes taking place there. The banks and savings and loans have managed to put even more distance between themselves and the blockbusters by making loans to them through fly-by-night mortgage companies set up for just that purpose by investors in mortgages generated by speculators. FHA, ordered to stop red-lining and start becoming active in the inner city, has now become the underwriter of these exploitive deals. In its effect on people and the community, blockbusting is unchanged. Whites are still pitted against blacks and Puerto Ricans in migration skirmishes that only the real estate dealers and their financial backers can win, while one neighborhood battleground after another is devastated.

Inner-city neighborhoods all over the country suffer from this exploitive manipulation of housing, although not all of them have yet fallen into such ruin as Bedford-Stuyvesant. The process is nevertheless quite debilitating in its earlier stages, as can be seen by comparing one of these neighborhoods with an almost identical section of the same city where the blockbusters have not yet struck. Two such neighborhoods exist in Baltimore, Maryland. A revealing comparison of census information and land and mortgage records for two Baltimore neighborhoods was made by a citizens' group, Activists, Inc., comprised of several hundred black families victimized by slum real estate dealers. These families organized to fight blockbusters and the financial institutions behind them through publicity and action in the courts.

The neighborhoods the group examined were a section of Edmondson Village in west Baltimore, where blockbusters have been active since the early 1960s, and a still predominantly white neighborhood along Bel Air Road in northeastern Baltimore, where black families have been kept out. Both neighborhoods were 99 per cent white in 1960. More than 90 per cent of the mostly single-family row houses in each tract was considered "sound" by city real estate tax assessors, although the majority of housing units in both neighborhoods were built before 1939. Even the average assessed value of a home in each neighborhood in 1960 was almost identical: $8,700 in the Edmondson Village tract and $8,900 in the Bel Air Road neighborhood.

Today, Edmondson Village is nearly 99 per cent black, while the Bel Air Road area remains nearly all white. The population of the Bel Air Road neighborhood has remained stable, actually declining a bit since 1960. However, the number of residents in an almost unchanged number of Edmondson Village houses has increased by nearly half, from 8,800 to 12,000 people in the census tract used for the Activists, Inc., study. Although part of the increase can be attributed to the larger size of the younger black families in Edmondson Village, many of the additional residents are extra families crowded into homes that some real estate dealers bought, cut up into apartments, and rented out. Among other newcomers are boarders taken in by Edmondson Village families who need help in paying off the huge mortgages they have been saddled with.

Because of this tremendous population growth, most schools in Edmondson Village have been running on double shifts. There are not enough after-school activities to occupy the growing number of children, and city services like garbage collection have fallen far behind the area's greatly increased need for them.

While the average selling price of homes in the Bel Air neighborhood had edged up by 1968 to only $9,500 (not including the ground under the house, which in Baltimore is often only rented to the buyer), prices in Edmondson Village were jacked up by blockbusters to an average of $12,000 per house. One real estate dealer, Morris Goldseker, who bought and sold 144 houses between 1960 and 1968 in the Edmondson Village census tract, paid departing white families an average of $7,000 cash each for their houses, which he then sold to incoming black families for an average of $13,200 each. Yet the real value of Edmondson Village homes, as determined by Baltimore city tax assessors, was only $9,500 on the average in 1969 and beginning to fall as more and more homes were found to be seriously overcrowded and poorly maintained. The average assessed value of a house in the Bel Air tract, on the other hand, was over $10,000 and rising.

FHA has remained active in backing new mortgage loans for the mostly white families buying into the Bel Air Road tract, where real estate brokers have generally refused to sell to blacks. FHA appraisers have helped hold sales prices to around actual home values there. But Edmondson Village, because of its changing racial makeup, was part of the area in Baltimore that had been red-lined as too risky altogether for conventional loan guarantees by FHA. So the savings and loan associations that continued making conventional FHA-backed loans at market interest rates to Bel Air Road homebuyers loaned money for mortgages in Edmondson Village only through blockbusting real estate dealers and at much higher interest rates.

Besides all these obstacles to black homebuyers, the inner-city real estate speculators in Baltimore use an ingenious scheme to increase profits in a neighborhood like Edmondson Village. They offer houses to black families on a tricky contract basis: Only a nominal down payment, usually $500 or less, is required if the black homebuyer signs a contract to purchase the house for a certain price, always way above what the speculator paid for it. In return, the dealer often requires that he first be paid rent on the house for a year or two "to see what kind of credit risk" the buyer is, according to dealers who have tried to justify this practice. None of the rent paid during that time is applied to or in any way reduces the purchase price.

At the end of that rental period, the buyer signs and begins payment on two mortgages covering the full stated purchase price—a first mortgage loan from a savings and loan association for about two-thirds the sales price and a second mortgage for the balance owed to the real estate speculator. The interest on both is usually higher than the going market rate. During the 1960s black homebuyers in Edmondson Village were agreeing to pay mortgages with 7 and 8 per cent interest rates, when homebuyers in other parts of Baltimore were paying 6 per cent or less. Many of the mortgages also had "balloons" at the end: When it came time for the homebuyer to make the final payment, he would find that it was much bigger than the others had been, that it might be for a balance of several thousand dollars. If the buyer were unable to make this big final payment, the house would revert to the dealer.

The buyer also could be easily evicted for being late with his rent during the rental period or for missing a single mortgage payment once he was supposedly buying the home. In many cases the savings and loan mortgage actually was made to the real estate dealer and not to the homebuyer. The dealer then collected payments, often on a weekly basis, from his contract buyers and, after collecting an extra $5 per month from each buyer for performing this service, made lump-sum monthly mortgage payments to the savings and loan association.

Because of all these contract devices, many Edmondson Village families have been homebuyers in name only. Several parts of their rent-and-purchase contracts violate sections of the Greater Baltimore Real Estate Board's code of ethics, but the board has not taken any action against inner-city real estate speculators, many of whom never bothered to join the board.

The most important ingredient in the contract sales scheme is the financial backing that Baltimore's inner-city speculators have received from savings and loan associations and banks there. In 1968, according to an Activists, Inc., study of city mortgage records, twenty-five major savings and loans in Baltimore made 827 loans totaling nearly $5.5 million for the purchase of homes in the Edmondson Village area. Nearly 85 per cent of those loans were traced directly to the deals of blockbusting real estate speculators

—deals in which the speculators marked up the prices of homes sold to black families by an average of 80 per cent. Sixty per cent of the loans, 482 of them, went directly to the dealers themselves.

Some Baltimore banks also have made large lump-sum loans for as much as $400,000 each to these speculators, who use the money to buy up houses with cash. When the speculator sells each of those houses under contract and obtains a savings and loan mortgage in the deal, he takes part of that money to pay off the bank loan he used to buy the house. He then pockets the rest, leaving the mortgage to be paid off by the homebuyer. The speculator also profits from whatever rent he collects before reaching the savings and loan mortgage stage of the contract, as well as from the proceeds of any second mortgage made out to him for the balance of the contract price, and finally, from the $5 per month service fee he frequently charges the contract buyer.

Although several blockbusting real estate speculators have been operating in Edmondson Village and elsewhere in Baltimore, one name—Morris Goldseker—stands out from the rest. For three decades he has bought, rented, and resold at huge mark-ups thousands of houses in Baltimore's inner city. Goldseker, a short, gray-haired, distinguished-looking man now of retirement age, has operated through a tangle of thirty companies that for many years made it difficult to trace or fully comprehend the enormity and immense profitability of his activities. In a 1971 court appearance forced on him by his own ultimately unsuccessful efforts to stop picketing of his offices by Activists, Inc., Goldseker testified that he himself did now know—"I can't remember their names"—how many paper corporations he used to funnel contracts and loans to himself. Among the many Goldseker companies that show up in the state of Maryland corporation records are Life Realty, Edmondson, Inc., Edgevale Realty, Kenneth Company, Reddy Realty, Linwood Realty, Liberty, Inc., Lee Realty, Jay Realty, and Eagle Corporation.

Activists, Inc., spent many months going through these and other records to reconstruct Goldseker's inner-city real estate empire. During the 1960s, Baltimore city land records show, Goldseker's companies bought 1,768 houses for nearly $10.9 million. They sold 742 of them for nearly $9.5 million and rented out or retained control through contracts the other 1,000. The 742 resold houses cost Goldseker an average of $6,868 each to buy and sold for an average of $12,700 each, a mark-up of 85 per cent. Rental income he may have collected on them first, any $5 per month collection service fees he may still be charging, and the mortgage interest on second mortgages still coming to him are not included in this already large margin of profit.

The Activists, Inc., study of Baltimore mortgage records also reveals close connections between Goldseker's blockbusting and several large Baltimore savings and loan associations and banks. During the 1960s Maryland National Bank in Baltimore loaned Goldseker a total of $1.6 million in a few lump-sum loans to finance his cash purchase of houses from white families leaving target neighborhoods. Equitable Trust and Uptown Federal Savings and Loan Association each loaned Goldseker just over $1 million for the same purpose during the same period. Between September 1967 and October 1968 alone Maryland National Bank advanced Goldseker companies $933,000 in six big loans, which he used to buy up 139 inner-city houses with cash. Uptown advanced him $581,000 in two loans covering seventy-one properties during the same thirteen months.

Another Baltimore savings and loan, Jefferson Federal, was the most active financial institution in making mortgage loans to and through the Goldseker companies. Of the $2,748,570 worth of mortgage loans made by Jefferson Federal throughout Baltimore between 1964 and 1969, $1,933,570—almost exactly 70 per cent —went to Goldseker for his deals. These loans made possible Goldseker's exploitation of black homebuyers, and, in many cases, they also improperly provided Goldseker with more cash from the savings and loan mortgages than he paid for the houses in the first place.

One of Goldseker's customers is Percell Woodrun. In 1966, when he was twenty-seven and he and his wife Sandra had an infant child, Woodrun began renting a house in the 1600 block of East Thirtieth Street in Baltimore from Goldseker's Lee Realty. Goldseker had bought the building a few months before for $6,000 plus ground rent of $96. After renting the house to the Woodruns for two years at $32.58 per week, Goldseker arranged a contract purchase deal for them at the price of $12,000, plus the ground rent, and obtained a first mortgage loan of $8,500 from Jefferson Federal. Goldseker took a second mortgage for the other $3,500, which he could collect as profit—plus interest—over a period of years. Moreover, Goldseker could immediately pocket, minus any sales or other expenses, the $2,500 of the $8,500 Jefferson Federal mortgage loan that exceeded the $6,000 he paid for the house.

The Woodruns' combined mortgage payments each month total $142. But FHA has since independently appraised the house at $8,800 market value, which means that with an FHA-backed mortgage the Woodruns could be making a monthly payment of $100 or less. The extra $42 each month means a lot to Woodrun. It keeps him from saving money or even keeping up his house as he would like to. "For one thing," he said, "you don't have enough money, like the sixty dollars to paint the outside, to fix up your problems . . . things that normally go wrong with the house. You don't have the extra money to put into it, and by the time you get to the point where you might have it, the house is in such bad shape that you'd rather move."

Finally, because the Jefferson Federal loan exceeded 80 per cent of the real value of the house, as appraised by the FHA, it could have been a violation of the by-laws of the Federal Home Loan Bank Board, which regulates federally chartered and insured savings and loan associations like Jefferson. Mortgage loans are supposed to be kept to less than a home's legitimate market value. Then, if the buyer defaults on his payments and the house must be auctioned off to recover the savings and loan's investment, the sale price can be expected to be big enough to keep the savings and loan and its depositors from losing money.

Land records in Baltimore show dozens of instances in which Jefferson Federal loans to Goldseker exceeded the actual value of the homes involved in the deals. They also show that Jefferson Federal violated Federal Home Loan Bank Board rules by tying up more than 10 per cent of its loan money in or through a single borrower, namely Goldseker. And they show that most of the rest of Jefferson's business during the 1960s was with other inner-city blockbusting real estate speculators, contrary to the Bank Board's guidelines on home mortgage financing, which stress making mortgages directly to homebuyers rather than to or through big-volume real estate dealers.

Jefferson Federal also was barely skirting regulations forbidding federally chartered and insured savings and loans from lending money to their own officers and directors, except for the mortgages on their own residences. One Jefferson director during 1968 was Martin L. Weinberg, a top employee of Goldseker and his companies. Jefferson did not lend directly to Weinberg, but 80 of the approximately 100 mortgage loans it made in 1968 went to or through companies run by Goldseker and Weinberg. It also happened that Jefferson was providing mortgage money for Calvert Realty Sales, the real estate company of William L. Siskind, Jefferson's chairman at the time.

What is there in this way of doing business to benefit Jefferson Federal Savings and Loan itself, beyond the obvious advantage to directors like Weinberg and Siskind of getting loans for their own real estate businesses? Nothing for the depositors, except the heavy risk inherent in some of these practices. Federal insurance protects the deposits themselves up to $20,000 per account, but the savers could suffer from reduced interest rates or, ultimately, a tie-up of their funds before insurance is paid in the case of massive defaults on such risky loans.

In the short run the savings and loan was enriched by the higher placement fees and interest rates that Jefferson Federal charged in speculative mortgage deals, higher charges that were passed along to the black contract buyers. This extra money increased the operating income out of which savings and loan officers drew their salaries, bonuses, and director's fees. Jefferson also charged exorbitant appraisal fees and closing costs for its loans, money that passed directly to the savings and loan officers and employees who did the appraising and other work covered by those fees.

Just as Goldseker is no small-time promoter with holes in his shoes, Jefferson Federal is no fly-by-night storefront, even though its lending was limited for years to a few blockbusting real estate dealers. From 1965 until early 1969 one of Jefferson's directors was Marvin Mandel, then speaker of the Maryland legislature's House of Delegates and now governor of Maryland. Mandel had been president of Oldetown Savings and Loan Association, which merged with another association to form Jefferson Federal in 1965. Oldetown, land records show, also frequently put up mortgage money for speculative blockbusting real estate deals.

When the Activists, Inc., study of Jefferson Federal and its predecessor associations was made public in 1971, Mandel said he served as president of Oldetown and as a director of Jefferson without pay as a favor to business associates and did not know that black families were being victimized by blockbusters in the deals that both Oldetown and Jefferson Federal helped finance. Mandel said, through his press secretary, Frank DeFilippo, that he thought the savings and loans, under pressure from the civil rights movement and encouragement by the federal government, were making it financially possible for lower-income black families to become homeowners. Although Mandel signed Oldetown mortgages as its president, DeFilippo said he did not remember much about their details. According to the press secretary, at Jefferson Mandel's "only function was to attend meetings. He was not on the loan committee or executive committee that made recommendations to the board." Sampson Green, a Baltimore civil rights leader who is chairman of Activists, Inc., and was a Mandel appointee to the Maryland State Human Relations Commission, responded that "the governor is either trying to cover up his own involvement in this mess or he is just plain ignorant."

Mandel had resigned from Jefferson Federal's board in January 1969, when he was appointed governor by the Maryland legislature to complete the term of Spiro Agnew, when Agnew became U.S. Vice-President. (Mandel has since been re-elected governor in his own right.) Two months after Mandel left Jefferson the Federal Home Loan Bank Board finally stepped in and placed two new people of its own choosing on the savings and loan's board with orders to stop making loans to blockbusters, but millions of dollars in loans made to and through blockbusters in the past are still due. The change in directors was alluded to but not elaborated on in a February 1971 letter from Preston Martin, chairman of the Federal Home Loan Bank Board, to Sampson Green:

> During recent years, we have been aware of the lending conditions you described with regard to Jefferson Federal Savings and Loan Association. Our past supervisory actions in this matter have consistently been directed toward curtailing further low equity home financing, lending to real estate speculators, and any federal violations by the association. The last examination of Jefferson as of March 13, 1970, disclosed that the association had ceased making loans to and for the type of speculators named in your report.

The Bank Board took no steps to punish personally anyone in Jefferson Federal's management for violating federal regulations. Nor did it do anything to alleviate the tremendous mortgage burden remaining on the shoulders of Baltimore's contract buyers.

The practice of contract buying is hardly unique to Baltimore. Would-be homebuyers in such cities as Detroit, Cincinnati, Milwaukee, San Francisco, Washington, D.C., and Chicago have found themselves exploited by the same kind of financial wheeling and dealing in all its lucrative variations. Among the hundreds of victims in the Lawndale neighborhood of half-century-old brick duplexes on Chicago's West Side—blockbusted in the late 1950s and early 1960s and now the home of 200,000 blacks—are Saul and Henrietta Banks. They signed a contract to buy their duplex in 1961. Although the dealer selling to them had just bought the house for $14,000, a price hidden from the couple, the contract they signed was for $25,500 at 7 per cent interest. After struggling for a decade on Banks's welder's salary and overtime pay, along with some extra money earned part-time by Mrs. Banks, to raise seven children and make the $200 monthly payment on the contract, they still owe $20,000. "We live in constant fear," Mrs. Banks says, "of missing a monthly payment and losing our home."

Another Lawndale resident, Charles Baker, found in 1960 that, despite his good record and years of steady work at the Campbell Soup Company, he could not get an FHA loan for an inexpensive new house in outlying areas of Chicago. Lawndale turned out to be one of the few places in the city where it appeared he could buy a home. The $26,500 contract price for a 2-story brick duplex on West Flourney Street did not seem unusual for the market he was limited to.

"I didn't know how to value property," Baker said later. "The price was about that of other houses in this neighborhood that were offered." And the real estate dealer selling the house lied to Baker in telling him that it had cost $21,000 to buy the house and more for improvements he made in it. Baker found out later that the dealer had just bought the house from a white family leaving Lawndale for only $15,250 and had obtained a mortgage loan on it from a savings and loan for $17,300. A later FHA appraisal showed the home to be really worth under $20,000, perhaps even less than $17,300. Under the 7 per cent interest rate contract he signed, Baker is obligated for twenty years to pay $220 monthly out of his approximately $500 in take-home pay to the dealer for principal and interest on the contract, taxes, and insurance on the home.

Before being able to obtain title to the house himself, Baker must pay a total of $48,000 in contract principal and interest alone.

That sum is three times what the dealer paid for the house—and at least twice what Baker would have had to pay himself, if he had been able to buy it at an FHA-appraised price with an FHA-backed savings and loan mortgage made directly to him.

"That's the part that burns you up," Baker said. "And I have no equity. I have to keep the house up myself, but I don't really own a part of it until all those payments are made."

By selling on contract rather than renting out the house, the real estate dealer also escapes the maintenance responsibilities of a landlord for a house that has reached the age when it needs a lot of repairs. To sell the house and the contract purchase idea, the dealer merely paints over the worst problems. These soon are found by the new resident, especially if he rents out half the duplex to help make his monthly contract payment, as Baker did. He had to have it inspected first by city housing officials, who found a dozen housing code violations from structural defects to improper door sizes. A neighbor, Baker said, had to have eighteen violations corrected.

In 1966 a group of Jesuit seminarians led by John R. Macnamara went to Lawndale to see what they could do about problems in the slum parish. Their survey of residents showed that the most common and bitter complaint was the sales contract on homes. The seminarians organized the unhappy residents into the Contract Buyers League (CBL), with Henrietta Banks and Charles Baker among the founders and top officers. Nearly two thousand families have belonged at one time or another to CBL, which sued fifty Chicago slum real estate dealers, nine banks, and fourteen savings and loan associations, charging that they had conspired to cheat black homebuyers in Lawndale. The suit, which has not yet come to trial, asked the federal court in Chicago to declare the contracts illegal.

Although the litigation persuaded a few real estate dealers to re-negotiate their contracts with Lawndale residents, thousands of contracts still remain in force throughout Chicago, and hundreds of families who could not maintain their payments have lost or abandoned their homes. Increasingly, the dealers holding the contracts have been unable to resell or rent these abandoned houses. Rather than dip into their past profits to keep up the buildings, the dealers have stopped making the mortgage payments they owe on them to Chicago savings and loan associations. In addition, the deaths of two of Chicago's most active contract sellers, Lou Fushanis and Richard Boston, left hundreds of mortgages for contract deals in default or tied up in their estates.

Boston's huge debt figured heavily in the collapse of one Chicago savings and loan, Gotham Mutual, which, like many savings and loans around the country, had dealt almost exclusively in mortgage loans to a few big contract sellers. This dubious, though widespread, role of savings and loan associations is particularly well documented in a little-publicized 2,000-page study of the savings and loan industry made in 1969 at the direction of Congress for the Federal Home Loan Bank Board by a team of academic experts led by Professor Irwin Friend of the University of Pennsylvania's Wharton School of Business. Parts of the study dealt with the damage done to the industry by conflicts of interest and mismanagement, including the financing of possibly illegal slum real estate deals at inflated prices.

Most savings and loans began in cities as neighborhood mutual savings societies in which each account holder had a vote in the direction of the association. The members pooled their savings to make home purchase loans to themselves and others, with the proceeds of the loans used almost entirely to pay themselves interest on their savings. Management of savings and loans was mostly part-time and nominally remunerated.

The majority of savings and loans today are still "mutuals," but they are no longer controlled by their shareholders, who have given their votes to the associations' officers, often in proxy statements unknowingly signed by the shareholders when they open their accounts. In this and other ways, the Friend study showed, the "vast bulk" of U.S. savings and loans have become "what amount to personal or family fiefdoms, or joint ventures controlled by small groups."

In one section of the Friend report H. Robert Bartell, Jr., of Washington University traced the rise and fall of Chicago's Gotham Mutual, which grew rapidly during the 1950s by taking in extra savings and making high-interest loans to the contract sellers who blockbusted Lawndale. Records made available to Bartell showed that Gotham made 108 mortgage loans totaling $1.3 million to real estate dealer Richard Boston before 1960, 67 more to him for $1.1 million during 1960, and another 175 for $1.3 million in

1961. By March 1963, Federal Home Loan Bank Board examination reports showed, Gotham had loaned Boston and one other contract seller in Lawndale a total of $8.2 million—one-fourth of the association's assets.

Bank Board examiners found that Gotham's president had cut himself in on the increased mortgage interest income during the boom years of high-interest lending to Boston and his friends by paying himself a bonus of 25 per cent of the association's annual net earnings. Thus in 1959 Gotham's president was paid a $32,937 bonus on top of a salary of $19,200—all for part-time work. The association's president, who was not named by Bartell or in any of the examination records he cited, also was active in a real estate business of his own.

The examination records indicated that Gotham's officers ballooned their net income by jacking mortgage interest rates up over 7 per cent, charging 5 per cent loan placement fees on top of that for contract sales deals, and, in order to attract more business from contract sellers, frequently loaning each dealer more for each house than he paid to buy it. Although Bank Board examiners continually expressed their dissatisfaction with the bonus fee arrangement, the practice continued, paying the association president a total of $90,883 in 1960: $20,400 in salary, $42,764 in bonuses, and the rest in miscellaneous fees also derived from the association's exorbitant loan charges.

By 1963 many of the inflated Lawndale mortgage loans already were running into trouble. Overburdened families were abandoning their homes, and speculators were letting their mortgages fall into default. By March of that year Boston alone was delinquent on 110 loans totaling $1.4 million in face value. Then, in May, he died, leaving behind millions of dollars more in unpaid loans. Meanwhile, another $2 million worth of loans made to other Lawndale contract sellers fell into default by late 1964. When it foreclosed on these delinquent loans, Gotham could not resell the houses it repossessed for as much as was still owed on the mortgages. Gotham itself tried selling some through contracts at inflated contract prices with no down payment, a practice that only got it into even deeper financial trouble. More and more houses were vacated and remained empty, soon falling prey to vandals. Finally, after millions of dollars of loans were written off and the loss made up by the Federal

Savings and Loan Insurance Corporation (FSLIC), Gotham was merged in 1968 with a sound savings and loan in Chicago.

Gotham Mutual's brief and spectacular period of plenty had ended, but not before Boston, other real estate dealers, and some of Gotham's own officers had had an opportunity to live well on the money they took from Lawndale's residents and the savings and loan's depositors. The depositors were all reimbursed by the FSLIC, but the vast majority of Lawndale families not already forced to abandon their homes are still suffering under those contracts.

Gotham was only one of many Chicago savings and loan associations financing these deals, and only one of nineteen that failed in that city alone between 1963 and 1968. (FSLIC paid out $122 million throughout the country to cover losses of failing savings and loans between 1963 and 1968, the Friend study showed, compared to just $8.5 million for all savings and loan failures during the eighteen years between World War II and 1963.) Meanwhile, a dozen or more Chicago savings and loans still collect on the mortgage loans they made to contract sellers, and some continue to finance blockbusters and speculators today.

Even after the blockbusters finish with a neighborhood, there is still money to be made by those who, like Goldseker in Baltimore, also are slum landlords. Not all absentee owners of slum housing are deviously exploitive. Many are little people who each own only a single house or building, usually places where they once lived themselves and never sold when they moved to new homes. Professional property owners also are sometimes left with buildings they owned and operated for years and failed to sell in time when the sudden drain of money from a blockbusted neighborhood around their property turned it into a slum almost overnight.

But there are many slum landlords who, like their brethren the blockbusters, have purposely bought slum property on speculation to generate big profits by inflating prices, obtaining overly generous mortgage loans, overcrowding buildings for extra rental income, and using accelerated depreciation deductions allowed on them to save on their income taxes. For a few years, they bleed a building of every penny they can, spending little or nothing on maintenance, until there is virtually no building left to exploit.

The scheme is to buy a run-down building for perhaps $100,000 and mortgage it at a friendly savings and loan for at least that much or perhaps a little more—perhaps $110,000 or $120,000—so extra money can be pocketed right away. Part of the savings and loan's justification for the big mortgage, which nevertheless violates Federal Home Loan Bank Board regulations, is that more living units can be carved out of the building, increasing its potential rental income. As many paying tenants as possible are then shoehorned in. Payments on the huge mortgage and real estate taxes are met by the rent collected, leaving what is left over as clear profit. All maintenance and repairs not ordered by housing inspectors or the courts are ignored. Meanwhile, rental profits and other income of the owner can be offset on each year's tax return by the maximum depreciation deductions allowed for the building by the Internal Revenue Service. Because the allowable deduction decreases with each passing year of ownership, the building should be unloaded after a few years—traded, if possible, for another building with another landlord in a similar position, so that each can start the depreciation cycle all over again.

Suitable property for exploitation—from individual homes, some of them abandoned by victims of blockbusters, to large old apartment buildings—is always available in a neighborhood going downhill. The first step is obtaining the mortgage loan. By paying extra high loan fees, which the landlord simply passes on to the tenants in higher rents, the landlord can usually find a savings and loan willing to loan him more money than he paid to buy the building used as security. This practice came to light in investigations of the exploitation of slum real estate in Washington, D.C., during the 1960s.

One Washington savings and loan association, Republic, had grown spectacularly—from $30,000 worth of assets in 1952 to $10 million in 1957 and a high of $57 million in 1967—by loaning large sums of money at high interest rates and fees to Washington's slum landlords. Republic was then able to pay higher dividends on deposits and draw steadily more savings, which, in turn, made it possible to lend still more money. The bulk of Republic's record asset total in 1967 actually was the money owed it on mortgages the association made to slum landlords.

Plenty of money was coming in to satisfy the rich tastes of Republic's top officers during the 1960s: president Pete C. Kalavritinos, a slum real estate speculator himself; executive vice-president John Kalavritinos, Pete's brother and another investor in slum property; and general counsel Russell Miller, a Washington lawyer and former counsel and treasurer of the Federal Deposit Insurance Corporation, the government insurer of savings deposits. These three men ran Republic with proxies signed by its depositors and cut themselves in on money from Republic's rapid growth in a variety of ways. Federal Home Loan Bank Board examiners later found that Republic's officers, in addition to paying themselves high salaries and fees, charged to the savings and loan their personal auto, restaurant, and credit card expenses, including $270 for each of the three every month for rental and parking of Cadillac automobiles.

Pete and John Kalavritinos also found ways to help their brother George and their sister Angelina Formant and her husband Dino. Republic loaned George Kalavritinos $900,000 and the Formants $960,000, all of which was spent on speculation in various slum properties. These loans to relatives barely skirted the letter of Federal Home Loan Bank Board regulations forbidding savings and loan directors from loaning association money to themselves, except for the mortgages on their own residences.

In addition, many of the mortgage loans to the Formants were for as much or more than they paid for the property securing those loans. They bought, for instance, a half-century-old apartment building on Twentieth Street, N.W., for $140,000 and mortgaged it at Republic for $155,000 cash. To make it look better to Bank Board examiners on paper, the Formants simulated a sale of the building to a company called 2415, Inc., of which they were the sole owners, for a stated price of $225,000—a typical maneuver used for this kind of deal that later was caught and criticized by the Bank Board examiners, although no one was ever prosecuted either for fraud or for violation of Bank Board regulations.

In time, as with Gotham Mutual in Chicago, the excesses caught up with Republic. The credit squeeze of 1966 pinched off the life line of Washington's slum landlords, who operate almost entirely on savings and loan and bank credit. They wound up with too little money at a time when more and more of their dilapidated buildings were being abandoned by tenants who found better housing elsewhere. A large percentage of Republic's loans fell into default, and in 1968 Republic was quietly merged by federal authorities into a healthy savings and loan in Washington.

The romance of the savings and loan associations and slum landlords is a drama played out of public view in many American cities. Washington, D.C., is one of the very few places where investigation has brought to light normally secret government examination of the transactions involved. In 1967 just forty slum real estate speculators owed Republic Savings and Loan a total of $21.8 million in outstanding mortgage loans, according to a report by a Federal Home Loan Bank Board examiner. The list included Washington's largest slumlord at the time, George Basiliko, who owed $1.5 million to Republic on 117 mortgage loans for slum row houses he had subdivided and rented out, and his brother-in-law John Swagart, also a landlord, who owed another $700,000. Basiliko had also obtained a few million dollars more from several other Washington savings and loan associations. Like many others of the slum speculator fraternity, Basiliko maintained a dingy hole-in-the-wall storefront office in a run-down slum building but lived in an expensive new home in the suburbs.

Other borrowers at Republic included realtor Leo Bernstein, who owed $600,000 in 1967, and his son Stuart, who owed $530,000. Stuart was still an active inner-city real estate speculator while his father, now a banker and investor in posh Georgetown rental property and living himself in a $300,000 Georgetown townhouse, was one of Washington's original blockbusters. Leo Bernstein describes himself, however, as having been an "agent" who performed an important "service for the underprivileged."

"Maybe they charged a lot for it," Bernstein says in referring generally to real estate speculators like himself, "but at least they housed people. It was the speculator's business to corral homes. The speculators gave the people an opportunity to buy houses at small down payments. And even if the Negro homebuyer had the down payment needed, he still wouldn't have the expertise to get a loan."

Leo Bernstein, now nearly sixty, an intent, handsome man with steely blue eyes, had the "expertise" and capitalized on it for millions of dollars in real estate profits, a prominent place in local Washington society, the chairmanship of a growing young bank (District of Columbia National), the presidency, in 1973, of the

District of Columbia Bankers Association, and, from the early 1950s until recently, control of his own local savings and loan, Guardian Federal. Bernstein built the savings and loan from $22 million in assets in 1962 to $41 million in 1967, rivaling Republic Savings and Loan in the booming business it did at the time bankrolling slum real estate investors.

Among the recipients of Guardian Federal money was none other than Pete C. Kalavritinos, president of Republic. Kalavritinos had formed the Sturbridge Investment Corporation, with an office in his home, to borrow $530,000 from Guardian in mortgage loans on nineteen slum properties. Kalavritinos could not legally borrow money for speculation from Republic, his own savings and loan. Nor could Bernstein borrow from Guardian. So they simply loaned money to each other, a practice known as "back-scratching" that the Friend study showed to be a widespread conflict of interest among officers of many of the nation's savings and loans. When the Federal Home Loan Bank Board found Republic on the verge of collapse in 1967, it criticized Bernstein and Guardian Federal, and other Washington savings and loans as well, for these dealings. But nothing more was ever done.

For many of Washington's slum landlords, however, the tight money years of the 1960s were not at all disastrous. These dealers had balanced their slum holdings with more lucrative real estate investments outside the inner city. Although the slum properties often continued to produce surprising rental profits themselves, partly because little or no rent money was put back into their upkeep, they usually were far more valuable as tax shelters. For the paper depreciation of their slum holdings, the owners could subtract huge deductions on their income tax returns; these offset both their slum rental profits and large amounts of income from other investments.

Although this perfectly legal practice is widespread throughout the country, the confidentiality of income tax returns usually shields it from the public. A revealing exception is the case of one of Washington's more active slum landlords, shrewd and pugnacious Sidney J. Brown. Among other controversies, Brown became entangled in a legal dispute in the District of Columbia tax court and at one point filed his 1963 personal income tax return in the court's public files.

The return showed that Brown had realized a gross income of $834,080.70 in 1963 from, among other things, 300 separate real estate investments in and around Washington: some of the city's biggest and most run-down slum apartment houses, other slum buildings he bought and sold, a suburban subdivision under construction, and a suburban shopping center he was developing. Brown's net taxable income for 1963, however, was only $6,431.45 —on which he paid just $259.20 in federal personal income tax.

Accounting for the big difference between Brown's gross and taxable incomes was the depreciation he deducted on his return. Not all of it showed up there, because Brown owned and depreciated many of his properties through several separate corporations, but $240,975 in depreciation deductions was listed on his personal income tax return. About $54,000 was deducted for one property alone, the Clifton Terrace Apartments, three huge brick and marble apartment buildings built on a prominent hillside in downtown Washington as luxury housing in 1915. Under Brown's ownership Clifton Terrace became known locally as a notorious example of slum real estate exploitation.

Brown, a rotund man, known by his rumpled, ill-fitting suits, thick glasses, and bellowing protests when publicly criticized, bought Clifton Terrace in 1963 for about $1.5 million, although he invested little of his own cash. He borrowed the purchase money and mortgaged the buildings heavily for it. His tax return showed that Brown made a profit of $9,463.67 out of the rent he collected at Clifton Terrace in 1963. The return also showed that he claimed a $54,000 depreciation deduction for Clifton Terrace in that year. This made his rental profit from Clifton Terrace and nearly $45,000 income from other real estate investments that year tax free.

Tenants at Clifton Terrace soon began complaining about an abrupt change in the maintenance of the buildings. "The decline became very noticeable after Brown had owned it about a year," said one tenant, Mrs. Viola Byrd. The previous owner, she said, had always made prompt repairs. "You called, and it was done immediately. There were flowers in the windows of the lobby. The apartments were painted before you took them. The elevators worked, the stairways were safe, there was excellent janitorial service. . . ."

Regular janitorial service came to an end soon after Brown bought Clifton Terrace. Apartments were no longer painted. The elevators in the 5-story buildings ceased to work. Leaking faucets and faulty electrical outlets were never fixed. The exterminator seldom came. And for much of every winter the heat never came on in Clifton Terrace; its residents lived and slept for days in their overcoats.

As might be expected, most of Clifton Terrace's old tenants moved out. Brown cared little about who moved in to take their places, as long as they paid some rent, enough in total to cover his mortgage payments. Otherwise, the primary importance of Clifton Terrace to Sidney J. Brown was as a tax shelter.

As the condition of the buildings rapidly worsened and the peeling paint, falling plaster, broken windows, missing doors, and hordes of roaches began to make newspaper headlines, Brown took to loudly complaining about the way the tenants behaved. "The minute we fix a window, they break it," he told reporters at a press conference. "The minute we fix plaster they break it in. . . . The minute we put a door in they rip it off. . . ."

Finally, in 1968, after he had taken the maximum allowable depreciation deductions for the buildings for five years, after Clifton Terrace had become so run-down that few rent-paying tenants were left there, and after Brown had been heavily fined and sentenced to sixty days in jail (the jail sentence was later vacated) for failing to heat the buildings and make necessary repairs, Brown managed to unload Clifton Terrace to a local nonprofit housing group, which later went bankrupt trying to renovate the badly run-down buildings. Brown has repeated the entire process—without the fine and jail sentence—with other large apartment complexes in Washington's inner city.

Slum real estate professionals like Sidney J. Brown are not the only investors attracted to slum property by its tax shelter possibilities. Doctors, dentists, lawyers, and other high-salaried professionals, as well as self-employed merchants like jewelers, hardware dealers, or opticians frequently invest some of their extra money in rental properties in the slums. They expect little or no profit out of the investment; instead they expect to use the depreciation deductions they become eligible for to offset much of the other income on their tax returns. Usually these investments are handled by brokers or bank trust officers who try, like the professional slum investors, to get the most building possible for the investor's down payment by swinging a big mortgage from a savings and loan or bank. Often several investors, law partners, doctors sharing a practice, or professional men who just happen to know each other, pool their money in a partnership (often known as a real estate syndicate) to buy one or several apartment buildings as tax shelters. They each are then eligible for a share of the allowable depreciation deductions proportional to the share of the down payment money they each provide.

This category of slum investors comprises a broad variety of people and motives. Some emulate the professional slum investor (who sometimes serves as the investor's adviser or broker) and cynically ignore maintenance of the buildings they own. Others fully intend to be responsible landlords, only to discover that they know too little about what to do or cannot afford the often very large amounts of additional money needed to make major repairs on older buildings or to keep up with the added wear and tear caused by lower-income tenants and their children. Often these investors simply turn the problem over to a slum property management firm for a percentage of the rent collection. These companies, usually 1- or 2-man operations using low-paid, unskilled maintenance labor, likely as not cheat the building owners of some of their money, while also failing to keep up the buildings themselves.

Not infrequently, naïve investors are taken in right from the start by a slum real estate speculator who either is the seller of the building they are buying or the organizer of the syndicate the investors join. One of these complicated sets of transactions was set into motion in Washington, D.C., a few years ago when Dr. Arthur J. Wilets, of Chevy Chase, Maryland, met Burton J. Dorfman, a Washington real estate dealer, at a party. Wilets said later that Dorfman persuaded him and some of his friends to invest in several large slum apartment buildings in Washington as tax shelters. Dorfman organized a separate syndicate of the investors for each of four buildings they bought. The businessmen put up a total of $256,000 to cover the down payments and other costs, while Dorfman contributed no money to three of the deals and only $3,000 to the fourth, according to District of Columbia records.

In each deal Dorfman decided what building to buy and handled the transaction himself. To one of the syndicates he sold for $275,000 a building he himself had bought for $250,000 and had mortgaged for the same amount. Without investing anything in that deal, he made an immediate $25,000 profit from his unsuspecting partners. Dorfman also mortgaged the other buildings the syndicate bought for large amounts of money, enabling him in each deal to pocket the difference between what he actually paid to buy a building for the syndicate and the much larger combination of the down payment raised by his partners and the mortgage loan he was able to obtain. As one might expect, Republic Savings and Loan in Washington made several of the loans to Dorfman-run syndicates.

It turned out that the rent from the buildings was not sufficient to cover the big mortgage payments due on them, much less pay for any repairs or maintenance. The buildings deteriorated rapidly and were soon abandoned by paying tenants. Their mortgage loans fell into default. Republic alone lost $1.1 million in unpaid Dorfman mortgages.

Dorfman already had taken his quick profits from these dealings and lost only the token $3,000. Dr. Wilets and his friends, however, lost almost everything they invested. "We all lost," said another partner, Joseph Orgel, a Silver Spring, Maryland, wholesale jeweler. "It is difficult," Dr. Wilets added, "for any of us to tell what happened."

The financial loss was hardly disastrous for Dr. Wilets, Orgel, and the others, however. It was conveniently deductible on their tax returns, as was the depreciation they were able to claim while they owned the buildings. But for the buildings that had housed hundreds of families, the Dorfman deals were the crucial events of their slide into ruin. They were left too run-down to live in and, ironically, too expensive, because of the large unpaid mortgages owed on them, to be bought and renovated or torn down and replaced.

In Washington, in many places within sight of the Capitol dome, and in nearly every good-sized city across the country, blocks of similarly exploited housing stand vacant and disemboweled. These shells are the depleted gold mines of slum housing speculators who have moved on to other neighborhoods to prospect, leaving behind broken buildings and embittered human beings.

Far from being the pitiful victims of unavoidable deterioration of inner-city housing, as they so often represent themselves to be, the slum speculators are cunning actors in a sophisticated real estate industry conspiracy aided and abetted by large, respected financial institutions and agencies of the federal government. With the discriminatory policies of FHA providing the market, and with banks, savings and loan associations, and other financial institutions providing the capital, blockbusters create slums out of still healthy older neighborhoods like Bedford-Stuyvesant, Edmondson Village, and Lawndale. With the help of the same financial backers and tax advantages offered by Congress, slum landlords plunder the newly created slums, taking as much money out of them as possible and putting none back into buildings now desperately in need of help.

The final abandonment of these buildings and the resulting loss of once lively urban neighborhoods are the visible costs of slum real estate speculation to society. It has been a high price for some cities to pay. In combination with other social and economic factors, slum exploitation has struck a nearly mortal blow to the old residential centers of such cities as Baltimore, Washington, D.C., Philadelphia, the boroughs of Brooklyn and the Bronx in New York, Cleveland, Detroit, Chicago, St. Louis, and many others. It is possible, of course, to rebuild buildings, but recreating vibrant neighborhoods has proven to be much more difficult.

A few favored slum neighborhoods, where the architecture or relics of history still kindle wide interest, have been "unslummed" (to use the term coined by Jane Jacobs) by speculators who bought out slum homeowners and landlords at low prices, evicted the low-income people then living there, thoroughly renovated the homes, and then sold them at large profits to middle- and upper-income families trying to buy their way into America's colorful urban past. Sometimes the incoming residents are the speculators, buying and renovating run-down houses themselves, knowing that their efforts and investment will pay handsome dividends when they decide to move again and sell their newly restored "townhouses."

Millions of dollars have been made in the unslumming of neighborhoods like historic Georgetown and Capitol Hill in Washington, D.C., Beacon Hill in Boston, Society Hill in Philadelphia, and the fashionable areas of Greenwich Village in New York. The spark of urban life continues to glow in these neighborhoods, but at a high price that can be afforded only by the reasonably well-to-do. The only reminders of the huge lower-income black population that inhabited Georgetown for many years are the domestics who return each day to serve the rich white society folks who live there now.

For all its appeal to the elite who can afford to enjoy it, unslumming may be the cruelest of all forms of slum real estate speculation. Old, run-down housing and neighborhoods are brought back to life, but there is no benefit for those who had to endure what had been those areas' dying years.

The greatest, although often hidden, cost of slum exploitation is in human victims. Today, they are predominantly black, Puerto Rican, and Chicano, although lower-income white families have been and still are exploited in some places. Many of these people already are the hard-core have-nots of society, for whom any real help must reach well beyond housing, but a surprisingly large number are steady wage earners trying hard to better themselves. They have been told that one way to get ahead is to own their homes, which should enable them to save money and earn a stake in society. They trustingly follow this advice, only to find the agents of middle-class, white society denying them homeownership opportunities and the agents of slum exploitation offering them only the illusion of homeownership. They invest what little savings they have and promise to pay as much each month as they can, only to discover they have been robbed, not with a gun but with a pen and the fine print of contracts and mortgages.

It is the "disinvestment" of these families that should concern us, not that of the real estate professionals who, when the slum gold mine peters out, can invest and profit elsewhere. These families trusted in the American Dream and were swindled. They lost the homes they thought they were buying or fell prey as renters to slum landlords. When a few of them complain, or withhold mortgage payments or rent, or go to court to seek redress, or simply abandon their wretched homes, the real estate industry howls and blames them for the deterioration of cities and their housing.

There are, of course, many destructive tenants and those who take advantage of naïve property owners who unintentionally become slum landlords. But their effect on housing and their threat to our cities is small indeed, when compared to the systematic exploitation of inner-city neighborhoods by the avarice of the real estate industry and the giants of finance and government who are their partners and allies.

2

Government Housing Programs: Builders' and Bankers' Relief

When George Romney, then governor of Michigan, was designated by President-elect Nixon in late 1968 to be Secretary of Housing and Urban Development (HUD), he was characteristically enthusiastic. It was "the exact position I wanted," he told reporters, and he was eager to get to work.

A year before, while touring a number of big cities during his abortive campaign for the Republican Presidential nomination, Romney had been genuinely shocked by the depressing slums he saw closely for the first time. As HUD Secretary he could do something about those slums and help provide a decent home for the one American in six who did not have one, just as he had helped revive American Motors years earlier as a young automobile executive.

Romney was confident that private business, with financial assistance from the government's wealth of housing programs, could help him at HUD. He was particularly counting on a large new batch of federal subsidies for private developers of housing for lower-income families. These new incentives were authorized by the Housing Act of 1968, which outgoing President Lyndon B. Johnson called a "Magna Charta to liberate our cities."

"So far as I can tell," Romney told congressmen considering his Cabinet nomination in January 1969, "the needed statutory tools are at hand. They may need some refinement, but certainly you've provided the tools."

But by 1972, his last year at HUD, a discouraged Romney was urging Congress to scrap that chest of tools, which he said had become a "statutory and administrative monstrosity," and White House budget officials were shutting off the flow of housing subsidy money until the programs' effectiveness could be reappraised during President Nixon's second term. Concerted use of the subsidies at great public expense during Romney's four years at HUD had failed to produce adequate housing for lower-income families and had made little impact on big city slums except, ironically, to help some of them spread. From inside HUD Romney learned that his experience was little different from those of federal housing officials who had served before him: All the public money spent on housing added up to "a $100 billion mistake."

"The truth is," Romney admitted just before resigning from HUD, "none of us are now sure what are the right things to do." The federal government, he said, was "throwing billions of dollars into these problem areas without making a dent on them"—a conclusion that by that time should have come as no surprise to the American public, which in 1972 had just gone through a year of government housing scandals. "There is graft. There is corruption. Kickbacks are a way of life," Romney told a national homebuilders' group when the scandals started to make headlines. "Thousands of the very families these programs were designed to help have been victimized by lax administration and unscrupulous operators."

The year had begun with revelations that real estate dealers in Detroit were defrauding the government of millions of dollars by selling virtually uninhabitable abandoned slum houses to unknowing poor families at highly inflated prices. In a typical case a real estate firm bought a run-down house in Detroit's east side slums in 1969 for $4,000, put a little paint on it, and sold it a few months later to a mother on welfare for $12,600. The woman did not actually pay that much herself, however. The dealer arranged for her to borrow the entire purchase price from a bank, with the Federal Housing Administration (FHA), a HUD agency, paying much of the interest on her mortgage to the bank and guaranteeing repayment of the entire loan should she default on her monthly installments.

As in thousands of similar transactions in Detroit, the real estate dealer had falsely certified that he spent several thousand dollars renovating this house and that the buyer was financially able to meet her share of the mortgage obligations. The house had not really been improved at all, and the welfare mother made only three mortgage payments on it before moving out of the dilapidated structure, leaving it empty and unsalable once again.

The deal's collapse posed no problem for the real estate dealer or the bank. The dealer had already collected his $12,600 from the mortgage loan made by the bank (minus an extra fee he paid the bank to get the loan) and had gotten out of the deal. The bank, in turn, was reimbursed the full $12,600 plus some interest by FHA under the terms of its loan guarantee. This left the government as the big loser. HUD repossessed the house but was unable to sell it to get FHA's money back. And after vandals gutted the empty structure, HUD had to pay to have it demolished, raising the government's total loss on the deal to $14,647.

In Detroit alone HUD already has lost $150 million on more than 10,000 repossessed houses like this one. Sixteen Detroit real estate dealers have been indicted on criminal charges, and several others have been suspended from further dealings with FHA for defrauding the government in these and perhaps 20,000 more slum home sales. HUD's financial loss in Detroit may double as it gets stuck with thousands more of these houses. So many have already been left standing empty or been demolished by HUD that large sections of Detroit's inner city are as empty of life and full of rubble as the ghost blocks of Bedford-Stuyvesant in New York.

When a congressional subcommittee headed by Representative John S. Monagan of Connecticut went to Detroit to examine the fraud firsthand, a subcommittee investigator said: "If what we found in Detroit is true only to a degree elsewhere, the residential areas of a number of large cities are in serious trouble and the FHA insurance fund [for loan guarantees] faces tremendous losses." Indeed, as 1972 went on, it became only too clear that the scandal in Detroit was typical of the way federal housing subsidies had been abused throughout the country.

In Washington, D.C., Ada A. Wabash, who earned $410 a month as a night cleaning woman in a federal government office, was offered a home in the southeast section of the city for $14,000. All she had to do was make a $50 down payment. The rest of the money paid to a real estate dealer for the house was a $13,950 loan from a local savings and loan association. Normally, the monthly payment on a mortgage loan that size would be $123, but Mrs. Wabash had to pay only $56 a month. The federal government was to pay the other $67, which was interest on the mortgage to the savings and loan. For Mrs. Wabash, who had been living with her four children in a dreary public housing apartment, this was an unexpected chance to "get out of the project."

But when she moved into her new home, which she had toured only briefly before, her dream was shattered. The new-looking furnace in the kitchen did not function and turned out to be unrepairable. None of the light switches worked, and only two electrical outlets could be found in the entire house. Floorboards were broken and loose, and window shades pasted on the walls hid huge cracks. Unknown to Mrs. Wabash, the real estate dealer who sold her the home for $14,000 had bought it a few weeks earlier for just $7,500 from a widow who had not lived in it for years.

Like Mrs. Wabash, low-income buyers of old houses sold with FHA mortgage subsidies and guarantees have frequently been greatly disappointed by what they found when they moved in. Not being experienced house hunters, they did not at first notice the wall holes hidden by flimsy new wallpaper, the rotted floors covered with cheap carpet, the leaky pipes that flood wall spaces as soon as the water is turned on, or the faulty wiring that makes the house a fire hazard. Nor have they any way of knowing that the real estate dealer is selling them the house for twice as much or more than he paid for it himself. One couple in Paterson, New Jersey, unknowingly paid $20,000 for a house a dealer bought four months earlier for only $1,800 after its previous owner, who had converted it from a tavern, was refused a city license to use it as rental housing.

Both the big mark-ups and poor condition of these houses must have been known, however, to local FHA officials who are required to inspect each house before approving it for an FHA loan guarantee and subsidy. When two real estate dealers and seven home repair contractors were indicted in Chicago for FHA home swindles in the slums there, they were joined in court by four local FHA officials, who were charged with accepting bribes to falsely certify that the homes had been inspected and approved by the Chicago FHA office. Forty individuals and ten corporations were indicted for defrauding FHA of $200 million in New York City. Among them were eight local FHA employees also charged with taking bribes and with falsely appraising slum houses sold under FHA auspices at far more than their real market values to support inflated prices being charged by real estate dealers. One New York FHA official was formerly vice-president of a Long Island savings and loan association that profited from the FHA-financed slum loan scheme. An officer of the well-known credit investigating firm of Dun and Bradstreet also was indicted in New York and charged with falsifying credit reports on black and Puerto Rican homebuyers to make them appear financially able to pay the inflated prices with FHA subsidy help. FHA had to repossess more than 2,500 slum homes in New York.

When Senator Philip Hart of Michigan held congressional hearings on the New York scandals, he was told some of the indicted real estate dealers there were old-fashioned blockbusters still operating in Brooklyn and Queens with the help of FHA. New York secretary of state John P. Lomenzo called FHA financing the "key" to present blockbusting in these areas; he said seventy-five slum real estate dealers were now operating where there had recently been only ten in the Crown Heights–East Flatbush neighborhood. The testimony also showed that New York banks, including Chase Manhattan, were financing many of the blockbusters' sales with loans made through middleman mortgage dealers, one of whom also was indicted for defrauding the government. Some of the mortgage dealers sold the FHA-backed mortgages from fraudulent slum home deals to other institutional investors, including labor unions, insurance companies, and a New York state employees' retirement fund. Whenever the deals went sour, of course, these investors were repaid their money and interest due on it by FHA. In this way the government has been guaranteeing unconscionable profits to slum real estate speculators and their hidden financial backers selling houses fit only for a wrecker's ball to the poor.

This also has been true of a matching program for the construction and sale of new homes to low-income families with mortgages guaranteed and subsidized by FHA. In Seattle several buyers of these homes have sued FHA, complaining that the plumbing in their new houses is faulty, their roofs leak, the electrical wiring is defective, plaster is already cracking, some ceilings are falling, and their heating is inadequate. Some of the houses were never finished, even though FHA inspectors approved them for sale. The builders used cheap, poor quality materials to keep their construction costs down to as little as half of the $15,000 to $20,000 they were paid for each home.

Staff investigators for the housing subcommittee of the House Banking and Currency Committee toured new houses produced under this program in Everett, Washington, and Elmwood, Missouri, and found the construction "of such poor quality and the cost so questionable that the projects can best be described as 'instant slums.'" The floors in the Everett houses sagged so much, according to a staff report, "they could best be described as trampolines." An investigator described how it was possible "to stand in the kitchen and move your weight from foot to foot and rattle objects in closets on the other side of the house." When the second floor bathtub was filled, water ran off from its drain inside the wall and poured out of first floor electrical outlets. Holes could be made in doors of the houses, the congressional investigator recounted, by simply leaning a hand against one of them "without exerting too great a pressure."

The Seattle families who have sued the government want to keep their homes and are continuing to make payments on them while demanding that someone correct the defects. But many other families in Seattle and elsewhere across the country have given up and left their brand new but shoddily built homes to be repossessed by FHA. In Everett the congressional investigator found that one entire subdivision of fifty-seven new subsidized houses had already been abandoned.

"Instant slum" also best describes thousands of apartment buildings that private developers have thrown up and rented to the poor under still another government subsidy program. The developer is assured a fixed profit from the proceeds of the project's construction loan, which is guaranteed and subsidized by FHA. Some builders also found ways to pocket some of the loan money earmarked for construction costs or have profited further by buying land for the project at a low price under a fictitious name, selling it to themselves at a big mark-up, and claiming a reimbursement for the higher price from the loan proceeds. After the apartments are built and rented out, the developer can claim large depreciation deductions for them on his income tax return and shield from taxation hundreds of thousands of dollars of income from other sources each year. Tax experts have estimated that in these ways developers can realize from the subsidized apartment projects benefits equal to a profit of from 20 to 50 per cent or more annually on the relatively small initial investment they must make.

One developer, Arthur L. Walters, who has put up federally subsidized apartment projects in the St. Louis and Washington, D.C., areas, created with several associates a miniconglomerate of interlocking firms that soak up all the profit from each project they invest in. Their own mortgage company, C. W. Cobb and Associates, makes the construction loan and collects the mortgage interest subsidy from the federal government. Their own development companies, Chesapeake Associates and Trans-American Research and Development Corporation, receive the mortgage money and develop the project, collecting the allowable developer's profit and realizing all the tax benefits. Their own construction corporation, P. G. Corporation, builds the project and keeps the allowable construction profit. Their own land firm, American Small Business Investment Company, buys the land for each project and sells it to the development companies at a paper profit that enlarges the project's subsidy from the government. And their own property management firm, Imperial Management, handles the initial rental of each project and keeps a fixed percentage of each month's total rental income.

"Here is a guy," one HUD official said of Walters, "who covers the whole field of construction, and he's getting profit out of every aspect available, and he's not unique in that regard."

Most of the developers do not necessarily expect any profit from the rental income and so do not care especially whether or not it yields enough money to keep up the buildings properly. They also do little to screen the buildings' tenants. If after a few years—once the project's tax benefits have been largely exhausted—the housing has deteriorated so much that steady tenants leave and the rent no longer covers the mortgage payments, the owner simply stops making them and allows FHA to repossess the project. Developers have pocketed their profits and then abandoned hundreds of subsidized apartment projects in dozens of cities, from Boston, New York, and Camden, to Chicago, Dallas, Wichita, and Seattle.

Fearing just this kind of exploitation of the program by some private developers, Congress also wanted nonprofit groups with enough money—usually large churches and labor unions—to sponsor projects and own them when they were finished. However, these groups have nearly always been inexperienced in real estate, so that, in addition to their difficulties with logistics and government red tape, they frequently have been at the mercy of the developers they hire to build and manage the huge apartment projects. Many of these developers have channeled as much construction loan money to themselves as they could, often by building cheaply and then spending little money on upkeep. If the nonprofit sponsor is not able to monitor all this and stop it, the church or union suddenly discovers that its intended good deed has become a terrible disservice to society and another burden for taxpayers when the government is forced to take over a bankrupt project.

Just outside Washington, D.C., in a lower-income neighborhood of suburban Prince George's County, Maryland, ground was broken in 1968 by then HUD Secretary Robert Weaver for Baber Village, an apartment project conceived as a model for nonprofit sponsorship of government-subsidized housing for the poor. The sponsor of Baber Village was the African Methodist Episcopal Church, a black denomination. But the actual development of the $2.9 million project was carried out by the Charles Burton Construction Company, headed by Charles S. Bresler, a former Maryland legislator, and the Soble Construction Company of Atlantic City.

By 1972, just three years after the clump of 3-story walk-up buildings containing 200 apartments had been completed, Baber Village was a slum. Its roofs leaked, its sewers backed up, the steep ground of its hilly site was eroding, the plumbing was a mess, and the cheaply built walls of its apartments were filled with holes. "This was an inferior, poorly planned project from the beginning," complained one county official, who said the builders had found in the church "a patsy to unload this place on."

Church officials did not know how to oversee the construction or how to screen the project's tenants, mostly welfare families whose rent was also partly subsidized by the federal government under the experimental rent supplement program. Management of the project was in Bresler's hands at the beginning, and somehow a number of disruptive tenants had gotten in, including drug addicts who terrorized the rest of the residents and the surrounding middle-class black neighborhood. Many rent-paying tenants moved out, and apartments in a number of the seventeen buildings were already boarded up. The church became financially unable to keep the project, and HUD had to repossess Baber Village.

Soon, Romney estimated in congressional testimony in 1972, HUD will be stuck with 240,000 mostly uninhabitable repossessed housing units "with little resale value except at catastrophic levels of loss." The government stands to lose at least $2.4 billion on these abandoned houses and apartments in cities all across the country. And that is just a fraction of the public money that has been sunk with little effect into the entire range of government housing programs, including FHA subsidies, public housing projects, slum clearance, and urban renewal.

In April 1972 Romney was asked by the House Appropriations Committee to explain why fifty-four row houses being built as public housing for welfare families in an urban renewal project in Washington, D.C., were costing the government an astounding $76,000 apiece. Romney could not speak about this case in detail, but one reason for the high cost was that the government, instead of building the housing itself, was paying several hundred thousands of dollars in subsidies above the actual cost of construction to private investors to build the row houses and turn them over to the local public housing agency. Another reason was the high price HUD paid private property owners for the land for the project: $1.5 million for 2.33 acres—more than $640,000 per acre and about $28,000 per row house—in a particularly run-down slum area partly destroyed by rioting after Martin Luther King's assassination in 1968.

Before the riots, in 1963, when the neighborhood's property values should have been higher, a New York–based real estate company bought a 1.2-acre parcel of the land in question for just $398,000. Knowing that the area was being designated for future urban renewal, the firm tore down the old buildings on the property and leased it as a parking lot, awaiting the day it could be sold at a sizable profit to the local HUD-funded urban renewal agency. Six years later, when that agency, with HUD's approval and money, bought the parcel as part of the land for the fifty-four townhouses, it rewarded the real estate firm's patience by paying its asking price of $755,000. That gave the firm a profit of $355,000 for slum property that, according to one local real estate expert, was probably worth little more than $200,000 on the private market. Romney admitted to the congressmen that slum property owners commonly receive such windfalls in urban renewal areas where the government's presence creates "an artificially high market for such land."

By the end of 1972 four congressional committees, Senate Judiciary, House Government Operations, House Appropriations, and House Banking and Currency, were investigating various HUD housing scandals. They were joined by the General Accounting Office (an arm of Congress that audits the government), HUD's own Office of Inspector General (revitalized and expanded by Romney), and assorted federal prosecutors and grand juries all across the country. Articles like one in *Fortune* headlined "Housing Subsidies Are a Grand Illusion" were featured in news and financial magazines. Another headline, in *House and Home,* a housing industry trade journal, summed it all up: "No biz like scandal biz: Housing becoming our most investigated activity."

If they were to look carefully enough beyond the obvious scandals, the investigators would find an expensive house of cards built by the real estate industry over the years with federal housing money. Even without outright fraud, nearly every government program since the 1930s has worked primarily for the benefit of the real estate industry, rather than the poor and ill-housed for whom they were supposedly intended. Property owners, realtors, builders, and bankers have all benefited from $11 billion in direct subsidies and tens of billions more in government loan guarantees.

When, for instance, the real estate industry was hit hard by the business recession and credit squeeze of the late 1960s, it was propped up with federal subsidy money conveniently provided by the Housing Act of 1968. By 1971 the federal subsidy programs were paying the real estate industry $1.4 billion a year and financing one of every four new housing units produced. Yet much of the housing built, sold, and rented with that money has turned out to be virtually uninhabitable. Far from being the generous welfare programs for the unfortunate depicted by both supporters and critics, the Housing Act of 1968 subsidies have proven instead to be builders' and bankers' relief.

The U.S. Government had first gotten into the housing business under similar if more dramatic circumstances during the Depression. Until then, housing was left entirely to "free enterprise." Buying a house meant making a down payment of at least a third of the purchase price and keeping up monthly payments on a high-interest, short-term mortgage that often left a balance of several thousand dollars due at the end of its 7- to 10-year term. Temporary unemployment, illness, or the inability to make the big final payment usually meant losing one's home and all the money that had been put into it. Mortgage holders about to foreclose became the villains of popular novels, plays, and silent films. Still, the private housing industry had boomed along with everything else during the expansive 1920s when so many people seemed to have so much money, and the banks overextended themselves by loaning out too much in their rush to collect more and more interest.

When the Depression came, millions of Americans were unable to keep up their mortgage payments and lost their homes. Banks and savings and loan associations could not collect on the mortgages or sell repossessed houses to cover the debt. They had no money to pay interest on savings or even to return all of every depositor's savings on demand. And with no market left, the construction and sale of homes dropped off sharply to almost nothing.

To help the real estate industry and banking community recover, the federal government first stabilized the lenders by assuming supervision and insuring the deposits of banks and savings and loan associations and by spending $3 billion to buy their problem home loans and lower their interest rates to levels that homeowners could afford. Urbanologist Charles Abrams called it a program to "bail out the lenders," because of the public money poured into private financial institutions, although it happened to help the average homeowner, too.

Then in 1935 the Federal Housing Administration was created to guarantee home mortgage loans made by savings and loans and banks. If the homebuyer defaulted on his mortgage payments and the house could not be sold for enough money to cover the outstanding balance and interest due, the government would pay the difference. As money was eagerly loaned out on this no-risk basis, realtors and builders prospered along with the financial institutions. Individual builders needed to invest little cash of their own because money was so easily borrowed. "The formula for providing new homes," Abrams observed, "was fashioned so that builders needed no investment to venture and lenders assumed no risk in lending," a formula, backed by government money, that is still in use today.

The middle-class homeowner has also benefited from these FHA loan guarantees. Not only is it easier for him to obtain mortgage money to buy a home, but the fast-growing market created by FHA loan activity has pushed prices steadily upward, creating for many homeowners sizable profits when they sell their houses. Thus, the homeowner himself has become a part of the government-supported real estate industry.

Homeowners are also subsidized through the deductions claimed on income tax returns for home mortgage interest and local property taxes. This subsidy is not available to renters, many of whom are lower-income families, even though they are usually charged in their rents for the mortgage interest and property taxes their landlords pay (and which those landlords can deduct from *their* taxable incomes). In 1971 homeowners alone were subsidized by a total of $5.7 billion in income tax they did not pay because of the special deductions they are allowed. This practice also acts as an indirect subsidy for builders and realtors who are able to build and sell more houses at higher prices because the tax deductions act as a potent incentive for homebuying.

The days of the Depression are nearly four decades behind us, yet the private housing industry and homeowners—middle- and upper-class America—are still being subsidized by the government through FHA loan guarantees and special tax benefits. For the "other America," the millions of poor and low-wage working-class families that author Michael Harrington reintroduced to our generation, government housing programs have been far less beneficial.

The first federal program for low-income renters began in 1934 when the Public Works Administration project started building public housing for the government to lease at low rents to the poor. Fifty projects with room for 22,000 families went up in thirty cities, but the project ran into disabling problems. The federal government paid so much for land, materials, and even labor that it was forced to charge rents that only better-off working-class families could afford. At the same time local governments and the real estate industry attacked the program, charging that the projects paid no local property taxes and competed unfairly with private rental housing. Several cities stopped projects from being built within their borders, and the real estate industry put great lobbying pressure on Congress to gut the program.

In 1937 a new arrangement was worked out and approved by Congress whereby local government housing agencies would pay private contractors to build public housing with money from the sale of tax-exempt municipal bonds. The federal government would repay the bonds and give the local public housing agencies extra money to help lower the rents for the elderly, the very poor, and tenants with large families. The local agencies were to use all the rental income they collected to pay for maintenance of the projects. There are now nearly 900,000 units of public housing in U.S. cities —space, if all of it were in good repair, for about one of every ten Americans who cannot afford decent private housing.

Although much of the real estate industry continued to oppose public housing as unfair competition, the program's built-in potential for financial and social failure was eventually to work to the industry's great advantage. Most public housing was built on cleared slum land still surrounded by decayed areas or on other sites nobody else wanted alongside railroad tracks or in warehouse districts outside the better neighborhoods, and many suburbs have refused to build any public housing at all.

Yet the land available for public housing has still been so expensive that cost-conscious bureaucrats felt they had to crowd it with as many living units as possible, first in egg-crate tenements and later in huge high-rise towers. Congressional watchdogs effectively prevented public money from being "wasted" on large lawns, trees, fancy playgrounds, balconies, air conditioning, or other amenities, especially facilities for the large numbers of children in public housing projects. In design and construction public housing has been consistently and depressingly spartan.

Even where local housing authorities have paid private developers to build public housing with special federal grants authorized by the 1968 Housing Act, most of the resulting projects have still been tightly packed instant ghettos of cheaply constructed buildings lacking such ordinary facilities as recreation areas, stores, and schools, much less the special social services needed for such large concentrations of large, poor families. The Atlanta Housing Authority, for example, recently paid $15 million to a private builder for a huge new public housing project, euphemistically called East Lake Meadows, where five thousand poor people, the overwhelming majority of them children, have been crammed into eight hundred low walk-up and high-rise units on just 59 acres of land in a remote corner of Atlanta that lies in suburban DeKalb County. When East Lake Meadows was opened, it had no schools, day-care centers, stores, playgrounds, medical facilities, or welfare services. Everything was a distant automobile or bus ride away. The school that was finally built is already badly overcrowded. Children must still play in the streets and parking lots that cover most of the ground not occupied by buildings. Because many of the families are fatherless and most of the mothers have several children, including scores of families with eight or more offspring, the older youths run out of control and terrorize the project, dealing in narcotics, bullying younger children, robbing adults, and sometimes shooting each other. DeKalb County's suburban police force, which did not ask for all this trouble, is purposefully slow to respond to calls for help, making matters even worse.

The wear and tear (and vandalism) from so many large, poor families jammed together has overwhelmed most public housing projects and their limited grounds. Many recently built projects are already slums and likely will not last half as long as it will take for their construction bonds to be paid off. Maintenance costs have soared so high that rental income can no longer cover them. Local public housing agencies have been forced to raise rents again and again, until some poor families are paying as much as three-fourths of their monthly income (often welfare checks) for shelter. Tenants of many projects have waged rent strikes to protest the increases, which has further reduced funds for maintenance.

To alleviate this problem HUD began, in 1969, giving local public housing agencies more subsidy money to reduce the rents of all tenants to a maximum of 25 per cent of their family income. But the unexpectedly large cost of this effort forced HUD to go back on its promise in 1972 and to cut off the extra subsidy payments. Local agencies had to raise rents again, more tenants went on rent strikes, and the deterioration of projects in one city after another accelerated. Tenants tiring of this vicious circle have been moving out of public housing in large numbers, even when it means returning to run-down, privately owned housing. They have left behind tens of thousands of public housing apartments no one else will move into, run by bankrupt public housing agencies that have become slum landlords.

There is no better single example of the failure of U.S. public housing than the Pruitt-Igoe towers in St. Louis. Designed and built in the early 1950s, when high-rise apartments were becoming quite popular with middle-class apartment tenants, Pruitt-Igoe's basic housing form was to be an 11-story high-rise apartment building with an elevator that stopped at every other floor (to speed up its trips) and a breezeway corridor on the outside of each floor, on which the architects expected children to play and their mothers to visit and enjoy the view. The designers envisioned the towers spotted on the 57-acre site amid low 2- and 3-story buildings, parks, and recreation areas. *Architectural Forum* praised the design in 1951 and predicted that it would "save not only people, but money." In the end it did neither.

The first mistake was imposing the trappings of vertical, middle-class housing on large, poor families, many just a generation removed from Southern farms. Middle-class tenants prize views from high-rise apartments and, when they feel cooped up, can always get into their cars or pay for transportation to stores, places of entertainment, or anywhere else. They can surround themselves at home with expensive self-entertainment gadgets. They also bring relatively few children into high-rise apartments. Poor families, however, depend more on easily accessible street life for their daily necessities and social intercourse. The absence of two parents in so many lower-income homes means that children are often left unsupervised when their single parent is at work. The breezeways at Pruitt-Igoe thus became dangerous places for unwatched smaller children, three of whom fell to their deaths, and the acquired turf of teenage toughs and drug addicts, who, particularly in the absence of adult men, often terrorized other tenants. Partly because of the extra floor between each stop, the elevators also became the haunts of muggers.

The problems in the design of the tower buildings were compounded by the housing authority's elimination of all the low-rise buildings and most of the park and recreation space from the plan in its effort to get the most for its money. Instead, more towers were built, and the project's population density doubled. Thirty-three 11-story towers eventually were built in dense rows on the cleared slum land. The only view from most windows was of the apartment building next door or the remaining slums that surrounded the project. Children had little place to play except in the building's stairwells and the dangerous breezeways.

The crowding was exacerbated by the concentration of so many poor families (at the beginning, 3,000 families—10,000 people—almost all of them poor and black) with all their social problems in one place. "It was clearly understood from the beginning that it was going to house only the poorest of the poor," one of Pruitt-Igoe's designers later remembered with regret. Most of the families had been displaced from slums torn down for urban renewal elsewhere in St. Louis and were unable to afford any other housing. "It was all one class," the designer said, "without even different gradations of poverty." Pruitt-Igoe, sociologist Lee Rainwater concluded, "condensed into one 57-acre tract all of the problems and difficulties that arise from race and poverty—and all of the impatience, indifference and hostility with which our society has so far dealt with these problems."

The Pruitt-Igoe towers began to disintegrate physically and socially almost immediately after the $100 million project was completed in 1955. By 1971 efforts to keep the buildings in good repair had run up a $2 million operating deficit (due in part to a 9-month rent strike in answer to increasing rents and decreasing maintenance in 1969). The buildings were in such poor condition and so beset by violence that four-fifths of the apartments were abandoned by their tenants. By 1973 all but six of the buildings, which were not yet twenty years old, had been boarded up or torn down. The 30-foot-high pile of concrete rubble from the demolished buildings remained on the site for months, serving as a ghoulish playground for children with no other place to go. The St. Louis public housing authority tried to get the federal government to take over Pruitt-Igoe and five other local high-rise public housing projects because, one commissioner said, "we're out of money." But HUD wouldn't take them.

In mid-1973 the St. Louis public housing authority decided to move the last 2,000 tenants from Pruitt-Igoe and tear down the remaining buildings by the end of the year. All that remained was to find other homes for the hard-core residue of residents (four-fifths of the remaining 587 families are on welfare)—in itself no easy job. "There must be an honest recognition," said Thomas Costello, executive director of the housing authority, "that this development, Pruitt-Igoe, has been a complete and colossal failure from a social, moral and economic standpoint."

Maintenance of public housing projects also has come to a virtual standstill in other cities throughout the country. Rent collections are sporadic. More and more buildings are being abandoned. At a time when the Census Bureau has estimated that 3.5 million

American families still live in essentially uninhabitable slums, the housing the government was supposedly providing as an alternative is itself a slum and increasingly stands empty.

Public housing should not be written off as an unworkable concept. It simply has not been given a fair chance in this country. It has been segregated in ready-built ghettos of problem families, naïvely designed, built as cheaply as possible, and given all the homeyness of prisons by government officials under constant pressure from real estate interests and homeowners who fear the alternatives. Public housing for families other than the very poor would compete with private housing. Public housing scattered throughout a city and its suburbs (as some public housing agencies have tried to do recently, only to run up against fierce opposition—the demonstrations in Forest Hills, New York, are a good example) would be bad for nearby property values. Public housing with balconies, air conditioning, attractive grounds, or swimming pools would seem an extravagant use of public money to the average homeowner, even though his own $40,000 split level is, through tax deductions, in effect, subsidized by nonhomeowning taxpayers. Clearly, public housing in the United States has been programmed to fail.

Predictably, spokesmen for the real estate industry have seized on the problems of public housing to argue that only private developers "tested in the marketplace" can provide livable housing for any segment of the citizenry. If the economics of that marketplace make it financially impossible for the private housing industry to serve poor and lower-income families on its own, the argument goes, then government should help it do the job. The federal government should put up the money in subsidies and private interests should build, own, sell, and rent the housing.

This argument has always sounded good, particularly to the ears of Congress. And literally dozens of different kinds of subsidy programs have been tried. But all have produced the same results as public housing—new slums for the poor and ill-housed and billions of dollars of public money wasted—but with one difference: The private real estate industry, from the bankers to builders to slum real estate speculators, has made a bundle every time.

After World War II Congress decided to subsidize the private development of apartments for returning servicemen through what became known as Section 608 of the housing laws. The FHA guaranteed loans made by banks and other financial institutions to private builders for this purpose. In addition to making the loans risk-free for the lenders, FHA allowed each builder to obtain loan money equal to the "estimated replacement value" of the new building. This meant the builder got as much money as he and the lender estimated the building would be worth when it was finished, *not* how much it actually cost to put it up. Since the actual construction cost would always be less than the market value of the finished product in a time of rapidly increasing housing prices, the builder would be assured a sizable profit without investing any of his own money. The lender also benefited from extra fees paid to it out of the loan money, in addition to interest. The rental income from the building was to pay off the loan plus interest to the lender over forty years' time. If anything went wrong, the government would repay the loan. The builder was not liable for a penny. It was a deal no clever developer could turn down.

The object of the 608 game was to keep construction costs as low as possible in order to have more loan money left over as profit. The program produced 446,000 apartments between the end of World War II and 1954, but it also produced more than its share of scandal. Many builders realized much bigger profits than anticipated by making rooms as small as possible, using cheaper materials, keeping costs down in other ways, and inflating the estimate of a building's value when finished.

In a typical example, the Congress Construction Corporation, controlled by E. C. O'Driscoll of White Plains, New York, received $7.3 million in construction loan money to build the huge Congress Park project of 670 apartments in southeast Washington, D.C., during 1949 and 1950. According to a suit later filed against the firm by the government, however, Congress Construction put only $5.9 million into construction of the 2- and 3-story brick buildings and kept the rest as a 25 per cent "windfall" profit of $1.4 million.

It was not long before the project's rental income was no longer sufficient to cover both the payments due on the huge construction mortgage and maintenance of the dozens of apartment buildings. When deterioration started, the apartments' original tenants moved out, and by 1970, when the project was just twenty years old and more than half of its construction loan was still unrepaid, Congress

Park was a ghost town of abandoned buildings with torn venetian blinds flapping through shattered windows on a windy hilltop in the nation's capital.

Discovery of the 608 program's exorbitant profits led to its repeal by Congress in 1954, but its legacy remains: tens of thousands of empty and uninhabitable apartment buildings, similar to those in many public housing projects. Like Congress Park, many of the 608 projects are now owned by the federal government, which repossessed them when their owners stopped paying on the mortgages and no one else would buy the buildings. Despite shocking congressional hearings at the time on abuses of the program, the lesson of 608 was quickly forgotten by congressmen and government officials, who continued to see some sort of public subsidies for the private real estate industry as the answer to the nation's persistent shortage of decent housing.

"A decent home" for every American was precisely the goal set by Congress when it produced the hefty Housing Act of 1949 after several years' gestation. Part of the bill authorized more government spending for slum clearance and public housing, which was strongly opposed by real estate interests in crowded public hearings. But that opposition was neutralized by another part of the bill, praised by several real estate industry spokesmen who correctly saw it as a potential bonanza.

This new program, which offered a different kind of subsidy to the real estate industry, was urban renewal. Under the 1949 legislation, a local government could use federal money to plan the redevelopment of any run-down or even partially deteriorated neighborhood of its choosing. A good early example is the area south of Washington Square in New York, where some houses and several old industrial and commercial buildings stood after World War II. The city of New York drew a plan for redevelopment of the area that met with federal approval, and the city bought the property for the $41 million considered to be its fair market value. The city then sold the land for only $20 million to private investors and developers who eventually built new apartment buildings on it.

The $21 million reduction in the price of the New York project's land is the big subsidy in urban renewal for private investors and developers. They have been able to buy land in prime locations at a fraction of its going market price, enabling them to make bigger profits by tearing down the old buildings and putting up new ones. They also have been able to buy the land in large tracts ideal for more lucrative, large-scale development projects without going to the trouble and additional expense of themselves buying it up from a number of small property owners, some of whom might not want to sell. The city has already done that, using its power of eminent domain to condemn and buy the property of holdouts. In recent years, most cities also have paid to clear urban renewal land, improve its utilities and roads, and make other public improvements that sometimes have included big public buildings (a new city hall in Boston, a government office complex in Cleveland) that enhance the profitability of private office buildings developed in the project area.

There are incentives in urban renewal for the city governments, too. The most important is that the federal government has put up most of the cash for the reduction in the price of land sold to private developers. The federal government is supposed to pay two-thirds of a project's cost and the city government one-third. But the city is allowed to count as part of its contribution any public improvements it makes in the urban renewal area, even if it would have had to make them anyway and even though it can pay for them through the sale of municipal bonds instead of cash from its coffers. In this way, the federal government has usually contributed much more than two-thirds of the huge amount of cash needed.

In Boston urban renewal director Edward Logue, a master strategist who learned how to play the game in New Haven, Connecticut, before moving on to Boston (and, more recently, to New York City), at one point had spent only $72,500 in cash from Boston's treasury to qualify for a $105 million contribution from the federal government. On top of this the federal government paid 90 per cent of the payroll and overhead for Boston's urban renewal agency, including all but $5,000 of Logue's $30,000 starting salary and 80 per cent of a $450,000 remodeling of the agency's office.

Another attraction of urban renewal for local governments has been the large increase in property tax revenue from redeveloped areas. Before renewal three particular blocks of slums on New York's East Side had been paying $205,000 a year in property taxes—and that much only when the city was able to collect it from elusive slum landlords. After redevelopment as the Kips Bay Plaza Urban Renewal Project, the 1,118 luxury apartments and a few small stores in the new high-rise buildings on the same ground paid $775,000 in annual taxes to the borough of Manhattan.

Conceived by some of its original congressional sponsors as a way of building better housing for slum dwellers, urban renewal instead became what the real estate industry and city governments wanted: a generous federal subsidy for the development of high-profit complexes of offices, luxury apartments, and grand civic improvements in or adjacent to local business centers. A survey of 1,155 urban renewal projects under way by June 1966 showed that two-thirds of them were in areas that had been predominantly residential. And many of those that remained residential, like Kips Bay Plaza in Manhattan, replaced low-rent housing with the most expensive luxury apartments the market would bear. Rents at Kips Bay turned out to be three times higher than the New York City redevelopment authority had promised the public. They ranged from $141 to $435 per month when the apartments were finished in the early 1960s and have nearly doubled since.

More than half of the urban renewal money spent in Philadelphia has produced new offices and government buildings, along with renovation of the Independence Hall area for tourists. Half of the balance that has gone for housing has produced luxury apartments for upper-income families. In an urban renewal project on Philadelphia's historic Society Hill, low-rent housing was demolished and replaced by luxury high-rises. These attracted to the area around them more upper-income families who bought old townhouses, evicted their tenants, and expensively remodeled them.

Inevitably, in addition to the built-in legal profit potential of urban renewal, there also has been scandal in the Philadelphia program. One of the owners of a "substantial interest" in the firm awarded the lucrative contract to manage the completed urban renewal office project across the street from City Hall was none other than the chairman of the city's urban renewal agency. Elsewhere in Philadelphia a federally funded urban renewal program for the renovation of run-down slum houses for lower-income families was exploited by slum landlords who made exorbitant profits selling the houses to the city for renovation and by contractors who overcharged the urban renewal agency, and ultimately federal taxpayers, for shoddy rehabilitation work. Forty-seven local firms and officials were eventually indicted for fraud.

People who were living in neighborhoods chosen for urban re-

newal in most cities have seldom been able to afford any of the new
housing that has replaced their old homes. Even if new housing had
been built in their price range, they would have had to endure years
of waiting between the time their homes were demolished and the
new buildings were finished. Studies by the federal government
have shown that many families displaced by urban renewal have
found improved housing elsewhere, but usually at much higher
prices. Hundreds of thousands of displaced families have simply
been forced to move from one slum neighborhood to another.
When new housing has been built for these urban renewal refugees,
it has generally turned out, like Pruitt-Igoe in St. Louis, to be public housing slums.

Because an area can be selected for urban renewal even if only
20 per cent of its housing is run-down, eager real estate promoters
and their allies in city government have, in the name of progress,
destroyed some neighborhoods that were still healthy places in
which to live. Such was the case of the 38-block West End neighborhood in downtown Boston. Between 8,000 and 10,000 people,
the majority of them Italians, had lived in the old low-rent, 5-story
apartment houses in West End. Although the buildings were
crowded tightly together, a condition criticized by Boston city
planners, there was plenty of room inside them because they had
been built at the turn of the century for larger families. The narrow
but lively streets were filled with neighborhood stores, and a good
part of downtown Boston's prime shopping areas and centers for
employment were within walking distance of West End.

Sociologist Herbert J. Gans, who made a landmark study of
West End's working-class residents in 1957 and 1958, shortly before the bulldozers invaded the neighborhood, concluded that West
End was anything but a slum. Thanks to a remarkable absence of
blockbusting and inner-city real estate speculation, the rents in
West End were lower than the average for Boston's public housing
at the time and allowed tenants to save money to extensively mod-
ernize and redecorate the insides of their apartments, as a majority
had done. The low rents also allowed older residents to stay in the
neighborhood after retirement, giving it a variety of age groups so
often missing in today's compartmentalized cities and suburbs.

Only the exteriors of the neighborhood's buildings were run-
down, Gans explained, "because West Enders pay little attention

to the status symbols connected with housing. . . . Nor do they regard the high density as a problem, except for parking. Privacy is not evaluated here as highly as it is in middle-class culture, and West Enders consider it more important to have large numbers of relatives, friends, and neighbors at hand."

But the worn building facades and crowded streets provided planners and developers with the excuse they needed to convince a middle-class public that West End needed redevelopment. They chose it over much more deteriorated and socially disintegrated neighborhoods that were truly slums because, as Gans explained, there was much more profit potential for new high-rent housing in West End's location between the Charles River and the downtown commercial and civic center of Boston. The city condemned and bought up West End's property for $7.40 per square foot and made it available at $1.40 a square foot to a private real estate investment group that included the former campaign manager for then Mayor John Hynes.

The wreckers came, and out of the rubble of what had been the vibrant West End arose stark apartment towers on lifeless pads of concrete and lawn. Lost to Boston, besides West End's social vitality, were its 2,300 units of rare low-rent, perfectly decent housing. Its residents, who refused to move into much less desirable public housing projects, had to hunt all over the city and its suburbs for new places to live. Often they could not find housing as well suited to their taste as their former dwellings. Usually the neighborhood was not nearly so congenial and included few of their old friends, who were now dispersed throughout Boston. And nearly always the price of the new housing was much higher than they had been paying in West End.

The trauma of relocation is no less severe for very poor black families living in acknowledged slums that have been cleared for other urban renewal projects. More than 10,000 such families—over half of them with annual incomes of less than $3,000, the official poverty level at the time—were pushed out of the southwest quadrant of Washington, D.C., during the 1950s to make room for new government offices and luxury apartment houses in the nation's largest urban renewal project. The 550 acres of delapidated row houses, separated by a railroad viaduct from the Capitol grounds, were all razed, except for several blocks of newer public housing that still stand there today, segregated from the new development in many places by high fences. The neglected condition of the public housing contrasts sharply with the expensively built and maintained apartment and townhouse homes of middle- and upper-income whites and blacks.

Black families who had been living in private housing in southwest Washington simply lost their homes. Their removal en masse was considered crucial to the economic success of the project. Developers feared that whites could not otherwise be attracted back into what had become known as a notorious "Negro slum." Rental agents became particularly irritated when former black residents would return on Sundays to curiously examine the model apartments of the posh buildings that had replaced their old homes; black employees were hired to tactfully shunt these people aside so that white prospective tenants would not get the wrong idea. Agents for many of the new apartment houses asked qualifying black prospects, including government officials and professional people, to wait until each building was half to three-fourths rented before moving in. It is not surprising that this was the project that earned for urban renewal the epithet "black removal."

There were feeble attempts to help the blacks of southwest Washington to relocate in decent housing elsewhere in the city. But most who had any money at all were left to become easy prey to blockbusters and slum landlords then exploiting neighborhoods just north of the Capitol. The poorest of the refugees were forced to move in with relatives and friends in other slums until their names came up on the waiting list for relocation public housing being built in less desirable locations.

The new southwest area was supposed to revitalize the center of the capital city. But despite all its fancy architecture it has failed to do so, primarily because it was designed for profit rather than liveliness. Apartment houses, stores, offices, and the meager public recreation facilities are all in separate locations in the project, which made it easier for builders and realtors to each develop and sell their own specialty. Most tenants of the new apartments must drive to the shopping center that contains the area's only stores. A huge concrete mall surrounded by new offices at the project's gateway remains eerily empty at night because no one lives around it. An especially attractive and comfortable movie theater located under the offices, with underground parking at its door, has failed to attract enough customers to make a profit under three different managements. Most residents of the housing developments in the south-west quarter turn inward behind the gates of their interior parking and the locks on their front doors. The streets are left to restless youths from the adjacent public housing projects and the patrolling police who watch them.

The programs may change, but the results always seem to be the same. The nation's housing problem and conditions in its central cities have worsened, while billions of dollars in public money have gone largely for private gain. This has been especially true of the widely heralded Housing Act of 1968, which provided every imaginable subsidy to the real estate industry to produce more and better homes for lower-income families: money to renovate old homes and to build new houses and apartment buildings, money to help make some poor families homeowners, and money to help others afford the rent for better housing. Every one of these programs has been marked by shocking scandals that ultimately contributed to the Nixon Administration's 18-month freeze on further federal spending for housing subsidies.

Even if there had been no fraud, however, these subsidy programs, by design, still would have put far more public money into the pockets of real estate industry middlemen than into decent housing for the poor. In addition to built-in profits for property owners, real estate dealers, and builders, billions of public dollars have been poured into banks, savings and loan associations, insurance companies, and other financial institutions who invest in real estate. Through subsidy programs authorized by the Housing Act of 1968, the government pays these financial institutions interest on loans they then make to housing developers and low-income home-buyers. It also guarantees them repayment of the loans in case of default.

The taxpayers are subsidizing the bankers to act as financial middlemen in the process of investing public dollars in housing. And they are doing so at especially great expense, because the government is being charged lofty interest rates at least as high as those charged other customers these days and because the government has had to assume repayment of billions of dollars in loans, which the bankers made, knowingly in many cases, for fraudulent, subsidized housing deals. U.S. Comptroller General Elmer B.

Staats has estimated that these subsidy programs cost the taxpayer $2 billion more each year than if the government could somehow directly finance production of the housing.

Richard L. Fullerton, an Atlanta consultant to developers of subsidized housing for the elderly poor, has claimed that by subsidizing the "inflated interest rates" of private lenders, the federal government is paying at least three times more than should be necessary for this housing. Each subsidized apartment for the elderly, Fullerton estimated, costs the federal treasury $1,000 in annual interest payments alone to a bank, insurance company, or other lender. "It is public money going to the lenders in huge amounts," he argued, "instead of public money going to the elderly in small amounts" that would be sufficient for them to rent or buy better housing themselves.

Of course, there could still be terrible waste and abuses if the government gave the money directly to developers or to the families who need it to buy or rent better housing (as is being tried in a small HUD experiment now). The developers could easily find ways to cheat the government directly, just as they do indirectly. And realtors could simply jack housing prices up much further to snare government money given directly to low-income renters and homebuyers without giving them any better housing. The possibilities of fraud, unconscionable profit-taking, and waste are probably as endless as the possible designs for federal subsidies for improved housing.

But fraud aside, much government housing money has gone directly to the real estate industry, banks, and other financial institutions because their powerful lobbies in Washington wanted it that way. When President Nixon temporarily stopped approval of new subsidy projects at the beginning of 1973 (projects approved before then are still benefiting from federal subsidies), he did not provide an alternative government housing program but left the field once again to the private real estate industry, with the continuing benefit of conventional FHA mortgage guarantees. Private builders were nevertheless very angry at having the flow of subsidy money slowed, and, when outgoing HUD Secretary Romney appeared at the National Association of Home Builders convention in Houston early in January 1973, the builders besieged him with hostile questions and complaints about the subsidy freeze. "It shows you how quickly people can feel deprived," Romney told reporters at the convention, "when their pipeline to the federal treasury is cut off."

Government has not come up with a workable way to provide decent housing for the millions of Americans who cannot now afford it, because that has never been the real goal of any program wholeheartedly supported by Congress. Aid for the private real estate industry and its financial backers has nearly always been the true object of federal housing programs. The one exception, public housing, has consistently been undermined by budget-cutting and niggardly administration to keep it so unattractive that it can never compete with private housing. It is undeniably difficult to design a government housing program that would dependably work for the public's benefit. But it is also certain that none will be produced until the public convinces Congress that it wants housing programs definitely intended to relieve the ill-housed rather than the builders and bankers.

3

The High-Rise Paper Empires

"Real estate," Big Bill Zeckendorf once explained back in the days of his 2-telephone Cadillac limousine and personal penthouse dining room atop a Madison Avenue skyscraper, "is one of the few businesses in which you can get into the big-time without much money."

And he should know. Zeckendorf, a college dropout who started as an assistant purchasing agent for a New York property management firm, built with other people's money and his own audacious promotion a real estate empire that made the burly, balding, and bushy-browed, 220-pound huckster an outsized folk hero.

Big Bill matched his life style to his impressive girth and boundless ambition. His salary at Webb & Knapp, Inc., which he had joined at $9,000 a year as a vice-president in 1938, surpassed $100,000, with himself in full control of the firm. He made the entire nation his own real-life Monopoly board by flying from city to city to close deals begun by long-distance telephone. When he worked from the swivel chair in his circular office, Zeckendorf bathed himself in a variety of colored spotlights from eleven bubbles overhead. The license plate of his limousine and the monogrammed silverware in his dining room bore the initials "WZ." Zeckendorf personified the term "tycoon." And he owed it all to real estate and the big buildings he built, bought, and sold with borrowed money.

At one time or another during the good years from the end of World War II until the early 1960s, Zeckendorf owned the Chrysler and Singer buildings and a handful of other Manhattan skyscrapers, the St. Regis, Astor, Chatham, Commodore, Manhattan, Taft, and

Drake hotels in New York, and the Sherman and Ambassadors East and West hotels in Chicago. He built the Denver Hilton and Mile High Center office tower on Courthouse Square in downtown Denver and the Place Ville Marie office complex in Montreal. He launched the Kips Bay, Lincoln Towers, and Park West Village high-rise apartment redevelopment projects in New York and controlled large chunks of urban renewal projects in Philadelphia, Pittsburgh, the Hyde Park area of Chicago, and the southwest section of Washington, D.C., where he originally proposed redevelopment of all 550 acres of slums. Zeckendorf conceived the mammoth Century City of high-rise offices, apartments, and hotels on a huge old movie lot bought for $43 million from 20th Century Fox in Los Angeles, and he assembled the land for the One Chase Manhattan Plaza headquarters of Chase Manhattan Bank in New York.

One of his most highly publicized deals began in the late 1940s, when Zeckendorf bought, for an estimated $7 million, six blocks of property covered with old slaughterhouses along the East River between Forty-second and Forty-eighth streets in Manhattan. He then announced with characteristic fanfare that he would build there a collection of skyscrapers, stores, hotels, and an opera house to be called "X-City." But one morning Zeckendorf read that the United Nations had been searching unsuccessfully for a place to put its headquarters in New York. He picked up one of his ubiquitous telephones and called the mayor to set in motion negotiations that led to the sale of the six riverfront blocks to the U.N. at what Zeckendorf considered a bargain price of $9 million.

If the $2 million profit in that deal went to Zeckendorf in cash, it would have been one of the few times he ever dealt in that commodity. Zeckendorf did most of his business on credit. He bought property and built buildings with money borrowed from the Rockefellers, big banks, and lesser lenders, to whom he sometimes paid 15 to 20 per cent interest to get extraordinarily large sums of money when he needed it immediately, although the prime rate (the interest banks charge their best customers on their safest investments) has fluctuated between 4 and 10 per cent. "I'd rather be alive at 18 per cent," Zeckendorf once said, "than be dead at the prime rate."

One of the most often repeated of Zeckendorf stories—which although probably apocryphal still best illustrates his way of doing business—concerns an occasion when Zeckendorf and his son, William, Jr., happened to be passing by the St. Regis Hotel, which they did not then own. According to the story Zeckendorf, Sr., estimated that they could probably buy the St. Regis for $50 million. "Yes," Zeckendorf's son is said to have answered, "but we would need $5,000 cash."

Only $5,000 cash to buy a building worth 10,000 times that much? Although the down payment necessary is usually a little larger than that, Zeckendorf and other big-time real estate speculators regularly buy and sell big buildings and pieces of high-priced downtown property with very little cash. Real estate professionals call it "leverage"—the investment of as little of one's own money as possible to buy an expensive piece of real estate. The rest is borrowed with mortgages.

In big cities in the United States, where well-located downtown property has always been outlandishly expensive, real estate empires of high-rise offices and apartments are built on leverage. Property is bought and, if necessary, developed with a little cash and a lot of borrowed money. The idea is to rent or resell the building for enough money to pay off the debt on it and still have money left over to buy more property with that cash and still more borrowed money. In this way an inverted pyramid of vast real estate holdings can be built on a relatively small initial cash investment.

But the pyramid is built on paper—the paper on which the mortgages to buy the buildings are written. If everything doesn't go just right, if the profit from one layer of investment fails to cover the debt owed on the next, the pyramid can topple and bury the speculator who built it. When he fails to repay the money owed on any one property, it can be repossessed by the lender. This takes away that building's potential to produce the profit the speculator needs to pay the mortgage on a second building, which means that it, in turn, will be repossessed and the money needed to keep a third building will be lost, and so on, as one domino pushes over the next, until nothing is left.

This is what ultimately happened to Bill Zeckendorf. He borrowed money at such high interest rates that he needed immediate big profits to keep up his huge mortgage payments. Too many of his ambitious construction projects moved too slowly, though, especially those in urban renewal areas where the government approval needed at every stage ate up month after month of Zeckendorf's expensive, interest-compounding time.

To raise needed cash, Zeckendorf sold some of his buildings at a dramatic auction held at the St. Regis Hotel in New York, but the sale did not bring in much more than he still owed on each of the buildings' mortgages. He also sold his interest in a multitude of uncompleted ventures, so that other developers wound up finishing Kips Bay and the other apartment projects in New York, Century City in Los Angeles, and the L'Enfant Plaza office complex in Washington, D.C. Zeckendorf maneuvered as only he could to try to cover each new debt that came due as his empire dwindled, but finally, in 1965, he was forced to allow his real estate company, Webb & Knapp, to fall into bankruptcy.

Zeckendorf was not one of a kind. Every now and then another flashy real estate speculator is catapulted to the top by a series of big deals. Perhaps the most dramatic rise was made by Jerry Wolman, a high school dropout and son of a fruit-stand operator from central Pennsylvania. At the peak of his success at age thirty-eight in 1965, Wolman was trading and building dozens of office and apartment high-rises in Philadelphia, Baltimore, and Washington and had begun construction of the 100-story John Hancock Center in downtown Chicago. He bought Connie Mack Stadium in Philadelphia and built an indoor sports arena, the Spectrum, there. Wolman had started out building cheap suburban apartments only twelve years earlier with just $5,000 capital borrowed from a friend, and he had accumulated $75 million worth of property and buildings, which, however, were mortgaged for almost as much—plus interest.

As long as he stayed a step ahead of his mortgage payments, Wolman had the money, as Zeckendorf did, to live well. Among other trappings of success, Wolman owned two Cadillacs, a Lincoln, a 55-foot yacht, and a $250,000 house with an indoor swimming pool and a separate bathroom for each member of the family, plus others for visitors. A fit, handsome, dark-haired man with a boyish face and wide, winning grin, Wolman identified his own rapid success with the flash stardom of professional athletes, particularly the Philadelphia Eagles football players he used to follow as a teenager by hitchhiking across Pennsylvania. In 1963 Wolman fulfilled "my childhood dream" by buying the Eagles and their stadium himself. He spent many afternoons during the next several autumns out on the Eagles' practice field in a sweatsuit working out with the team.

But Wolman's high-rise paper empire also wound up dismantled in bankruptcy court. He, too, had piled up too many mortgages in the effort to rapidly pyramid his holdings. Delays in construction of the John Hancock Center in Chicago had left him so far behind his debt on that project alone that after pouring the foundation he had to sell out his interest at an estimated $5 million loss. By 1968 Wolman had even lost his beloved Eagles.

Not that Wolman or Zeckendorf is in the poorhouse now. Zeckendorf still has his penthouse apartment in Manhattan and a variety of investments; Wolman held on to a Philadelphia cab company and part of a downtown Washington office building, and he is now back to developing houses, apartments, and recreation land communities in Maryland and Virginia. Besides, it is the initial ostentatious success achieved by the Zeckendorfs and Wolmans, not their later falls from the top, that continues to attract others to gamble at getting rich quickly in high-rise real estate speculation. This keeps ever-bigger buildings rising in most big-city downtowns, even as nearby slums are dying from "disinvestment."

Thanks in part to the new World Trade Center twin towers that now dwarf the Empire State Building on the New York skyline, lower Manhattan is where the downtown high-rise empires are being built in that city today. And the man behind several big new office buildings due to rise soon in Battery Park City, also in lower Manhattan, is the apparent successor to Zeckendorf and Wolman at the top of the "big time." In his mid-sixties and decidedly not flamboyant in dress and life style (despite his expensive penthouse apartments in New York and Florida), Harry Helmsley is a new-style high-rise tycoon, although he has been in the real estate business for half a century and, like the others, has built his empire largely on borrowed money.

Helmsley, who worked his way up from office boy and rent collector, is more diversified than Zeckendorf or Wolman ever were. In addition to owning, along with numerous partners in complicated syndicates, literally hundreds of office and apartment buildings throughout New York and in several other cities from Washington to San Francisco and Los Angeles, Helmsley controls firms that profit from managing most of the buildings and one that even washes all their windows. His income is widely estimated in real estate circles at several million dollars each year, much of it sheltered from taxation by the operating expenses, mortgage interest, and depreciation deductions he can claim on his share of the buildings and businesses he has invested in.

But to keep fueling his empire—which includes ownership, with partners, of the Empire State Building itself—Helmsley is constantly borrowing more money and placing new mortgages on his holdings. And, in the now familiar pattern, he must keep buying, building, and renting at an ever-increasing rate just to keep up with what some say is now a half billion dollar mortgage debt. Helmsley already has built several large new office buildings in New York City and traded half a billion dollars' worth of existing office and apartment projects there, including three giant projects of several thousand apartment units each—the Parkchester, Fresh Meadows, and Tudor City complexes—whose tenants are fighting plans by Helmsley to turn the buildings into condominiums and sell the apartments off individually at a huge mark-up over what he paid for them. Moderately priced rental housing in better central-city neighborhoods throughout the country is being lost this way as speculative owners no longer needing them as tax shelters and seeking to avoid expected increases in maintenance costs turn older, big apartment buildings into condominiums at very high profits that can be plowed back into their highrise empire building.

What kinds of central cities do Zeckendorf, Wolman, Helmsley, and the others build? Their plans, unfortunately, are master plans for profit—not for people or for thriving communities. Even the buildings they put up are only the necessary by-products of their speculation, in which money and mortgages are the important commodities.

New buildings usually go up in the place of old—no matter how sturdy and serviceable the old may be—because the profit potential of new construction is greater, and more generous depreciation deductions are allowed for new buildings. They are built as tall as possible to produce the greatest amount of usable rental space on the relatively small amount of ground under them. They usually are offices or, in some places, luxury apartments because these bring in the most money. Their design is plain, and their construction often overly cheap to cut costs. Older buildings, mixed neighborhoods, and the 24-hour downtowns that have always made urban life attractive all are destroyed to make way for these cold, monstrous by-products of the high-rise paper empires.

In nearly every U.S. city, there are notorious examples of the speculator's handiwork. Courthouse Square in Denver was a park before Zeckendorf dug it up for construction of the Mile High Center offices and the Denver Hilton. Local businessmen in Los Angeles boast that they have "revived" that city's historic downtown, now a confluence of freeways, by building a cluster of once-rare Southern California skyscrapers filled with offices but neglecting to provide any place in which to live. New business-district skyscrapers threatened the celebrated human scale of San Francisco, prompting *San Francisco Chronicle* columnist Herb Caen to lament that the city's new skyline is "almost indistinguishable from Pittsburgh's, Houston's, or Atlanta's . . . the San Francisco of yesterday has been lost in the crush." Real estate speculators leveled much of downtown Detroit only to fail to refill it with new buildings because too much of its economic vitality had been swept away; instead they black-topped acres of downtown as parking lots for the cars of suburbanites commuting to work in those new office buildings that had been finished.

Among several central cities that have been undergoing great changes in recent years is Washington, D.C., where speculators have thrown up big office buildings as quickly as they can to profit from the ever-expanding appetite of the federal bureaucracy and its supporting services for office space. In several downtown Washington neighborhoods, housing that had served a wide income range of residents has been destroyed and replaced with offices or, in places where offices were not permitted, with high-rent luxury apartment buildings. As a result, Washington now suffers from an acute shortage of usable housing, particularly for middle-income families, which is driving up prices and rents at a record rate, while in 1972 the city wound up with a surprising surplus of unrented office space—equal to half of the Defense Department's huge Pentagon.

The temporary overbuilding of office space forced some speculators to charge lower rents than they had planned to attract tenants to their buildings, while they were being charged higher interest on their mortgage loans. The squeeze was tight for some, and it helped topple at least one local high-rise real estate empire—that of the Pomponio brothers of Arlington, Virginia, a suburb of Washington. Their father, Louis Pomponio, Sr., had built up a successful plumbing business, which the three sons, Louis, Jr., the eldest, and twins Peter and Paul were to take over. But Louis, Jr., was interested in real estate development instead. He wanted to turn the section of Arlington just across the Potomac River from downtown Washington into an extension of that downtown by filling it with high-rise office buildings.

"Lou got the bug," one acquaintance remembered. "He had been to college and here he was hustling pipe and driving a truck around at three o'clock in the morning, and he said to himself, 'There must be a better way of making a living.'"

With money borrowed at first on their father's name, the Pomponios went on to build fifteen big office buildings in Arlington and plan similar redevelopment of a section of downtown Washington itself. Louis, Jr., impressed New York bankers with the speed at which his buildings were going up and with the lavish entertaining he did at Washington's finest and most expensive French restaurant. The plumber's son now was also able to show off a new home equipped with two swimming pools, a skating rink, and a tennis court.

To keep up their dizzy pace and meet their obligations as they came due, the Pomponios had to finish and rent buildings fast. When the market turned against them in the late 1960s and early 1970s, they had to offer prospective tenants, including government agencies, rents much lower than other local builders thought economically prudent. In a very short time the nay-sayers proved to be right. The reduced rental income from their finished buildings plus delays in completing and renting out others left the Pomponios without enough money to make all their mortgage payments, pay their real estate taxes, or pay subcontractors. Since mid-1972 they have been losing their buildings one by one to creditors.

It also turned out that the Pomponios were paying kickbacks to a prominent New York banker who arranged construction loans from his and other banks. The banker was indicted in March 1973 and charged with accepting from the Pomponios $278,000 in cash, $17,000 worth of interior decorating services, and two automobiles, a 1968 Cadillac and a 1972 Lincoln.

The Pomponios refuse to talk about it all now. But a more conservative Washington developer said of them and other overly ambitious local real estate speculators: "They think they can build the world, buy the world, develop the world."

Many real estate speculators, however, have successfully avoided overextending themselves and managed to make and keep fortunes in Washington, where real estate is the biggest business outside government itself. One who has almost succeeded in "developing the world" is Charles E. Smith, the most prominent of Washington's real estate speculation "syndicators." Smith spreads the risk of speculation among the well-to-do partners he finds to invest with him in high-rise development projects. All together, these investors put up several hundred thousand dollars, which enables Smith to borrow perhaps ten times that much or more for each project.

For example, in a Smith syndicate ten partners may each put up $10,000 of a $1 million project (the other $900,000 is borrowed); thus each partner's investment amounts to only 1 per cent of the total capital, including the borrowed money. Yet each partner has a full one-tenth share in the project and is eligible for one-tenth of the profits. Even more important for most of the high-income investors in Smith's syndicates, each partner is able to claim 10 per cent of the building's depreciation each year on his income tax return—a deduction that makes a large chunk of his other income tax-free. Owners of newly constructed apartment buildings are also allowed to accelerate a building's depreciation. Oversimplified, this means they can assume that its useful life on paper is only twenty instead of forty years and can deduct twice as much for its depreciation on their tax returns as they could for an older building worth just as much. Thus these real estate syndicates are ideal tax shelters, especially since the several partners the developer finds to invest with him are always protected from liability for any losses beyond their original investment.

In the Washington area and nationally, real estate syndicates have become the latest investment rage for the rich, who have been attracted to them by their unique tax shelter possibilities, the syndicator's promises of easy profits on relatively small capital investments, and what appears these days to be a much safer risk than the wildly fluctuating stock market. Shares in publicly offered real estate investment syndicates, virtually unknown on Wall Street before 1970, are now being sold in large volume by the biggest brokerage houses. In 1972 publicly offered real estate syndications accounted for 10 per cent of all new security offerings. Before the Nixon Administration slowed the flow of federal subsidies for the construction of big new apartment projects for low-income families, partnership shares in publicly offered syndicates developing scores of subsidized projects were especially hot Wall Street items.

Among the investors in Smith's syndicated high-rise office and

apartment projects in downtown Washington, Arlington, and elsewhere have been other local real estate figures, doctors, lawyers,
judges, and even politicians. They include former U.S. Supreme
Court justices Abe Fortas and Arthur Goldberg, Judges David L.
Bazelon and J. Skelly Wright of the U.S. Court of Appeals in the
District of Columbia, and Senator Abraham Ribicoff of Connecticut. Judge Bazelon, for instance, at one point had a total of $300,-
000 invested in eight Smith syndicates, with each syndicate involved
in a different project.

Smith and his friends also have occasionally invested in projects
of a local real estate team—Dominic Antonelli and Kingdon Gould,
Jr.—whose daring speculation has had an even more profound
effect on life in central Washington. Antonelli and Gould are, in
effect, blockbusters—but of a different kind than the real estate dealers who push black families into previously white neighborhoods.
Antonelli and Gould break up old but thriving downtown residential neighborhoods with parking lots.

Their aim is to replace quiet townhouse neighborhoods with
much more profitable high-rise office and apartment buildings.
They usually find that the residents do not want to give up their
convenient, in-town homes and that the city will not allow big
buildings to replace them. That would normally be that, except that
Antonelli, a high school dropout who started out as a parking-lot
attendant, and millionaire Gould, great-grandson of railroad and finance magnate Jay Gould, are also in the parking-lot business.
They run Parking Management, Inc., the largest parking firm in
Washington and one of the largest on the East Coast. And they
figured out how they could kill a good neighborhood and move in
big buildings by blockbusting it with parking lots.

As Dan Morgan, a reporter for the *Washington Post,* described
it in a detailed study of the methods of Antonelli and Gould, the
two needed to buy only enough houses in a neighborhood to tear
them down for the first parking lot. After that lot appears, Morgan
reported,

> . . . the chain of events is predictable: Residents find the new neigh-
> bor unpleasant. It causes noise. People gather on the lot when the
> attendant goes home. Heating bills rise in the winter in adjacent
> rowhouses, whose sides suddenly have been laid bare to the cold.
> Land developers offer residents handsome prices for their properties,

in hopes of extending their holdings. The stepped-up buying activity in the area catches the tax assessor's eye, and real estate taxes, to conform with rising sale prices, rise—an added inducement to residents to sell out.

Lot by lot, houses are purchased, razed and the land blacktopped in a chain reaction. Finally, as downtown's growth overtakes the once-residential street, and the zoning is changed, the lot is sold to a development syndicate and a tall building sprouts on the site.

Antonelli and Gould bought the houses to be replaced with parking lots by borrowing the money—even for a millionaire borrowing money has its advantages, such as freeing his capital for other uses —and then making the mortgage payments and paying the real estate taxes on the ground with the income from parked cars. Once they had bought out a block and won the rezoning (the zoning officials were told this time that a new high-rise building would replace an ugly parking lot and not an attractive residential street), they sold the property profitably to their own speculation syndicate. Among the investors in Antonelli-Gould syndicates—besides Charles Smith, Senator Ribicoff, and Judge Bazelon—have been the president of the Washington area's largest construction company, the owner of a dozen local restaurants, and Werner G. Puppa, a retired employee of the U.S. General Services Administration, the federal agency that, among other responsibilities, decides which new private office buildings the government should rent.

At one time or another during their 20-year partnership, Antonelli and Gould have controlled 1 million square feet of downtown Washington. They own a hundred parking lots with space for more than ten thousand cars, in addition to having the exclusive parking concession for Washington's National Airport. They have developed two dozen downtown office and apartment high-rises, put up five big buildings in Arlington, and have assembled large packages of central-city land for development by others.

With their parking-lot blockbusting techniques and the help of developers who have followed them, Antonelli and Gould have replaced old central-city, townhouse neighborhoods with new high-rises in Foggy Bottom (the city's old Irish neighborhood near the State Department) and on both sides of Connecticut Avenue, which had been Washington's most diverse boulevard of commerce and housing. Inroads are now being made into other residential neighborhoods in an ever-widening circle out from the center of downtown Washington. Affected areas can easily be spotted by the yawning cavity of a parking lot or the towering hulk of a new high-rise smack in the middle of a block of turn-of-the-century row houses.

The sad story of the demise of these in-town neighborhoods is reminiscent of the fate of West End in Boston. Where there had been diversity and vitality—commerce and housing, buildings and trees, indoor life and people on the streets at all hours, young residents and old, a sprinkling of income levels, and, unlike West End, both black families and white—there soon will be uniform sterility: big, bland buildings, cold, empty sidewalks, silence and darkness in the office buildings after five, and predominantly white, upper-income tenants locked away in the luxury apartment high-rises.

In Chicago's Uptown area, halfway between the Loop and Evanston on the North Side, where the rich tenants of new high-rise apartments are pushing lower-income blacks, Puerto Ricans, Indians, and East European ethnics out of what had been an unusually polyglot neighborhood, the Rev. Iberus Hacker, president of the Uptown Neighborhood Association, lamented: "We've been squatters on someone else's plantation."

It is difficult even to concede that the new construction really adds to the economic value of the central city. The buildings and their owners are so encumbered by mortgages even from before the time construction begins that their materials and workmanship are often substandard and their maintenance is not adequate. These deficiencies and high rental costs, especially in a city as overbuilt with offices as Washington is, leave many new buildings empty for long periods of time. And because most of the investors in these projects are interested in them primarily for short-run profits or the tax benefits that decline sharply after the first few years, their ownership turns over quickly, which also militates against consistent upkeep.

The speculators continue to build their high-rise paper empires ever higher. One topples every now and then, but new holdings are always being pyramided by new entrants in the race to make it into Zeckendorf's "big-time." And every day, even as more and more new high-rises are built and traded, the city suffers a little more under the weight.

4

The $ in $uburban $prawl

For nearly two hundred years no more than 20,000 people lived at any one time in the gentle, green hills of Loudoun County, Virginia. Although Washington, D.C., is only an hour's drive away, Loudoun always seemed somewhat isolated, with the Blue Ridge mountains and West Virginia to the west, the Potomac River and Maryland to the north, and the flat land of what became the Virginia suburbs of Washington to the east and south. Settled by farmers and hunters who founded little hamlets like Snicker Gap and Lucketts, the county was the home of wealthy horse breeders, dairy farmers, and fox-hunting owners of large estates reminiscent of English country manors. They were joined in recent years by government workers and retired military officers from Washington, who intended to live out their days raising a few cows and growing their own vegetables on anywhere from a dozen to two hundred acres of land. Loudoun's market town and county seat is Leesburg, population 4,821 in 1970.

One of the city people who pursued the agrarian American dream to Loudoun is Jim Swart, now nearly seventy. Loudoun was to be the last refuge of his forty years' retreat from skirmishes with Washington's rapidly advancing suburbs in what is now the nation's fastest-growing metropolitan area. While he was still a government worker in Washington in the mid-1930s, Swart moved to then rural Arlington County, Virginia, across the Potomac River from the capital. Soon, however, came the first of the subdivisions and apartment houses that now blanket Arlington, and Swart moved further west to an 11-acre farm in Fairfax County. There a crossroads not far from his land began to attract the kind of attention from real estate speculators that later was to bring shopping centers and even office buildings to the area. So in the late 1940s, two decades before Fairfax County's population would reach 500,000, Swart sold his little farm to the speculators for a big profit and bought a 200-acre dairy farm just over the Fairfax line in Loudoun County. He quit his government job and settled down to farming.

Once again, however, Swart had not moved far enough. The suburban growth that consumed much of Fairfax County by the early 1960s soon reached the edge of Loudoun, attracted in part by the new Dulles International Airport on the Fairfax-Loudoun line and by lower land prices in the more distant county. The day came in 1962 when Swart climbed a hill on his property and just to the west saw bulldozers scraping bare land in preparation for the construction of hundreds of subdivision houses. Where fifteen separate farms had been on 1,777 acres of land, an entire new community called Sterling Park, which eventually is to house 25,000 people, was started.

Swart was being surrounded by the city again, and he was besieged by speculators who wanted his farm. By his own count he was visited by prospective buyers more than 350 times before he finally gave in and contracted in 1971 to sell his property for around $6,000 an acre, contingent on the buyer's receiving county zoning approval. That adds up to more than a million dollars for Swart, but he does not know what he will do with the money—or himself—without that farm.

"I was never anxious to be a millionaire," he said. "Farming's my life. The life I can handle. . . . You tell me I'm a millionaire, but I cannot do what I want to do"—keep the farm and keep away crowded subdivisions.

Swart looked sadly at the property all around his, where neighboring farmers had already sold and moved out. Scruffy little wild cedar trees were growing in clumps in the empty, neglected pastures and no longer cultivated fields. "I hate to see the land go like that," Swart said. "Once those little trees start coming up, it never goes back."

Little cedar trees are now growing in fields all over eastern Loudoun County, where speculators, including at least one Wall Street investment firm, have bought up most of the land and are waiting for permission and the right time to start development. Loudoun's population, which had risen from about 20,000 to 24,500 between 1950 and 1960, jumped dramatically to 37,150 in the 1970 census. A big share of the increase came from families moving into Sterling Park, where nearly 10,000 people, many of whom work at Dulles airport and elsewhere in Washington's Virginia suburbs, now live. The local builder who began the project has since sold out at a big profit to U.S. Steel, which is completing the construction. Just north of Sterling Park, another large development planned for 8,000 people was started in 1969 by Boise-Cascade, the lumber-land-housing conglomerate.

The sudden growth of the county upset many more Loudoun residents than Swart. City people who had moved there to be in the country also felt betrayed. And longtime Loudoun farmers and big landowners were particularly displeased by a 500 per cent increase in their property taxes in 1970. The money was needed, the county government explained, to pay for schools, police and fire protection, and other services for residents of Sterling Park and even newer developments. The $572,765 in property taxes paid by Sterling Park residents to the county in 1970 fell far short of the $736,000 county officials estimated was needed merely to educate the development's 2,500 children. And the county tax rates were likely to rise again, because it was already $20 million in debt for the construction of new schools, firehouses, and sewer and water lines.

Loudoun County residents could not help but notice the even more steeply rising taxes, vanishing farms, overflowing sewers, eroding soil, and increasingly congested traffic of adjacent Fairfax County, where the government has gone $320 million in debt building sewers, schools, and other public facilities for its hundreds of thousands of new residents. A growing number of Fairfax subdivision dwellers have become outspokenly critical of their county's rapid growth. One of them, Gilbert Ryback, bought a home in Fairfax in the early 1960s. Today he is unhappy about the doubling of his property taxes, the traffic congestion that has extended his commuting time from twenty to forty-five minutes to and from work, the sedimentation from soil erosion that has ruined nearby streams, and the confusion in his children's school caused by shifts of students from other overcrowded schools. Ryback was one of the

Fairfax voters who in 1970 turned down a bond issue to allow the county to go further into debt to build more sewers for more housing developments and who in 1971 elected a new group of county supervisors who promised to slow the growth of Fairfax County.

With the Fairfax example clearly in view, even newcomers to Loudoun's Sterling Park are worrying about the consequences of more growth in the county. "Look at the strain another development would put on existing medical and shopping facilities," one Sterling Park homeowner, Bert Hawkins, said. "This county has not gotten over Sterling Park yet," added another, Jim Care, who advised, "They should adjust to Sterling Park before they start growing and growing and grow too fast."

Now that they are feeling threatened by the development around them, the Rybacks, Cares, and Hawkinses—like a surprisingly large number of people on the fringes of suburbia across the country—want to keep everyone else out. In Loudoun County the new suburbanites of Sterling Park joined with the gentleman farmers to slam the door there with a bang heard by real estate developers and suburban governments throughout the nation.

Levitt and Sons, one of the largest builders in the United States, had asked Loudoun County officials for permission to build a $125 million "planned community" of homes, apartments, shopping centers, and parks for 13,000 people on 1,270 acres of land. Although the county's supervisors agreed that the plan was particularly impressive—it appeared to guarantee a minimum of environmental damage and had been repeatedly changed during years of negotiations to meet every specific objection of the county's planners—they voted in 1971 to refuse Levitt the rezoning it needed to build on the land. "It just seems to be the time for somebody to say 'whoa,'" explained Loudoun supervisor James F. Brownell, a farmer from Round Hill.

Levitt went to court to argue that the Loudoun supervisors had no legal right to disapprove a plan it had no objections to in detail, but a county judge upheld the supervisors' decision. In the meantime the supervisors also passed an ordinance requiring developers to pay a large share of the cost of new public facilities, including schools, necessitated by their projects. So Levitt, resubmitting its rezoning request, agreed to pay nearly $900 to the county for every home in its planned community. But the builder was again turned down in 1972, this time by the county planning board, with its two members from Sterling Park joining in the majority vote to reject the plan. Planning board member Richard K. Bishop said that Loudoun just was "not at the stage right now where it can tolerate a large increase in population in a very short time."

Levitt may yet build its project in Loudoun County. But the precedents set there for local government control of suburban growth have helped focus national debate on the wisdom of the "growth is good" policies that always prevailed in the past and allowed greedy suburbs to continue eating up land until they became even larger than the unwieldy cities that spawned them. In 1967 the population of the nation's suburbs surpassed the central cities. Three-fourths of the U.S. population growth in the 1960s occurred in the suburbs, while many central cities lost residents in large numbers. Philadelphia dropped below 2 million for the first time in twenty years, and St. Louis, which lost one resident in five to its suburbs, fell to its population level of the turn of the century. The largest U.S. "city" today is actually the ring of more than seven hundred suburbs around New York, which contains 9 million people, a million more than New York itself, and covers 2,100 square miles, 600 more than Los Angeles and its suburbs combined.

Jobs, shopping, and services have moved to the suburbs, too. Three out of every four wage earners living in Nassau and Suffolk counties, Long Island, in the New York suburbs, also work in those counties. While retail sales increased 50 per cent and manufacturing employment 13 per cent in the St. Louis metropolitan area during the 1960s, the increases in the suburbs of St. Louis were 96 per cent for sales and 41 per cent for jobs, while the city itself suffered a decline in both. Even in a newer big city like Denver, the sales increase of 63 per cent and jobs expansion of 38 per cent for its entire metropolitan area were dwarfed by the 158 per cent jump in retail sales and 91 per cent increase in manufacturing jobs in its suburbs alone.

These jobs, shopping areas, and services, however, are like pieces of a city scattered across the suburban landscape. A woman in Nassau County described, in terms once applicable only to the sprawl of Los Angeles, how her family spends much of its time traveling the highways:

> We live in East Meadow. I work in Garden City. My husband works in Syosset. We shop for clothes in Hempstead. My husband's Pythias

Lodge meets in Great Neck. Our temple is in Merrick. The children's doctor is in Westbury. And we pay our parking tickets in Mineola.

Scarcely surprising, then, are the 1972 federal Environmental Protection Agency figures demonstrating that the suburbs of New York City suffer much more seriously from air pollution, caused primarily by auto exhaust, than does the central city itself. The figures show both hydrocarbon and carbon monoxide emissions present in the air over the northern suburbs in Westchester County, New York, and Fairfield County, Connecticut, the western suburbs of Bergen, Middlesex, and Monmouth counties, New Jersey, and the eastern suburbs in Nassau and Suffolk counties on Long Island at levels two to three times higher than those in the air over Manhattan and the Bronx.

In Los Angeles the roads and parking lots for the cars needed to get from one part of that scattered city to another have consumed more than a third of the land area. And despite all those roads, many of them wide freeways, rush-hour traffic still comes to a dead stop twice daily. The new federal standard for allowable air pollution—a maximum of .8 parts of hydrocarbon per million parts of air—was exceeded on 220 days in Los Angeles County in 1971, in large part because of its auto traffic. In order to enforce that standard by 1977 the federal government is considering gasoline rationing in Southern California to reduce automobile traffic by 86 per cent during the smoggiest half of the year. Although the housing density in the Los Angeles area is the lowest of all big U.S. cities —just five homes per acre on the average—there is little real open space, parks, farmland, or forest. To be nearer nature it is necessary to drive great distances to expensive "vacation home" areas that now are also overflowing with people—places like Lake Tahoe on the California-Nevada border, which in summer months is encircled by a perpetual traffic jam.

Unhappy paradoxes like these have led Lewis Mumford to describe U.S. suburbia today as "the end of a dream." The American middle class migrated to the suburbs for the same reasons that upper-class people have maintained suburban villas for as long as there have been cities: They wanted to get away from the congestion, noise, dirt, blight, poverty, and crime of the city and enjoy greenery, clean air, and independence in the countryside. But in suburbs like those of Los Angeles or New York the congestion, pollution, and traffic are now nearly as bad as in the city, and the average suburbanite is farther away from the countryside than ever before. Crime in the suburbs, much of it burglary, vandalism, and drug offenses, is rising faster than crime in the cities, and suburban police and courts, largely overlooked among the many demands on the property tax dollar, have been overwhelmed.

City planners, sociologists, and journalists commonly diagnose suburbia's ills as the predictable consequences of unplanned rapid growth. They say the U.S. suburbs have developed more or less spontaneously, without rhyme or reason. Of course, that is how the suburbs look.

But suburban development has not been happenstance. In fact, it has been exactly as real estate speculators, builders, bankers, and even many suburban homebuyers have wanted because it has been so profitable for them. They have forced government at all levels to plan suburban growth their way through the administration of zoning laws, construction of highways, laying of sewers, writing of tax laws, and supervision and subsidy of mortgage banking.

The suburbs have sprawled inefficiently, because the farther out the speculators go into the countryside the cheaper the land is. The natural environment has been defiled, because more careful development would cut into profits too much. Houses are free standing and lots wastefully big, at the expense of parks and other public open spaces, because that brings homeowners more profit on resale. Individual homeownership is also encouraged by preferential tax treatment and government backing for home mortgage loans. Most of the houses are built cheaply by developers cutting corners to maximize profits, yet they still sell easily to buyers who expect to change homes frequently—"buying up" to a better house with the profits from the sale of the last one—and who are more interested in short-run profit potential than a home's lasting value as part of the community's housing stock.

The suburbs are not planned for attractiveness, efficiency, social vitality, or protection of the environment; they are planned for profit—the maximum profit for everyone concerned, including the homeowner—which comes primarily from speculation in suburban real estate. The housing itself is only a by-product of that speculation.

The process begins when the speculators go out beyond existing suburbs and start buying up farmland. "On the moon," reporter

Jack Rosenthal wrote in a *New York Times* examination of suburban growth around New York City,

> the "terminator" is the moving line between light and dark. In many suburbs, a similar line marks the contrast between development and farmland. In Westchester, the line moves one mile a year. . . . On Long Island, the urbanization line is instantly visible from the air. That line, planners say, moves even faster—two miles a year. In Middlesex County, N.J., the line is not so easily visible, says George M. Ververides, a planner. "There's no front. It's like Vietnam. It's happening all over."

Nationally, suburban growth eats up 1.5 million acres of farmland every year now, compared to about 1 million acres taken in 1964. California alone, which produces one-fourth of the nation's fresh food, loses 375 acres of farmland a day to suburban sprawl. At this rate experts estimate that half of California's presently productive farmland—often the best farmland, because developers and homebuyers favor the same flat land in areas of good climate that produces the best crops—will be taken by developers in the next thirty years. Already avocados, brussels sprouts, and artichokes are in danger of disappearing from California altogether as suburbanization crowds them off the land best suited to their soil and climate requirements.

Land speculators are able to buy out many farmers immediately by offering them $2,000 to $6,000 and more per acre for land they had bought at $200 to $500 an acre. The rest of the farmers are eventually forced to sell when the development going on all around them begins to seriously damage both their crops and their finances. Their property taxes are often increased 500 to 1,000 per cent in a single year, as their land is revalued by local assessors to match the skyrocketing prices of nearby acreage bought and sold for development. Their crops are thinned by the poisonous emissions of the cars of their new subdivision neighbors and by flooding rain water that no longer can be absorbed by ground now covered with the concrete of streets, freeways, and home foundations. As the land rapidly increases in potential sales value for development, its value for farming declines steadily. Eventually, it is all sold to the speculators.

The next step is zoning. The newly bought property is worth nothing to the speculators as farmland. Rezoned to allow construction of houses, apartments, or a shopping center, however, land bought for $2,000 to $6,000 an acre immediately jumps in value to $20,000 to $50,000 or more per acre. The speculator can collect his windfall profit immediately by selling to a developer, or he can contract for the construction himself and take his profit when he sells or rents the finished houses, apartments, or stores. The change in zoning is so important that many real estate speculators refuse to buy outright land still zoned only for agricultural use. Instead, they contract with the farmer to buy it after the rezoning has been won, with the price contingent on the kind of land use permitted.

In what may be the ultimate in real estate speculation, a four-year-old New Jersey company is doing a profitable business assembling cheap parcels of land into usable tracts for big developments and then obtaining the necessary rezoning for that development before reselling the land at a huge mark-up to a builder. Officials of the firm, Building and Land Technology Corporation, call their business "land packaging," and it is all they do. They do not engage in any development themselves. The key to their impressive success thus far is their ability to present a builder with the size tract he is looking for with the zoning his proposed development requires. And although the company also takes care of other arrangements, such as sewer and water authorizations, the land assembly and vital rezoning are what it is really selling.

Local governments began the zoning of land half a century ago theoretically to stop reckless developers from doing whatever they pleased with it. Some builders had put up houses next to factories, and their residents wound up living in permanent clouds of poisonous smoke. Others stretched the crowded gridiron street pattern of central cities out into the open countryside. Staten Island, isolated by water from Manhattan, was still an untouched rural sanctuary in the 1920s when speculators, counting on ferry boats to carry commuters, began buying up the island and marking off on official city maps a gridiron of 200-by-600-foot blocks delineated by wide 60-foot streets. The Staten Island land boom of the twenties was snuffed out by the Depression, and the streets were not built then, but they remained on the maps. When the speculators returned to the island after World War II, they forced the city government to honor these maps, stripped the land of its greenery, and covered it with long, wide streets and endless rows of uniform, 2-story boxes. This is what zoning laws were designed to stop.

But two Chicago lawyers who have studied zoning law, Fred Bosselman and David Callies, have written in *The Quiet Revolution in Land Use Control,* a report to the Presidential Council on Environmental Quality, that the promoters of zoning regulations in the 1920s actually "made no attempt to conserve land for particular purposes or to direct it into a specific use." Instead they "only sought to prevent land from being used in a manner that would depreciate the value of neighboring land." Thus, the two lawyers argued, the early real estate industry zoning advocates wanted to keep smoking factories separated from housing developments only to maintain the value of the residential land, not to protect the environment or make better use of the land. In reality, the Staten Island development was consistent with these ends. And today, even with strict and complicated zoning laws almost everywhere in the country, real estate speculators are able to do what they please by seeing that the zoning laws work for them.

Realtors and developers turn up on local zoning boards and local governmental bodies and consistently rule in favor of themselves and their buddies. Or they steer campaign contributions and, sometimes, bribes to officials who decide zoning cases their way. Several suburban officials on Long Island were recently convicted of accepting zoning bribes after being exposed by *Newsday,* a Long Island newspaper. One of the nation's largest homebuilders, Kaufman and Broad, Inc., was fined $50,000 in late 1973 after pleading no contest to charges of conspiracy and bribery of officials of a Chicago suburb in return for favorable changes in the suburb's zoning laws in 1968 and 1969. Two former mayors and a village trustee of the suburb, Hoffman Estates, pleaded guilty to the same conspiracy charges, as well as to charges of filing false income tax returns.

Bribery is not really necessary, however, in many places where developers are simply able to convince their fellow businessmen on the zoning and planning boards that their hardware store, bank, building supply outlet, or law practice, will profit considerably, if more people are moved into the area on farmland rezoned for residential development. The amounts of money riding on rezonings are enormous: In Montgomery County, Maryland, an affluent area just north of Washington, D.C., an estimated $100 million was added to the value of 4,000 acres of land by rezoning in 1963 and 1964, making possible $500 million worth of construction on that land.

After rezoning come roads, water lines, and sewers—the lifelines of the suburbs. The roads are easy. The nation's drivers, many of them suburban commuters, want more and bigger highways, vote for officials who build them, and pay for them with gasoline taxes. Wide highways and freeways now branch out from most U.S. cities in every direction; all the speculators and developers have to do is follow them or, more profitably, get out first to where they know the freeways will go. Inside each new housing development, most builders put in the roads themselves and include the cost in the sale price of their homes.

Few builders, however, can lay expensive and complicated water and sewer lines on their own. Huge water and sewer bureaucracies have grown up in suburban localities to do that job. They sell tax-exempt bonds to pay for laying the trunk lines and then charge each developer a sizable fee for connecting each new house or apartment building onto the pipes. The developers, of course, also pass this cost along to homebuyers and renters.

To a large extent, suburban growth is shaped by where water and sewer agency officials decide to put the pipes. The farther out they go and the more pipe they lay, the bigger their multimillion-dollar bureaucracies grow and the more connection fees they collect from developers, so they tend to encourage and provide the plumbing for increasing sprawl. Most water and sewer agencies operate on the policy that anyone who gets the necessary zoning should get water and sewer lines, too, even if it means laying pipe through miles of cow pastures to reach the rezoned land. And to collect as much as it can in connection fees on that pipe, the agency is soon pressuring zoning officials to allow the cow pasture to be rezoned as well. In some places, water and sewer agencies draw up master plans projecting the extension of their lines far out into the undeveloped countryside. When such a plan is approved by the local government, speculators gain just the excuse they need to go before the zoning and planning agencies: Because the sewers are already planned to reach the distant farmland they just bought, they argue, it should be rezoned to permit development.

Not infrequently, local officials making sewer decisions are also speculators themselves, as in the case of a former supervisor of Fairfax County, Virginia, Stuart T. DeBell, who funneled a $3 million land-sale windfall for himself and a sister through the pipes of new sewers. DeBell had already been on the Fairfax County board for eight years when his mother died in 1960 and he and his sister, Mary T. DeBell, inherited the 500-acre family farm, valued for estate purposes at $350,000. The farm, in then rural western Fairfax County, was a long way from the rapid development already eating

up the eastern part of the county. But DeBell, a realtor and insurance broker as well as a county supervisor from 1952 until 1966,
helped organize his farming neighbors to vote to make their area
a special sanitary district supported by their taxes to install sewers
in the area. "I hasten to say they all understood it would enhance
the value of their land," DeBell later told *Washington Post* reporter
Kenneth Bredemeier. He also helped petition the county court for
its approval of the district.

As a county supervisor, DeBell then proposed and voted with a
six-to-one majority that the county sewage authority draw up plans
for a complete sewering of the remote area containing DeBell's
farm, even though that would mean bypassing a large part of the
middle of the county where there were no sewers and little development at the time. DeBell also voted for approval of the final
sewage plan for his own sanitary district and for the spending of
county and bond money to build the sewers themselves. Three
years later, in 1964, DeBell abstained and sat in the audience while
the rest of the county supervisors, impressed by the argument that
sewers were already being built in the area, rezoned much of De-
Bell's property to permit high-density residential, commercial, and
industrial development. Two years after that DeBell and his sister
sold their 500 acres to a developer for $3.4 million—ten times the
value placed on the land when they inherited it eight years earlier.

A shopping center surrounded by apartment houses and single-
family subdivisions now stands on part of DeBell's former farm.
The tightly developed little sanitary district, carved by DeBell out
of farmland where Civil War battles were fought, is now a problem
for the rest of the county. Schools and other services were not adequately planned for in advance, and, because developers leap-
frogged still undeveloped parts of the county, it now costs more to
provide police and fire protection and road maintenance to this
distant area. Fairfax officials now lament that the area was developed and populated with 19,000 residents before the county was
financially ready for it. And on top of everything else, partially
treated sewage from DeBell's sanitary district now pollutes a
creek that feeds the reservoir from which much of the county's
drinking water is drawn. "There wasn't any such word—what's that
word?—ecology?—in those days," DeBell said recently, remember-
ing the years when he and his fellow supervisors sewered and rezoned the bulk of Fairfax County.

Many other sewer agencies have knowingly allowed their sewers to become overloaded with waste from too many new connections, even though they are usually the local public bodies charged with controlling water pollution. The overflow bypasses limited-capacity sewage treatment plants and spills directly into nearby streams, rivers, and lakes, polluting them with untreated waste. The Potomac River around Washington, D.C., where there is almost no water-polluting industry, is so fouled by residential sewage that the federal government has warned people not to go boating on it, lest they be splashed by some of the bacteria-filled water. Rather than forbid the new connections that overload the sewers, the agencies continue to allow more developers to hook on, collecting from them lucrative connection fees. When both Maryland and Virginia state officials ordered a moratorium on new connections in the Washington suburban area in 1972, the local sewer agencies fought the ban alongside angry developers and violated its spirit daily by granting scores of special exceptions that allowed most developers to continue connecting to sewer pipelines.

The final link in the suburban real estate development chain is financing. Like almost everyone else in real estate, the suburban developer works on a shoestring. He borrows the money to buy the land, and he puts off payment of his subcontractors and bills for building materials until the house is finished and sold. The money he receives for the house he uses to satisfy his land loan and construction debts.

Because nearly all their interest income comes from home mortgage and apartment construction loans, savings and loan associations are the most active financial institutions in the suburbs, where greater interest can be earned on more new mortgages. Savings and loans began, however, in the cities and still collect much of their savings deposits there. The Bronx Savings Bank in New York—where savings banks are the equivalent of savings and loan associations elsewhere—has five offices in the Bronx, and most of its savings deposits come from that borough. The bank also has two new offices in affluent Westchester County, where most of the money from the city goes into suburban home mortgage loans. Throughout the New York area money deposited by lower-income savers, many of them blacks living in the city, where the savings banks no longer want to make home loans, goes to upper-income homebuyers in exclusive suburban enclaves.

It is so important for suburban speculators and developers to find savings and loans that will do business with them and the buyers of their homes that some of them take control of savings and loans themselves by proxy, just as some slum real estate speculators have done in the cities. The same conflicts of interest also result. Some suburban speculators operate both their real estate business and a savings and loan out of the same office, a practice especially prevalent in California. In a Philadelphia suburb the largest borrower of construction money from one savings and loan a few years ago turned out to be the wife of a director of the association, and she was the front for her husband's real estate company. In the Houston area federal examiners found in 1969 that the officers of fourteen savings and loans were lending tens of millions of dollars of their associations' funds to each other's suburban land speculation and development projects.

Money is the beginning and end of the suburban development process. The construction of the housing itself becomes an obstacle to be overcome in the creation of new land values and profits, rather than a carefully fashioned product. Because the developer is working with borrowed money, he wants to finish and sell each house as quickly as possible to pay off his loan and construction debts. Because his profit comes primarily from marking up the value of the land under the house—if a home on a quarter-acre lot sells for $40,000, the buyer is likely paying $8,000 to $10,000 of that price for the lot, which the developer bought for about $2,000 —the house needs only to be built well enough to sell reasonably quickly. Any construction costs not absolutely necessary simply cut into the developer's profit or force him to raise the price of the house to a level that may discourage buyers.

Most developers therefore have not taken the time nor spent the money to take care of the ground on which they build. They cut down the trees, bulldoze the land as flat as possible, and scrape off the topsoil and pile it to one side during construction. As a result, much of the soil washes away before it is replanted with grass and small shrubs or young trees. Without grown trees to anchor the ground and with the soil haphazardly rearranged so that it drains badly, the newly built-up area remains liable to undergo massive soil erosion for years. Nearby streams and rivers become choked with silt, and the water table is irreparably damaged. Heavy rains eat away at high ground and flood lower areas, where no damage occurred before development took place.

In recent years the public's growing concern about the environment has produced many local laws requiring developers to show more respect for the land: to keep more full-grown trees, to grade the site so that it drains properly and erosion is reduced, to stay away from stream valleys and other places where development would do too much damage to natural water flows. Predictably, developers are fighting these new standards, arguing that they unreasonably increase both development costs and the selling prices of new homes. In its lobbying for abolition or relaxation of the new regulations in several states, the National Association of Home Builders (NAHB) calls them "problems which have grown out of environmental and 'no-growth' movements."

The NAHB has even put out a table of the estimated extra cost per lot to developers complying with the new requirements of each state: $185 to put utilities underground in Virginia; $300 to save a minimum percentage of trees on building sites in Florida; $500 to meet silt-control requirements in Kentucky; $800 to comply with open space, flood control, and tree preservation regulations in Georgia; up to $1,000 to meet drainage standards in Texas; and as much as $1,500 to obey laws on water quality, site grading, and landscaping in California. The majority of the new laws have been limited to the South and West, where land prices are still somewhat lower than in the crowded Northeast and where developers had not fought the regulations so fiercely. They are coming a little late for many suburban areas, particularly in California, where too much countryside has already been ravaged, and the enforcement of the laws has until now been far from uniformly strict.

Where they have not been closely regulated, some developers have built entire subdivisions on river flood plains, where seasonal overflows from heavy rains regularly flood the homes. Others have built homes with septic tanks instead of sewers in inappropriate places. The waste water from houses in subdivisions without sewers is supposed to be chemically treated in septic tanks buried in their backyards. From the septic tanks it seeps gradually into the ground. But if the water table in the area is too high, the ground already is saturated with water. So the septic tanks back up, and raw sewage oozes up through the neighborhood's lawns, endangering the health of everyone in the area and polluting the ground water for miles around.

Even when septic tanks are functioning properly, they discharge a lot of treated water into the ground, which can pose another kind of problem. Where homes with septic tanks have been built on shallow soil on top of rock, there is only so much soil to absorb the water. In the Portuguese Bend subdivision on a steep hillside south of Los Angeles runoff from septic tanks eventually saturated the soil down to a layer of shale just below the surface. This made the shale slippery and sent the soil that had been clinging to it sliding downhill, taking with it more than 150 houses costing $25,000 to $50,000 each.

In a rush to finish and sell houses quickly builders also have moved people into sloppily built and even unfinished new homes in the suburbs. Buyers of many of the 340 new houses in the Sugarbrook development built outside Chicago by Kaufman and Broad, one of the nation's largest developers, won newspaper headlines in that city with their complaints of cracking foundations, sinking driveways, chipping and peeling paint, and water seepage into their homes because of the poor grading and drainage of their lots. Some Sugarbrook homeowners put up large yellow, lemon-shaped "open house" signs in their front yards to show prospective buyers of other houses in the subdivision what they had found wrong with their homes.

Kaufman and Broad fired the president of its Chicago division and promised immediate improvements in Sugarbrook. "We've learned our lesson" about forcing homes to hasty completion, said Eli Broad, chairman of the firm's board. "We got burnt; it's a new day, and we hope the consumer and the whole industry will benefit." But newspapers and even building trade journals increasingly report the same kinds of complaints from families buying new homes from all kinds of developers in subdivisions scattered throughout the country.

A survey of residents of some of the new suburban subdivisions of attached townhouses on both coasts, published in mid-1973 by the nonprofit Urban Land Institute in Washington, D.C., is filled with complaints about the construction quality of new homes in all price ranges: "These houses are so poorly put together it's a crime . . . there isn't a square or straight wall in the whole house" (owner of a $30,000 home). "Noise comes through the walls, including bathtubs filling and toilets flushing from both sides. My basement leaks in heavy rains" ($33,000). "Hot water ran in our toilets and ruined the insides, which had to be replaced. The cheapest of everything possible was used. You can see we are very disappointed" ($35,000). "Walls and woodwork are crooked and poorly finished. Plywood floors are loose and squeak. Plumbing repeatedly leaks or is stopped up. The basement leaks" ($40,000). "Construction workmanship is very poor! Floors are bouncy. Drywall is poorly installed . . . The houses are nothing more than plywood boxes" ($45,000).

Others complain about the developers' unfulfilled, grandiose promises of attractive community amenities. Brochures for homes in the huge Dale City development of 3,000 houses in Prince William County, Virginia, thirty miles south of Washington, D.C., advertised that the community would have a lake, two golf courses, several swimming pools, tennis courts, nature trails, bridle paths and stables, baseball diamonds, and plenty of schools and stores. But the lake, golf courses, and bridle paths and stables have not materialized, and spokesmen for developer Cecil D. Hylton admit that they never will be. The only baseball diamond is a Little League field graded by the U.S. Army Corps of Engineers at the request of Dale City residents, and the short hiking trail, laid out by local Boy Scouts, also was financed by the residents. The only swimming pool and two tennis courts are located in a private membership club controlled by Hylton.

Hylton's only provision for schools was the donation of land for them to otherwise rural Prince William County, which could not afford to build schools nearly as rapidly as families were sold houses in Dale City. So the community's children attended classes only half a day each for the several years that Dale City had only one elementary school. More schools have since been built, but there still are not enough to eliminate persistent overcrowding. Instead classes continue all year round, with the pupils' "summer" vacations staggered throughout the year.

For the first three years in Dale City there were no stores at all, and residents had to drive five miles to buy a loaf of bread or a bottle of milk. Since there is no public transportation, wives without cars of their own were trapped in Dale City's forest of houses all day long. One woman said that living in Dale City was "like being in prison," compared to her previous home in Arlington, Virginia, where she could get everywhere by bus.

Most Dale City residents, however, do not seem sorry they moved there, despite Hylton's broken promises, simply because the price of the houses was right. In the tight, high-priced suburban home market around Washington, the $20,000 to $35,000 charged for Dale City's large, reasonably well-constructed if nondescript houses was almost a bargain. Most buyers also were required to put only a few hundred dollars down and could pay all the rest in mortgages to Hylton and a bank. "We came here because it fit well with our finances at the time," said a civil engineer who worked miles away in another Virginia suburb of Washington. "It cost me just $100 to get the key and move in."

Because of the continuing shortage of medium-priced housing in Washington's suburbs, Dale City residents have been able to sell their houses for much more than they paid for them. Dale City has been quite profitable financially for everyone.

In their own way suburban homeowners are speculators, too. They buy houses to make a profit. They hope to buy at the lowest possible price, watch property values in their neighborhood rise steadily, and sell at a much higher price. They do not have to pay tax on that profit, not even capital gains tax, as long as they reinvest it in another house costing at least as much as they were paid for the one they sold, which most families want to do anyway. Meanwhile, all the mortgage interest and property taxes they pay are deductible on their income tax returns.

University of California researchers who surveyed buyers of new homes in a variety of suburbs outside San Francisco and Los Angeles found that "most people on the suburban housing market seem to have two overriding concerns—class image of communities and the investment potential of homes." The two considerations are obviously related. "Rather than talking about what *they* like or dislike about a location, home, or community, they often talk about what the *market* tends to prefer or reject, thus transforming 'houses' into 'commodities' that are being bought to resell but which function as 'homes' during the interim," concluded the final report of this remarkable study in 1965.

"What were you looking for when you started looking for a new place?" the researchers for the university's Institute of Urban and Regional Development asked the suburban California homeowners. "Primarily . . . we weren't looking for a house that would suit us but for something that would make a good investment," answered an automobile salesman in a Los Angeles suburb. "There are of course a lot of features we were looking for, but the most important over-all factor would be investment. We wanted something we could sell for a profit in a few years after we have lived here awhile."

"We decided to move here for a profit," a roofer living in a San Francisco suburb said simply. One of his neighbors, an engineer, explained that he was buying a house for the first time and that "the people that I knew who bought homes were buying them at $19,000 five years ago and they are now worth $28,000." He hoped to make a similar profit "so I can someday be able to afford something just a little bit better, although I am pleased with this house." Another neighbor, a pilot, said he had already "made a few thousand dollars on our last home, enough to pay a $6,000 down payment on this one." Two-thirds of the scores of homebuyers interviewed in the California study estimated that they made a profit of $4,000 or more above their built-up equity when they sold their previous homes.

Many of them talked about house-hunting in terms of square feet of living space: "We wanted a home with over 2,000 square feet" or "This was a good price for 2,200 square feet." Some said they purposely bought homes bigger than they needed because they would bring bigger profits on resale. "We expect the value of this house to appreciate in the next few years, and this was our primary consideration because we don't need a house this size," said the automobile salesman. "We bought this size house because the people moving into this area later will be people with growing families," he added. Buyers of homes with both a living room and a large "family room" frequently said they used only the family room, either because they could not afford to furnish both or because they wanted the living room left unmarked as a showpiece when it came time to sell the house.

Other homebuyers said that for investment purposes they purposely sought out the least expensive house they could find in the highest priced subdivision they could afford. "Now, if you buy in a tract and buy the cheapest in that price range you could afford, where the other houses around you cost more," an electronics engineer explained, "that way your value will come up and you will protect your home, and we have found that the profit will be better that way." It was considered even better if your subdivision bordered a much more expensive one. "Although all the homes here are pretty much the same price, the surrounding homes are higher priced," another electronics engineer pointed out. "That means our property should go up in value. We are looking at it sort of as an investment."

On the other hand, none of the homeowners wanted any less expensive homes than their own located nearby, nor, for that matter, corner stores, gas stations, or anything else associated by the survey's respondents with lower-class neighborhoods. "Some of the people out here feel they are not going to hold their value because they are surrounded by cheaper homes," a computer specialist outside Los Angeles said. An IBM repairman said he would not want houses below a certain price in his area because "that brings everybody and anybody in. . . . I think they would bring down the value of my house. The labor force—the people who work on the line—the majority don't keep up their homes like you or I would."

The biggest threat to many of the homebuyers was the possibility that a black family might move near them. "Well, a couple of them bought houses on the block where we were living in Sunnyvale," said a pilot who moved to a new San Francisco suburb.

> I tried for eight months to sell that damn house. I finally had to sell it for $2,000 under the market value. Nobody wanted to buy with Negroes in the neighborhood. I must have had a hundred people look. They would say it was a nice house, and would like it, but then they would see the kids playing in the yard next door and that would be that.

As a result, the suburbs are segregated by both income and race —for investment purposes as well as in response to social prejudices. White middle-class suburbs are kept that way by, among other things, the same zoning powers that were used by developers and homebuyers to invade the countryside. Homebuyers, for example, are restricted to expensive large lots and single-family houses (a process called "snob zoning" by its opponents). Local building codes are written to prohibit less expensive "prefab" home construction. Subtle but effective discrimination against unwanted homebuyers is practiced by the real estate industry: Realtors quote higher prices to black buyers, for instance, and savings and loan associations and banks find ways to deny them mortgage loans. Laws in many places outlaw this kind of discrimination, but they are seldom vigorously enforced.

In fact, the 1970 census shows a marked decrease in the percentage of black residents in the suburban rings around many U.S. cities, including Detroit, Baltimore, Houston, Dallas, Atlanta, Kan-

sas City, and New Orleans. The suburbs of Cleveland, a city with
a large black population, are nearly all white, with the exception
of predominantly black East Cleveland. For some of the other
Cleveland suburbs the 1970 census figures show North Royalton,
population 12,800, with no black residents at all; Fairview Park,
population 22,000, with just 5; Lakewood, right on Cleveland's
western border, with only 21 blacks in a population of 70,000; and
Parma, south of Cleveland, with 50 black residents in a population
of more than 100,000.

Only the suburbs outside Washington, D.C., Los Angeles, Chicago, and New York show sizable increases in black population,
and, with the possible exception of those in the Washington area,
most of the new black suburbanites have been segregated in older,
close-in suburbs. Like some inner-city residents, they are often victims of blockbusting and end up paying exorbitant mortgage payments or rents for houses that were poorly built to begin with in
neighborhoods that have nearly always lacked a strong social structure. These black families—and Puerto Ricans in the New York
area, Cubans in Miami, and Chicanos in the Southwest—have been
trapped, along with 1.7 million poor families (40 per cent of the
urban poor) in suburban slums that are rotting away faster than
some even older parts of the cities.

For many of the white suburbanites who manage to "buy up"
from one house to a more expensive one, the goal is a home in
those prestigious suburbs where the lots are the biggest and property values the highest. Census figures show that in these suburbs—
the kind for which Westchester County, New York, has become a
national symbol—nearly everyone is white and in the top quarter
of the nation's wage earners. These suburbs also have the best
schools and local services, even though it is well known that "bedroom suburbs" of single-family homes cannot generate enough
property tax revenue to adequately support such local government
services.

The answer to this seeming paradox is that more and more suburbs, like many of those in Westchester County, are no longer
bedroom communities at all. They have brought in shopping centers, offices, and even light industry to help share the property tax
burden. All across the country businesses have left the central
cities for the comparatively cheaper building sites, lower property
taxes, access to freeways, and locations near their executives' homes

in the distant new suburbs. Retailers of all kinds have built new stores in shopping centers with acres of free parking nearer their best customers in these same suburbs. Westchester County now has nearly as many jobs as working residents. Although 116,000 workers still commute out of Westchester, 81,000 people, many of them from New York City itself, now commute from elsewhere into the county to work.

New real estate fortunes are being made by speculators who buy inexpensive farmland and have it rezoned for the development of new high-rise office buildings, sprawling industrial parks, and massive mall shopping centers on 400- and 500-acre sites. Southdale, one of the first enclosed, air-conditioned, "regional" shopping malls, was built in 1956 in the suburbs of Minneapolis. The land under it increased in value from $2,200 an acre when the center was being developed to $283,000 an acre for land sold on the edge of its site in 1970. Real estate speculator and mortgage banker James W. Rouse, who is developing the suburban "new town" of Columbia, Maryland, has built his real estate empire on a foundation of twenty mammoth regional shopping malls in the United States and Canada, including the one in Columbia. Rouse's chief financial backer, the Connecticut General Life Insurance Company, now holds $1 billion worth of shopping mall mortgages.

Chain retailers also have an enormous financial stake in suburban shopping centers. Montgomery Ward, for instance, reported in 1972 that 65 per cent of its $2.4 billion annual sales volume and 70 per cent of its profits came from stores in suburban shopping centers. Sears also profits from shopping centers as real estate ventures by itself investing in the development of twenty-six of them and retaining ownership rather than renting its own stores in the centers. This enabled Sears to deduct from its 1971 taxable corporate income $105 million in depreciation, an amount equal to nearly one-fifth of its after-tax profit.

An increasing number of planners and journalists now see more than just profit in the big new suburban shopping centers. They are describing them as the new downtowns of America—exciting social as well as commercial phenomena—and they are comparing them with the covered markets of the Roman Forum, the market squares of medieval Europe, the surviving piazzas of Italy, and the nineteenth-century shopping galleries of European cities. "To an amazing degree," Gurney Breckenfeld has written in *Fortune* magazine, the big suburban shopping malls "are seizing the role once held by the central business district [of U.S. cities], not only in retailing but as the social, cultural and recreational focal point of the entire community."

For all the exterior ugliness of the monolithic malls and their acres of paved parking lots, they are flashily decorated on the inside and frequently jazzed up by the color of "sidewalk sales," art, flower, fashion, furniture, boat, and auto shows, and even occasional evening events like senior proms. Most malls now also have movie theaters and a variety of restaurants, making them an oasis of public activity and personal interaction in the compartmentalized, automobile-dominated suburbs.

But unlike public piazzas of Europe or the old town squares of this country, there is little activity in the suburban shopping malls that is not directly intended to produce profits; all those shows, and even the senior class prom, pay rental fees. Just plain mingling and loitering are being increasingly discouraged by merchants and shopping center developers, who are competing frantically with all the other malls for sales volume. The teenagers who hang out at the shopping centers—instead of the neighborhood drug stores, playgrounds, and street corners that don't exist in the suburbs—are seen as shopper-discouraging nuisances with their scruffy appearance and boisterous manner. The general manager of the huge South Hills Village shopping mall outside Pittsburgh has given his ubiquitous uniformed security guards strict orders not to permit teenagers to collect in groups larger than four and, if they are not shopping, to keep them moving along. With the authority given them by a 1972 U.S. Supreme Court decision, operators of many malls have posted signs pointing out that "Areas . . . used by the public are not public ways, but are for the use of tenants and the public transacting business with them. Permission to use said areas may be revoked at any time. No trespassing."

"Retailers don't want anything in the center that will interfere with retailing," explained Bob Guthrie, public relations director for the International Council of Shopping Centers in New York. Quite contrary to the rosy expectations of *Fortune*'s Breckenfeld, James Johnson, advertising manager for Seattle's Southcenter shopping mall, said, "We don't try to duplicate the downtown community. . . . We don't do anything unrelated to our main purpose, which is merchandising."

The fact remains, however, that the duplicate retail function of the suburban shopping malls is killing the central-city downtowns, both financially and socially. Phoenix has 125 shopping centers around it and only one downtown store, J. C. Penney's. Neither Newark nor Cleveland has first-run downtown movie houses. The jazzed-up pedestrian-only main shopping street of downtown Minneapolis is quite attractive, but its stores still lag far behind their own suburban branches in sales.

Similarly, all those businesses that have moved to the suburbs have taken capital out of the cities and left problems behind. Many of the lower-income workers for those businesses cannot afford housing in the suburbs or, if they are black, are blocked by other barriers. Part of the critical unemployment problem in the cities can be traced to many of these workers, who lose their jobs because they have no transportation to get them from their homes in the cities to factories in the suburbs. In Westchester County there are 82,000 more jobs for low- and middle-income workers than there are houses for them, and, as a result, some relocated businesses are now finding themselves desperately short of workers in a period of rising national unemployment.

Suburban sprawl—planned for profit—has not produced livable or workable communities. More and more suburbanites are dissatisfied with the chaos, time-consuming transportation problems, inflated home prices, high property taxes, increasing pollution, disappearing open space, and surprising social problems. Many of them are also finding that they can no longer afford houses in the nicer suburbs; inflated real estate values are breaking the chain of buying up to better homes.

Only the real estate speculators can win in this situation, which is why some local governments, like those of Fairfax and Loudoun counties in Virginia, are trying to say "whoa" to further growth. This may seem a short-sighted and selfish answer to the problem. Slamming shut the doors to these suburbs exacerbates the over-all housing squeeze, making it still more difficult for lower-income and minority families to find decent places in which they can afford to live. But the alternative to "no growth" offered by the real estate industry is to allow whatever kind of growth is the most profitable. And that has already proved to be much more disastrous. This can be seen clearly by examining in detail the recent development of two very different and yet similarly exploited suburbs at opposite ends of the country: Santa Clara County, California, a suburb of San Francisco, and Prince George's County, Maryland, outside of Washington, D.C.

5

A Tale of Two Suburbs: Santa Clara County, California, and Prince George's County, Maryland

A mustard-colored haze hides all but the shadowy outlines of the mountains on either side of the long, flat valley. Automobiles push and shove through crowded concrete corridors of stores, service stations, car lots, and taco stands. Isolated groves of the last surviving fruit trees fight asphyxiation from the polluted air and strangulation by the surrounding homes, shopping centers, factories, and freeways. The houses huddle together, back to back and side to side, in cities of subdivisions without open spaces, parks, or even sidewalks. Many homes just ten years old slouch in ready-built slums, their gravel roofs leaking, concrete slab foundations cracked, flimsy veneer doors and walls warped, stick fences rotting, and sparse dirt yards alternately flooding and heaving. This is Santa Clara County, California, a jigsaw puzzle of intertwined suburbs beginning forty miles southeast of San Francisco.

The once unusually fertile Santa Clara Valley stretches almost due south from the southern tip of the San Francisco Bay for about sixty miles between low ranges of wooded mountains. Its balmy Mediterranean climate has always produced sufficient rainfall in a few weeks each year for the thriving agriculture and left the sun shining warmly the rest of the time. Not so very many years ago, residents of Santa Clara County called it the "Valley of Heart's

SANTA CLARA COUNTY
CALIFORNIA

Delight," and not without good reason. "It was beautiful," remembered Karl Belser, who once was the county's chief land planner, "it was a wholesome place to live, and it was one of the fifteen most productive agricultural counties in the United States."

In a retrospective analysis written after he resigned his post in dismay over the ravages of suburbanization, Belser described in detail what the real estate speculators were destroying:

> The land in the valley was of the very highest quality. Two alluvial fans had been laid down over the millennia by systems of streams which had coursed from the mountains to the sea during the rainy season, flooding the lowlands almost every year. Topsoil of fine loam thirty to forty feet deep in places overlaid water-bearing substrata of gravels and clays. A tremendous underground water storage basin with a capacity of roughly one million acre-feet spread itself out beneath this wonderful soil. In many places the water gushed forth from artesian wells. Here was nature's handsome gift: soils second to none in the state and perhaps the world, indigenous water enough, if properly used, to serve that soil adequately, and a mild climate with a year-round growing season.

For centuries this gift of nature was used appreciatively and conservingly by man, first by the Indians who fed off the land, then by Spanish settlers who grazed cattle there, and finally by European immigrant farmers who introduced into the valley grapes and prunes from France, and pear, apricot, and other fruit trees. For a time the valley produced a third of the world's prunes and became nationally known for its fruit and nut orchards. Its population of about 150,000 people in the 1920s and 1930s was divided primarily between those who tended the 100,000 acres of orchards and those who worked in the more than two hundred food-processing plants.

Although World War II brought many newcomers to Santa Clara's Moffett Field naval air station and the new electronics firms associated with the military and Stanford University, the county grew gradually and relatively smoothly. Its largest towns—San Jose, Santa Clara, and Palo Alto—expanded slowly without disturbing much of the agricultural area around them. Their residents took Sunday drives through the orchards when blossoms were in bloom. Early in the 1950s a book called *America's Fifty Best Cities* described the "verdant" valley as "one of the most beautiful in America" and growing San Jose as "a tidy, bustling metropolis of twenty-two square miles, but still a garden city famed for its liveability, hospitality and healthful climate."

At that time there still were only about 300,000 people living in all of Santa Clara County. But the valley's oasis reputation, unusually agreeable climate, and easily developed flat land beckoned to the suburban masses moving south from San Francisco, who had already filled most of the usable land in neighboring San Mateo County. Soon, 4,000 new residents a month were moving into the valley. From 1950 to 1960 Santa Clara County's population more than doubled to 640,000. By 1970 it exceeded 1 million people.

"Wild urban growth attacked the valley much as cancer attacks the human body," said Belser, who found himself virtually powerless to slow or channel that growth. "What so recently had been a beautiful, productive garden was suddenly transformed into an urban anthill."

Today the majority of the orchards are gone. The paving and building over of so much absorbent soil has brought about serious flooding of many populated areas during the rainy season, while the heavy demand for water the rest of the year threatens to exhaust the underground supply. The water table already is so depleted in many places that the land over it is sinking. The once-clean air has been discolored and poisoned by the glut of automobiles and some of the county's not-so-clean industry, and smog from San Francisco and Oakland, trapped by the mountains, adds to the pollution.

The cost of borrowing money to rapidly install sewers, pave streets, build and staff schools, and provide police and fire protection for so many people over so large an area has put the county and several of its cities deeply into debt and burdened their residents with steadily increasing tax bills. No money is available, for instance, to pay for a mass transit system that could eliminate some of the automobile congestion. The welfare rolls are lengthening with the names of fruit packers, canners, and other low-paid and otherwise unskilled agricultural workers who cannot find jobs in the county's new highly skilled, technical economy. Crime has increased so much that all of the county's jails are overcrowded, and its officials have borrowed space in an underused facility in San Mateo County.

The views of the mountains, the deep green of the orchards, and bright colors of the fruit blossoms have almost completely disappeared, and little public park land has been developed to replace them. Indeed, the most scenic spots left in the valley may be the carefully tended and regularly watered tropical greenery along the shoulders of the county's many freeways. A private park advertises its trees and flowers for those who wish to pay to wander among them for a few hours. Otherwise, only the giant, enclosed shopping center of Eastgate, with its artificial climate, gaudy metal sculpture, concrete and tile terraces, and man-made fountains is left for families who once enjoyed weekend drives through the lost outdoor beauty of the "Valley of Heart's Delight."

Santa Clara County has become the mass media's favorite symbol of the evil of rapid suburbanization. "Urbanists cite it as the archtypal slurb, a sprawling confusion," *Business Week* noted. "Growth came so fast . . . and with such disastrous results," *Newsweek* concluded, "that the experience serves as a dire warning of what can happen if residents fail to watch what is happening to their community."

Yet what has happened in Santa Clara cannot be neatly explained by the clichés of suburban sprawl. The county is not a single-dimensional bedroom community for San Francisco; Santa Clara has its own industry and other economic resources, including the huge plants of Ford, Lockheed, General Electric, and IBM, which Nikita Khrushchev toured during his 1958 visit to the United States. The valley was not unused, valueless land before the speculators arrived; it was one of the most productive and profitable agricultural regions of its size in the world. The rapid residential and industrial development of the valley has not taken place in a vacuum, without governmental planning; Santa Clara County and several of its cities have had strong governments, model planning and zoning laws, large staffs of professional planners, and citizenries that include academic leaders at Stanford, top corporation executives, and a highly skilled, well-paid labor force. Tract houses and cheap apartments alone have not filled the county; there are also whole communities of substantial homes costing $50,000 to $100,000 and up on lots of one-half to several acres each.

Even if Santa Clara could not have escaped some degree of urbanization, the process need not have destroyed the valley and its agriculture. One study has shown that all the county's growth since 1947 could easily have fitted into 30 square miles with residential densities no greater than they are now; vast orchards and open space could have been saved, and the cost of public services for a more compact urban area would have been lower. But because development jumped from here to there as the speculators found farmers who would sell their land quickly, there is now a subdivision, factory, or shopping center on nearly every one of the approximately 200 square miles of once premium soil on the valley floor. Scattered throughout the county are swatches of barren vacant land, passed over by the developers for one reason or another and now orphaned from nature by the development all around them.

What happened in Santa Clara is that speculators, developers, other entrepreneurs and homebuyers systematically ravaged the valley for their own benefit. And government at all levels helped them. The large planning staffs and powerful governments of Santa Clara County and San Jose—now by far its largest city, with a population of 500,000—reviewed and approved all the rezonings, annexations, and building plans that were necessary before the land could be developed and the big profits realized. Independent water and sewer agencies extended the utilities the developers needed into previously untouched areas. State and federal officials located and paid for the freeways that crisscross the county. State and federally supervised savings and loan associations and banks provided the financing for developers and homebuyers, and the Federal Housing Administration (FHA) and the Veterans Administration guaranteed thousands of those loans and approved the houses they paid for. As a Stanford University study concluded about San Jose's apparently chaotic growth, Santa Clara County is not an "unplanned" suburb, it is "a misplanned one."

The officials who could have planned it differently were under great pressure from speculators who looked at the flat valley of spindly fruit trees and imagined huge profits. Little investment was needed to clear or level the land for construction. The mild climate eliminated the need for basements, so thin concrete slabs served as adequate, cheap foundations. Nor were expensive heavy insulation, elaborate roofs and eaves, or weather-resistant exterior finishes necessary. One builder, who cut his costs and increased profits by substituting cheap flat tar and gravel roofs for the conventional built-up, peaked, and shingled variety, set a Santa Clara Valley trend and earned for himself the nickname "Flattop Smith."

Developers found they could supply new housing quickly in Santa Clara County, and buyers, attracted by the reputation and climate of the valley—and not realizing that the orchards they expected to see would be replaced by other newcomers' homes—created a spectacularly heavy demand. One builder sold 2,000 houses in Santa Clara with only a model on the roof of Macy's department store in San Francisco. Speculators rushed to every corner of the valley to buy land from farmers and turn it over at a big profit to onrushing developers.

The farmers were more than willing to accept $2,000, $3,000, and more per acre for ground that had seemed valuable at $400 and $500 an acre. Many of them also were experiencing financial problems at the time: The groves in some parts of the valley were a century old and were due to be torn up and replanted. For some farmers that meant living off their savings, or going heavily in debt, until new trees matured and produced profitable harvests. Other orchards were being threatened by an unusual fungus that attacked and killed pear trees. Many farmers, moreover, were hurt by the higher tax assessments on their land after lots near them sold at comparatively high prices to speculators; older men feared that death taxes on the higher paper value of their land would make it impossible for their heirs to hold onto it. "Everything," Karl Belser said, "worked against saving the land."

So more and more farmers took the speculators' profitable offers. The speculators, in turn, sold the land for up to $10,000 an acre to developers, who parceled it out in lots to homebuyers at prices equivalent to $20,000 and more per acre. "It was not unusual," Belser remembered, "for land to double in price while changing hands in a single day. Everybody wound up speculating in land."

Speculating in land also meant speculating in official planning and zoning decisions that allowed agricultural land to be developed with houses, stores, and factories. Determined officials could have used their power over these decisions to carefully stage the valley's development, shape it along the lines of a rational master plan, and conserve more of its open space, orchards, and natural assets. A fierce struggle between these officials and the greedy land speculators and developers should have occurred. But it never did, because they were never really opposing interests. With few exceptions the local officials were also involved in real estate speculation, had other vested interests in the rapid development of the valley, or, like Karl Belser, as he later admitted, simply were unable to make a strong stand against the powerful development interests and their allies in local government.

Belser remembered how his county planning office was overwhelmed with requests for its preliminary approval for zoning changes all over the county. "Every day, someone would come in and say, 'Karl, you have to approve this because it's good for the county.'" What was "good for the county" was what was most profitable for its speculators, developers, realtors, and merchants, who contributed heavily to the political campaign funds of local officials supporting rapid growth.

The chamber of commerce of Santa Clara County campaigned hard to convince unknowing voters to repeatedly approve bond issues to borrow money for the installation of the water lines, sewers, and streets needed for sprawling new development. The voters were not told about the heavy property taxes that would have to be levied to pay off those bonds. One of the most persistent supporters of these bond issues and development generally was the county's largest newspaper, the *San Jose Mercury*. Its publisher, when asked some time ago why he so strongly supported the rapid growth that was destroying the valley's orchards, replied in a widely repeated quote, "Trees don't read newspapers."

Continuing breakneck development also meant windfall profits for many of the local government officials themselves. The Stanford researchers found from city records that four of the five members of the planning commission in San Jose from 1950 to the early 1960s had financial interests in the development boom: One was a realtor, another a general building contractor, another an electrical contractor, and the fourth a two-time president of the San Jose Merchants Association, a vociferous booster of continued San Jose population and business growth.

San Jose's city manager for its two decades of most rapid expansion was A. P. Hamann, who openly admitted that he speculated in real estate in and around the city during the boom years and used his position to promote untrammeled growth of San Jose. "They say San Jose is going to become another Los Angeles," he once testified before a state board. "Believe me, I'm going to do everything in my power to make that come true." Again and again in the official annual reports he wrote for the city, beginning in 1950, Hamann emphasized his belief that even wider expansion was needed "if San Jose is to fulfill its appointment with destiny."

A few years ago, Hamann, other San Jose officials, and various local developers were found to be meeting regularly in a local hotel for what they called literary discussions. It turned out, however, that they were trading information about where the next public improvements, zoning changes, and development starts were to be. These "book of the month club" meetings, as they came to be popularly called, caused some scandal at the time, but Belser, the Stanford researchers, and a Ralph Nader task force study of Santa Clara County all place relatively little blame on outright illegal activity for the rape of the valley.

"We believe that less blameworthy motivations have been the cause," the Stanford researchers wrote. "Human beings tend to sympathize with those with whom they deal . . . planners, engineers, planning commissioners and councilmen deal daily with people who represent development interests. Advocates of the public interest are rarely seen."

A master plan was drawn up for Santa Clara County, but only

after a state law was passed requiring it. Although the plan itself consisted primarily of vaguely worded platitudes about orderly growth and loosely mapped suggestions of land uses for various parts of the county, Belser's staff used it as an excuse to recommend against many of the requested zoning changes. Nevertheless, they were nearly always overruled by the planning commissioners and the county's board of supervisors.

Exasperated farmers finally decided to act on their own to protect their orchards. They lobbied successfully for a change in the county's zoning laws that authorized the planners to designate large sections of the county "exclusive agriculture," putting them off limits to everyone else, as long as they were controlled by county zoning. The speculators and developers then turned to the officials of the proliferating cities in Santa Clara, who simply annexed and took over all zoning control of areas where the developers wanted to build.

In this way, during Hamann's twenty years as city manager, San Jose alone annexed hundreds of parcels of land and multiplied its area more than eightfold to 137 square miles. Because developers searching for the cheapest land they could find often went far beyond the nearest built-up or incorporated area, San Jose simply annexed whichever street led from its existing outer boundary to the noncontiguous piece of land, along with the parcel itself. The map of the city became an irregular spider's web reaching far out in all directions with large gaps of unwanted, unincorporated territory left inside it.

Other Santa Clara cities, concerned that San Jose would gobble up everything, joined the annexation competition. They began relaxing regulations on lot sizes, site preparation methods, sewage disposal, industrial pollution, and store locations to attract more developers and their unannexed land holdings. In the rush, many $100,000 homes were built with septic tanks instead of sewers. Residents of areas that did not want to be swallowed up by one of these bigger cities incorporated themselves as municipalities instead.

Soon Santa Clara County had fifteen cities of widely varying sizes and populations—San Jose, Santa Clara, Palo Alto, Sunnyvale, Milpitas, Los Altos, Mountain View, Los Altos Hills, Cupertino, Saratoga, Campbell, Monte Sereno, Los Gatos, Morgan Hill, and Gilroy—wrapped around each other and still unincorporated county

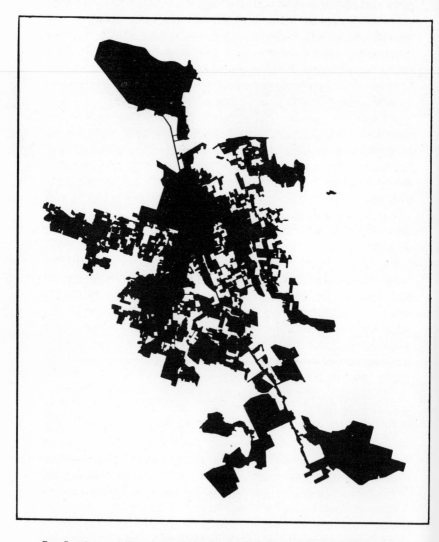

San Jose's sprawling, meandering, wasteful city map is a result of sense-less annexation and expansion policies to accommodate the whims of developers.

areas in a cartographic confusion with no discernible boundaries or, for many residents, any sense of community. To this day, many residents have admitted not knowing in exactly which city or unincorporated part of the county they live, work, shop, or vote. In a survey of 250 residents made for a Ralph Nader task force study, *Land and Power in California,* most respondents living in unincorporated areas mistakenly thought they lived in a nearby city where their post office was located. And only one-fourth of those respondents who lived in one of the cities knew the form of their local government and the name of one member of its governing body. Santa Clara's geographical and political chaos thus effectively prevented many of its citizens from exercising any real control over their local officials.

Among the choicest land parcels for municipal annexation were the sites for industrial plants and stores, since this meant expansion of the community's tax base. In the end officials rezoned so much of the valley for industrial use that 3,000 acres of this ground now stands empty, much of it neglected patches right in the middle of built-up areas. On the other hand, so many stores, small businesses, and shopping centers have been built in strips along main traffic arteries in the county that the equivalent of a new strip seventy miles long is added each year.

"This offends more than aesthetic taste," the Nader task force report concluded.

> First, it is wasteful in terms of transportation. Businesses are not clustered in available centers for easy pedestrian access after parking. Second, it is wasteful of land. For example, everyone must have more parking facilities to satisfy possible store capacity. More total land must be concretized for parking . . . than if stores were clustered with one lot serving them all. Third, it is extremely dangerous. Every twenty feet there is a possible entrance or exit from the main thoroughfare.

El Camino Real, the old Spanish road that connected the missions along the California coast and now runs through most of Santa Clara's larger cities, has been transformed into a linear parking lot flanked by strip development. It and so many other old thoroughfares in the county became so congested in this way that it has been necessary to pave over 40 per cent of the valley with more streets and parking lots.

Much of what was not paved over turned out to be in low areas that frequently flooded during the winter and spring rains. This posed no problem for the fruit trees when the ground was still covered with orchards, but the flooding has been disastrous for some of the housing subdivisions that have replaced them. Because knowledgeable higher-income buyers could be expected to know or find out about the flooding and would refuse to buy expensive homes in these areas, developers put up much cheaper housing instead. These homes were sold to lower-income families for no money down and no payments for the first six months on 30-year mortgage loans guaranteed by FHA. The developers made a little less profit on each of these houses, which sold for $8,000 to $12,000 from the mid-1950s to the mid-1960s. But the FHA loan guarantees made that profit risk-free for them and the savings and loan associations that made the mortgage loans to the homebuyers, many of whom were blacks and Chicanos.

The developers also were able to take advantage of a special exception to the county's normal zoning laws for so-called planned developments. The measure had been considered quite a progressive step when it was proposed: It freed developers from normal lot-size minimums and other restrictions so they could try new street plans, place stores within walking distance of homes, provide more park land and public open space, and, by grouping them more tightly, lower the prices of the homes to make racial integration possible. But developers in Santa Clara used the relaxed restrictions only to cut costs and maximize profits. They crowded the houses together on small lots but left no compensating open space or parks. The stores, packed together into one little shopping center in each huge subdivision, are accessible only by car. The houses themselves have proved to be no bargains, even at their low selling prices, because their construction was so slipshod that they literally began falling apart almost as soon as they were occupied.

One of the largest of these "planned developments" in Santa Clara is Tropicana Village, built alongside the freeway to San Francisco in the eastern part of the valley. Its single-story, rectangular box houses on concrete slab foundations line streets with such exotic names as Bermuda Way, Sea View, Cathay, Harbor View, Biscayne, and Jamaica, though no body of water, palm tree, or inviting scenery is anywhere in sight. The developer, A. L. Branden, marketed houses there and elsewhere under a dozen company names like Westbury, Mandarin, Revere, and Montclair Homes, and his plans and finished homes were approved both by local officials and the FHA.

Although Tropicana Village was built just over a decade ago, it is now nearly a slum. The houses are deteriorating rapidly, and most of their owners cannot afford necessary major repairs. The cheap roofs of tar and gravel have failed to hold up even in Santa Clara's mild climate. The low-quality wood trim is rotting, and the overhanging garage doors are so warped they can no longer be closed. The thin aluminum siding has buckled in many places and failed to keep out water that then wears away the cardboard-thin walls inside.

All these deficiencies are exacerbated by the seasonal flooding of Tropicana Village and by what happens to the "cracking adobe" soil when the rainy season ends. As the ground dries out in the summer sun, it heaves and separates in wide cracks that, in turn, have caused the shallow slab foundations of many houses to crack. During the next rainy season, water seeps up through these cracks into the homes. Many Tropicana Village residents have simply abandoned their wretched new houses, turning their backs on their relatively small investments. Some of these houses could not be re-sold and had to be boarded up or demolished, with FHA, the guar-antor of the unpaid 30-year mortgage loans, taking the loss.

While students of urban problems have descended on the Santa Clara Valley to document its demise, an increasing number of its residents, those professors, scientists, and engineers who had not bothered to notice before, have belatedly become concerned about what has gone on around their homes. A collection of civic leaders formed a committee to find ways to cope with the valley's problems. But they have been hampered by its unwieldy multiplicity of local governments and their own individual preoccupation with their business affairs in San Francisco, Los Angeles, New York, and Washington.

Too many influential Santa Clara citizens also remain more con-cerned with their own interests and property values than with the more universal problems of pollution, congestion, crime, or welfare in the valley. Stanford University's trustees are still fighting to put large housing and industrial developments on hillside land around the campus, even though environmentalists warn that it would create serious erosion and pollution problems. Citizens of wealthy Santa Clara communities—Los Altos Hills, Campbell, and Palo Alto, among others—are trying to keep the problems of the rest of the county out by strictly enforcing their big-lot, "snob zoning" laws, even as they continue to allow their rich residents to move their 2- to 5-acre "ranch" homesteads farther and farther up the once untouched foothills that line the valley. Meanwhile, officials of the other local governments have ignored the Nader and Stanford reports and stepped up their competition for new development that they hope will expand their property tax base and meet the steeply rising cost of community services. Office and apartment buildings and still more shopping centers are being squeezed into the gaps left between subdivisions. The rest of the orchards are steadily disappearing, as are the mountains behind the smog. Growth is still the one goal in Santa Clara County, as it continues to rush headlong toward its "appointment with destiny."

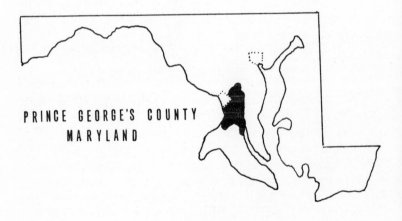

PRINCE GEORGE'S COUNTY
MARYLAND

Ralph D. Rocks, tall and dignified in an expensive suit, his fifty-four-year-old figure trim, his skin richly tanned from his many Florida trips, and his receding, graying hair carefully groomed, embodied the American real estate success story as he stood before federal Judge Alexander Harvey, II, in May 1972. Rocks was, indeed, a "self-made man," Judge Harvey noted as he examined the financial statement Rocks filed with the court. "Your personal wealth," the judge told the defendant, "is in excess of $11 million."

Much of that wealth came from speculation in real estate in Prince George's County, Maryland, a huge suburb just east of Washington, D.C., that fell victim to perhaps unmatched exploitation of land, people, and the environment during a decade of overwhelming population growth in the 1960s. Rocks gained his biggest profits buying, selling, and developing farmland that he had gotten rezoned for the construction of 3-story, walk-up "garden apartments." But he won many of those lucrative zoning changes in part by bribing one of the county's top officials.

Jesse S. Baggett, a stocky, tough-talking stonemason and farmer was twice chairman, and for sixteen years a key member, of the Prince George's Board of Commissioners, the county's governing body and final zoning authority until a reform government was elected in 1970. Baggett had been convicted at a separate trial of accepting a $3,500 bribe from Rocks and was sentenced in early 1972 to serve fifteen months in prison and pay a $5,000 fine. At that time the prosecutor told Judge Harvey that Baggett had received about $100,000 altogether from Rocks from 1962 through 1967, a period when the county commissioners approved twenty-eight requests (out of thirty) by Rocks for rezonings covering 714 acres of land scattered throughout the county.

A few months later, as Rocks stood before the same judge's bench with his wife and four children seated in the courtroom behind him, he also was sentenced to fifteen months in prison. His fine, $10,000, was double Baggett's, Judge Harvey said, because Rocks "profited more" from the crime. "You stood to gain more than he did," the judge told the defendant. "It is clear to me that you made a very substantial profit."

Testimony at the trials and other revelations before and since show that the Rocks-Baggett bribes were part of a pattern of corruption, conflicts of interest, and influence-peddling in the wholesale rezoning and development of Prince George's County. A Prince George's paving contractor who also speculated in real estate testified that he spent $1,100 paving the long driveway of Baggett's farm with 130 tons of asphalt without charge when he filed a rezoning application in 1963. Baggett told him, "I can help you" on the rezoning, the contractor testified, and it was subsequently approved. Two other developers were indicted for bribing Baggett with a $500 sauna installed in his farmhouse, in a case in which Baggett was not charged. Earlier Baggett had been tried and acquitted of being bribed by still another developer, who testified that he put a new addition on the farmhouse as a payoff for a favorable rezoning in 1962.

From 1963 to 1967 Baggett also was a paid officer, along with Rocks, of a local savings and loan association that made mortgage loans to developers in the county, and he was an investor, along with Rocks's zoning lawyer, in a local bank that also did business with Prince George's real estate speculators. Another county commissioner, Frank Lastner, who served on the county board from 1954 until 1966, was a partner with Rocks in at least one land deal in the county. And another commissioner, Francis J. Aluisi, who served from 1966 until 1970, was himself an active developer who built hundreds of houses in the county.

Several of the representatives from Prince George's in the Maryland legislature also were developers who freely voted on state bills that affected their speculation in county real estate. In particular, three of the legislators, delegates Xavier Aragona and Gilbert Giordano and state senator Fred L. Wineland, fought hard against state approval of a scenic drive and park along the Potomac River in southern Prince George's County, where they wanted land they owned on and near the riverfront to be rezoned for and developed with apartments and a shopping center. All three were Democrats, as were a solid majority of the county commissioners during the most active rezoning years from the late 1950s through the entire 1960s, a time when the majority of money contributed to the county's Democratic Party and its candidates for local offices, according to official reports, came from Prince George's developers, real estate speculators, and lawyers who handled their rezonings. Political power in Prince George's County was deeply rooted in land speculation.

When Ralph Rocks, then a gangling young man in his late twenties just out of the U.S. Coast Guard, first came to Washington, D.C., after World War II, Prince George's County was still rural countryside: meadows, marshes, woodlands, and modestly productive farms and tobacco fields. But the Washington area's population had already increased dramatically with the expansion of the federal bureaucracy during the New Deal and war years, and Rocks correctly foresaw a continuing development boom. "There seemed to be an obviously terrific demand for housing here," he later recalled, "so I got into the business."

He chose suburban housing development because the land outside the city was less expensive. And although he eventually built in nearly all of Washington's suburbs, in addition to such distant places as Florida, Rocks concentrated on Prince George's County, where the land was cheapest.

Prince George's, surrounding the eastern half of the District of Columbia, was definitely on the city's wrong side of the tracks. The main thrust of previous growth had been from Washington's more fashionable western and northern neighborhoods out into Virginia and Montgomery County, Maryland, where the higher, more attractive wooded ground was. But a growing demand for less expensive housing for younger families, new residents in the area, and lower-income whites running from an expanding black population eventually sent developers like Rocks out to the less desirable low ground of Prince George's.

Fortunes were made and the face of the county changed in a generation. Nothing of such obvious value as the orchards of the Santa Clara Valley was destroyed by the exploitive development of Prince George's. Instead, it was the potential for decent living that was ruined. Today, the county's streets are congested with traffic and dangerous to travel, regular public transportation does not serve most of the county, nothing can be reached on foot, and sidewalks themselves are nonexistent in many places. Schools are still overcrowded in some neighborhoods, there are far too few parks and recreational facilities, raw sewage from overloaded sewers and septic tanks flows into streams and rivers, and poorly graded denuded soil has eroded so badly that some parts of the county look like abandoned strip-mining sites. Housing just a decade or two old is deteriorating into slums. Unemployment is rising steadily in a suburb with little industry, and local taxes have been raised to the highest levels in the high-tax Washington area in a nevertheless ineffectual attempt to cope with these problems. Even before its staggering population expansion slowed, Prince George's County had rapidly become the poor man of the Washington suburbs.

From 200,000 people in 1950, the population of Prince George's grew to 350,000 in 1960. Most of the newcomers moved into new, inexpensive, frequently prefabricated, single-family, detached and duplex homes in subdivisions developed by Ralph Rocks and several other builders. That increase, however, was dwarfed by the jump to more than 700,000 residents in 1970, after a decade in which the number of apartment units in the county mushroomed from 8,000 to more than 80,000, the majority of them cheaply built garden apartments clustered around parking lots.

Although the growth in Prince George's County was exceptionally dramatic, apartment construction boomed throughout the country during the 1960s. Speculators had just realized that the liberalized depreciation provisions of the 1954 federal tax law could be combined with the lower income tax rates for capital gains on real estate to produce bigger after-tax profits from the development of apartment projects than from the construction and immediate sale of houses. And because banks and savings and loan associations had plenty of money to lend in the 1960s, developers needed little cash of their own to put up apartments. In fact, many financial institutions were willing to lend them all the money they needed for construction; the steady rise of construction costs and the still unmet demand for housing, including apartments, in the suburbs promised high rental incomes and selling prices when the buildings were completed.

In addition to Ralph Rocks, one of the most active speculators in Prince George's County was Jerry Wolman, who used the profits he made on garden apartments he built there in the late 1950s and early 1960s as a foundation for his briefly held empire of high-rise buildings in the downtowns of several Eastern cities. Prince George's land records show how Wolman usually borrowed enough money to pay for the land and construction and then sold the completed apartments to syndicates of buyers, which usually included himself, at sizable profits. Through the syndicates Wolman also shared in the depreciation deductions on them until they were no longer sufficiently lucrative. Then Wolman sold off the rest of his interest in the buildings.

Among other Prince George's projects, Wolman built the Sunview garden apartments with a $1.6 million loan from the American National Bank in Maryland and sold the completed buildings to a syndicate of investors he organized for $2.1 million. The Parkway apartments, built with a $1.2 million loan from the General Motors Retirement Fund, were sold for $1.4 million; three other garden apartment projects, built with loans of $2.3 million, $2.4

million, and $2.6 million from local banks and mortgage firms, were sold for $3 million, $2.8 million, and $3.1 million, respectively. A few years later all these projects, containing several thousand apartment units in all, were sold by the Wolman syndicates to a New York real estate firm for $20 million.

Garden apartments were built most frequently in Prince George's County because they promised the biggest profits for the smallest investment. Three stories was the height limit under county regulations for a building without elevators or expensive deep foundations. Fireproofing, parking, open space, and other requirements were also much less stringent, and hence less costly, for these buildings than for high-rises. The garden apartments, moreover, could be built on ground too steep or otherwise unsuitable for single-family houses.

Of course, when costly precautions were not taken, steep ground eroded badly when trees were uprooted and dirt bulldozed around. Buildings constructed as cheaply as possible, and then traded among owners interested in them only as lucrative tax shelters, also were bound to deteriorate quickly. Predictably, some of the apartments in Prince George's County came almost to resemble South American hillside *barrios*. But profit, rather than sound housing or environmental protection, was the goal in Prince George's, and the key to the largest profits was zoning.

Short of outright bribery, the best way to get land rezoned in Prince George's County in the 1960s was to hire zoning lawyers who were former county officials themselves or personal friends of various county commissioners. How they then influenced the outcome of zoning cases was described in detail at Jesse Baggett's second bribery trial by zoning attorney Blair H. Smith. Smith was himself a former county prosecutor, the official who represented the public interest in county zoning cases, and a former chairman of the local water and sewer agency, which doubtless helped him get sewer lines installed to his clients' properties.

Smith told of representing developers Ralph F. Triska and Edward J. Cook, who wanted their waterfront property rezoned to permit the construction of apartments and a shopping center near an existing community of single-family homes and a country club they owned. As was the custom, Smith testified, he invited Baggett, then chairman of the county commissioners, to see the project site and to play a round of golf at the country club. Baggett brought with him two other lawyers, William L. Kahler and Samuel J. De-Blasis, at that time partners in one of the county's more successful zoning law firms. Both also were quite active in and substantial contributors to the county Democratic Party.

At the country club outing, developer Cook later testified, Baggett "told me, in effect, 'You've got the wrong lawyer' or the wrong law firm or the wrong attorney for the zoning." Triska quoted Baggett as saying, "You'll never get it [the rezoning] with that law firm"—meaning Blair Smith. Both developers testified that they took these remarks as obvious hints that they should also hire Kahler, who later testified at Baggett's trial that the county commissioner was "probably the closest friend I've got."

Smith followed the advice and took several assisting lawyers to help him represent Cook and Triska before the county commissioners: Kahler; Herbert L. Reichelt, a former county commissioner who was closely associated with another sitting commissioner at the time, M. Bayne Brooke; and Leonard Collins, an acknowledged close friend of still another commissioner, Gladys N. Spellman. The strategy worked, and the rezoning was approved by a four-to-one vote of the county commissioners. Only the selection of Collins as a co-counsel "obviously didn't work out," Smith said, because Gladys Spellman voted against the rezoning.

Kahler's influence, however, was unquestionably effective. He was the only zoning attorney for Ralph Rocks when Rocks won so many rezonings for his speculative deals from 1962 through 1967. Kahler also was an investor—with a 16 per cent interest in each of seven deals and an 8 per cent interest in one other—in the partnerships that Rocks formed to develop the rezoned real estate. These investments were in addition to his legal fees for representing Rocks.

The Rocks-Kahler partnerships profited from several land deals in one particular area of Prince George's County—the northern tip just south of the small city of Laurel—which Rocks almost singlehandedly changed from rural land to a hodgepodge of hastily built apartments. South Laurel had been a buffer of woods, marshes, and ponds between Laurel and the Fort Meade military post to the north and the U.S. Agricultural Research Center and the U.S. wildlife refuge on the Patuxent River to the south. Only a few private homes had been built in South Laurel when, in the very early

1960s, Rocks put up the first apartment project there, the largest to that date in Prince George's, the 450-unit Snow Hill apartments.

While finishing Snow Hill, Rocks leased 250 acres of nearby farmland from two families, the Dawsons and the Staggers, with an agreement to buy their land outright at a set price if rezoning for apartments could be won. Rocks and Kahler then went to the county commissioners in late 1962 to seek rezoning for the Dawson tract, promising to "preserve some trees" and build just 700 apartment units, though the land could hold more. The apartments, they assured the commissioners, would be "an improvement on our Snow Hill development," where Rocks had kept an old farm barn and a large pond, as well as considerable open space, although there were few trees or recreation facilities for children.

One of the South Laurel homeowners, the late Arthur Vogts, testified against the rezoning request, arguing that if Rocks and Kahler got their way, "others are sure to follow in their wake and . . . an imbalance of apartments will develop."

"There should be some effort at conservation," Vogts told the county commissioners.

> This is virgin area which will soon be lost to the apartment-type developers. Spot zoning. Poor planning. Giving in to the developers who are out for the most profit zoning-wise. . . . Wholesale deforestation continues throughout the country for the good of a few developers interested only in a quick profit, and not for the good of the community.

Testifying on behalf of Rocks, however, was William J. Stevens, vice-president of the Prince George's Board of Realtors, who claimed that the project would be economically good for the county. The commissioners approved the rezoning, and the action immediately doubled the Dawson property's value over Rocks's contractual price. Rocks then began construction of 800 apartment units in buildings considerably less attractive and more congested than those at Snow Hill. Some trees were saved along the edge of the site, but the bulk of the land was bulldozed bare.

Long before this project was finished, Rocks and Kahler were back before the county commissioners asking that the Staggers farm be rezoned for the development of 1,400 more apartments. Rocks promised to protect the "very beautiful," heavily wooded, steep site there from unnecessary harm and said he would add to it a pitch-

and-putt golf course, tennis courts, a softball diamond, and other amenities. This time there was no opposition, and the rezoning was speedily approved. On October 1, 1964, under his agreement with Mrs. Staggers, a widow, Rocks and some partners, including Kahler, bought full title to about 88 acres of land for $4,000 an acre.

Two months later Rocks and his partners sold the property to another developer, John Gordon Bennett of New York, for $1.4 million—or $16,000 an acre—a profit of more than $1 million in just two months' time. What made this unusually lucrative deal possible was a large construction loan to Bennett from Loyola Federal Savings and Loan of Baltimore, out of which Bennett paid Rocks for the land. Actually, the loan to Bennett was arranged by Rocks himself, who had borrowed frequently from Loyola and worked closely with its president, Rogers H. Israel. Israel personally won approval for the Bennett loan at Rocks's request, according to later court testimony.

A few days after completion of this highly profitable deal, Rocks and Kahler left for a vacation in Florida. And they took with them Jesse Baggett, Rogers Israel, and William Stevens, who was by then the chairman of the county planning board. According to testimony at Baggett's bribery trial, the bill for $1,152.97 at the Doral Beach Hotel in Miami Beach was paid by Rocks on his Rocks Engineering Company checking account, and the $781.20 air fare was covered by another of his companies, Allen and Rocks, Inc.

It was a violation of federal savings and loan regulations for Bennett to pay Rocks for the Staggers land with Loyola Federal loan money earmarked for construction, and both Rocks and Israel were later indicted for loan fraud when Bennett turned state's evidence and testified against them. The two were acquitted, however, when they were able to prove that other officers at Loyola knew about the money diversion plan. Thus, the savings and loan was technically not defrauded, even though its depositors' money was misspent.

Partly because of this misuse of loan money and the diversion by Bennett himself of more of the construction funds to such private pursuits as his polo ponies, Bennett was not able to finish the apartments on the Staggers site. Although Bennett kept his polo ponies and the rest of his private fortune, he lost title to the project when Loyola had to foreclose on its mortgage and pay out still more of its depositors' money to finish the construction itself. The apartments now stand among swampy pools, deep drainage ditches, and a labyrinth of steep parking lots on the despoiled site. Most of the trees were cut down or badly damaged during construction, and the hillsides are washing away. The promised golf course, softball diamond, and tennis courts have, needless to say, never been built.

Just as Arthur Vogts warned, South Laurel has been overrun by garden apartments, as other developers rushed to profit from the rezoning precedents set by Rocks, who also eventually built more apartments there. When the Prince George's County planning board belatedly attempted to draw a master plan for the area in the late 1960s, it concluded that "an ideal design concept for the development of the area" was no longer possible. The planners admitted they had already been defeated by the county commissioners' approval of an "avalanche" of apartment rezonings.

South Laurel now suffers "potentially serious problems," according to the planners, because of "disorganized land use," overcrowded schools, highway bottlenecks, eroding soil, disappearing woodlands and park sites, and overflowing sewage treatment facilities that are poisoning fish in the federal wildlife refuge on the Patuxent River. Government services of all kinds are inadequate in South Laurel, which is isolated by the nearby federal government preserves from much of the rest of Prince George's. And the planning board predicted that continuing population growth there will "far outstrip the ability of proposed facilities to serve the community efficiently and properly within the limitation of reasonable public expense."

Even when planners beat speculators to an area in Prince George's County, they were unable to significantly change the outcome. For the watershed of Henson Creek, an area of woodlands and streams at the opposite end of the county from South Laurel, the planners spent many months drawing up a master plan for orderly, restricted growth that would protect many of the farms, trees, and stream beds from encroachment by developers. When the plan was presented at a public hearing in 1964, it was praised by representatives of the few families living there and by citizens' groups concerned about environmental protection in the county.

But one witness at the hearing—William Kahler—raised an objection to the Henson Creek master plan. Together with Ralph Rocks he had contracted to buy 138 acres of wooded land right in the middle of an area reserved in the master plan for farms and single-family homes on large rural lots. Kahler now asked the county planners to change the designation of the 138-acre tract to allow apartment development there.

The request seemed outrageous; granting it would gut the plan and could cause serious physical damage to the area. Not only did the Rocks-Kahler property abut Henson Creek, which could be filled with eroding soil if the tract were completely developed and its trees cut down, it was also miles away from the nearest sewer lines. The few existing houses in the area, built on lots of several acres each, used septic tanks for their sewage, which is impractical for a large apartment development. One Henson Creek resident at the hearing remembered thinking at the time that Kahler's requested change "was nothing to worry about," that it would never be granted because "it would have been absurd to put apartments there."

But when the final Henson Creek master plan was published a few months later, there it was: authorization for an island of high-rise and garden apartments in the middle of a huge area of agricultural and rural resident zoning. The outline of that island corresponded exactly to the perimeter of the 138 acres that Rocks, Kahler, and their partners had bought. Soon after, the speculators won final zoning approval for the apartments from the county commissioners, who explained to an audience of surprised, angry citizens that they were simply following the Henson Creek master plan approved by the county planning board.

The chairman of the planning board at the time of the Henson Creek master plan change was William Stevens, Rocks's supporter at the South Laurel rezoning hearing when he worked for the Prince George's Board of Realtors. As a spokesman for developers, Stevens seemed an unlikely choice for planning board membership, but he was another friend of Jesse Baggett's and owed his planning board appointment in mid-1963 to the county commissioner's clout. Stevens served until mid-1966, when Baggett's attempt to keep him on the board was overruled by a majority of the rest of the county commissioners.

The planning board, in addition to drawing up master plans, investigated every request for rezoning in Prince George's County, and advised the commissioners which requests to approve and which to turn down. Under Stevens's leadership, the planning board recommended approval of the vast majority of the record number of rezoning requests submitted during that period by developers and speculators, including all of those that had been submitted by Ralph Rocks.

Stevens was convicted and sentenced to nine months in prison for income tax evasion in 1971. He pleaded guilty to evading payment of $8,200 in federal income taxes by understating his income by about $25,000 between 1963 and 1967, which included the years he served on the Prince George's County planning board. The unreported income Stevens received was in addition to his planner's salary, according to the federal indictment.

Witnesses at Jesse Baggett's bribery trial testified that after Stevens took office as a planner he was paid $1,000 by Kahler for his testimony months earlier in favor of the Rocks South Laurel rezoning. At the trial Stevens himself admitted accepting loans from Kahler for uncounted hundreds of dollars during Stevens's chairmanship of the planning board, when Kahler's clients, including Rocks, had a number of rezoning requests pending before it. Stevens testified that he eventually repaid Kahler all but "less than $1,000" of the money lent him.

Stevens also testified that during his term as planner he had all his expenses paid on many of his estimated ten trips to Florida, Puerto Rico, the Bahamas, and New York with Kahler, Rocks, and Baggett. One of those trips was the December 1964 vacation after the South Laurel million-dollar deal was closed. Also included among those free jaunts was a Florida vacation Stevens took with Rocks, Kahler, Baggett, and Baggett's son-in-law after Rocks and Kahler won rezoning of their 138-acre Henson Creek watershed tract.

The development of the Henson Creek land continued in the established Rocks-Kahler-Loyola Federal pattern. Rocks and Kahler and two other partners had paid $415,000 for the land. After the rezoning they sold it for $2,752,000—at a profit of more than $2.3 million—to the same John Gordon Bennett of the South Laurel deal. Again, a mortgage loan from Loyola Federal for $6.3 million—actually obtained by Rocks for Bennett from Rocks's friend Rogers Israel—enabled Bennett to pay Rocks for the Henson Creek site. This time the Loyola Federal loan contained $1.1 million, more than $1.5 million short of the actual price to be paid Rocks, that was legally earmarked for purchase of the land, and funds were again diverted from the remaining $5.2 million loaned for construction.

Because Bennett, as a relative outsider from New York, did not have the necessary local political connections, he also counted on Rocks to obtain approval from the water and sewer agency for a new $500,000 sewer line to the apartment site. Rocks was successful in doing this, on the usual condition that he pay a $130,000 "developer's contribution" toward the sewer's cost; it was never made clear just where this money came from—Rocks's or Bennett's funds—but it was paid to the sewer agency. Such contributions, critics have charged, give big developers the leverage to have pipes laid where they want them in the county, while small builders and families living in relatively isolated areas cannot. Families living in the rural area near Henson Creek have tried for years to get sewage lines to their homes, and they still are not hooked up to the sewer that now runs to the Rocks-Bennett apartment site not far away.

Even before that sewer was completed, Rocks obtained permission for Bennett's apartment construction to go ahead. For about eighteen months after tenants had moved into the apartments, their waste went through a "temporary sewage treatment plant" that was actually no more than a nearby open field where the raw sewage was sprayed into the air with a mixture of chemicals. It then settled to the ground and ran off into Henson Creek and down to the Potomac River. Residents of the area can still remember the foul odor emanating from the field and the creek.

Construction of the apartments has also filled Henson Creek with silt. The steep embankment that runs down from the site to the creek, designated a "park" by the developer, is littered with dead trees and discarded construction materials. And residents of the apartments complain that the nearest store is two miles away, a situation other developers say could be remedied if they were allowed to follow the Rocks-Bennett rezoning precedent and given the right to build shopping centers and more apartments on nearby farmland.

Rocks and Kahler also got into the business of financing other speculators and developers in Prince George's County. In 1963 they founded Fidelity Federal Savings and Loan Association, with Rocks as chairman of the board, Kahler as vice-president, and Jesse Baggett as a member of the board of directors. Baggett also worked as an appraiser for the savings and loan, which meant that developers paid him fees to estimate for mortgage loan purposes the value of their properties; that value was dependent, of course, on the zoning decisions that Baggett participated in as a county commissioner. The general manager of the savings and loan was Peter J. O'Malley, a law student at the time who later became a partner in Kahler's zoning law firm, a prominent figure in the Prince George's County Democratic Party, and an adviser to Maryland Governor Marvin Mandel.

Fidelity Federal, with the money collected from its depositors, made some loans that helped enrich its own officers. Among these were five loans, totaling more than $500,000, made in 1964 to a development company called the Rev Corporation for the purchase of land from Prince-Mar Builders, a partnership controlled by Ralph Rocks. The loan made it possible for Rocks to collect a sizable profit on the land sale, but the Rev Corporation ran into financial trouble while building houses on the land and could not repay the loan.

Other loans also went sour, and in 1967 U.S. officials who supervise federally chartered and insured savings and loans ordered that Fidelity Federal be absorbed by a healthy savings and loan in Maryland. The merger was necessary, a government spokesman said later, because the savings and loan was not being operated prudently, although Rocks insisted that Fidelity was "well run and growing" and that "there is no sensation" or scandal in what happened. "I just didn't have time to run it," he said.

William Kahler and his other law partner, Samuel J. DeBlasis, also founded a Prince George's county bank, the Southern Maryland Bank and Trust Company, in which they are still involved. DeBlasis was president of the bank and Kahler its lawyer. In 1969, when DeBlasis was named a county judge by Governor Mandel, he stepped down as president of the bank but remained a member of the board of directors—despite adoption by the Maryland court system in July 1971 of a code of judicial ethics that directed judges not to hold directorships of banks. In April 1972, however, after his colleague and former law partner, Kahler, was thrust into the headlines by revelations at the Baggett-Rocks bribery trials, De-Blasis, then fifty-one, resigned from the bench for what he said were health reasons. He rejoined his old law firm and was again elected president of Southern Maryland Bank and Trust.

In late 1973 William Kahler, who was still the bank's lawyer, was convicted of perjury the government accused him of committing during the bribery trials of Baggett and Rocks. He was charged with lying when, among other things, he testified that the Florida vacations for Baggett and planning chairman William Stevens had no connection with decisions favorable to Kahler and Rocks.

Ralph Rocks is still dealing in land and building apartments in Prince George's County, and since the late 1960s he has been supported by the federal government. Rocks has specialized in the development of apartments for moderate-income families with mortgage loans subsidized and guaranteed by the FHA. These multimillion-dollar projects have been reviewed in detail and approved by FHA, which has insured and paid much of the interest on the loans made to Rocks for the projects.

Each loan has paid for everything for a particular project: the price of the land, all construction costs, and a guaranteed 6 per cent construction profit for the builder, Rocks himself. On top of that, Rocks also has siphoned off from the project loan money huge profits on the land bought for the apartments.

In one series of transactions Prince-Mar Builders, the Rocks-controlled partnership, bought up ninety acres of farmland in South Laurel for $8,000 an acre. After getting the land rezoned for apartment development and winning FHA approval and financial support for the projects, Rocks divided the land into three parcels for three different groups of subsidized apartments. He then transferred each of these parcels to one of three other Rocks-Kahler partnerships at stated prices per acre of $18,000, $21,000, and $26,000, respectively. FHA valued the land at these higher prices and approved mortgage loans based on those figures. This meant profits for Rocks and his partners of $10,000, $13,000, and $18,000 per acre on the three land deals—nearly $500,000 altogether.

Rocks has done just as well financially on several other FHA-subsidized apartment projects in Prince George's, as have other developers there and in lower-income suburbs all across the country where local officials have allowed the projects to be built. FHA officials have defended the profiteering possible in this housing program as a necessary incentive to developers who build the badly needed inexpensive housing. But the big built-in profits have inflated the subsidized mortgage loans for the projects—which must be repaid from rental income. Even with the FHA paying much of the interest on the loans, it has become necessary either to raise rents beyond the reach of needy tenants (as has been done in many places) or to leave little of the rental income for maintenance, which allows these projects to fall quickly into disrepair.

These subsidized projects also have burdened Prince George's County with other woes. Because it was one of the few Washington area suburbs to allow FHA-subsidized apartments, it has wound up with nearly all of them—several thousand apartment units in all. Thus, rather than being integrated into the suburbs generally, the lower-income families moving into these projects have once again been concentrated in a few areas, where, as usual, community services for them are inadequate and social problems have festered. The county, moreover, did not provide new schools or recreational facilities in adequate proportion to the large numbers of children moving into these projects, and school overcrowding, delinquency, and vandalism resulted.

The years of rampant real estate exploitation have left a legacy of problems for the new Prince George's County government—which consists of new personnel working under a reorganized governmental structure that was approved by the Prince George's voters in 1970. In addition to the environmental damage and the shortage and high cost of necessary government services, the county, despite the large number of relatively new dwellings, is facing a growing housing problem. The apartments of the 1960s and the little box houses of the 1950s, built both hastily and cheaply by speculators, are wearing out quickly. Blockbusters have already invaded many of Prince George's neighborhoods of single-family houses. Slum landlords who had before operated only inside Washington are now buying run-down Prince George's apartment buildings that have changed hands three and four times in a decade.

Unfortunately, the only answer Prince George's reform government has proposed is more development of the county's dwindling supply of undeveloped land. Only this time the officials want what they consider to be higher-class development: luxury homes and high-rise apartments, light industry, and big office buildings. In the autumn of 1972 the new county council approved the private development of an 18,000-seat sports arena, restaurant, and other facilities in a huge complex with parking for thousands of cars on seventy-five acres of land owned by the local park authority. To make development of the arena legally possible the council opened all 10,700 acres of county park authority land to the possibility of similar "commercial recreational" use, although other projects would still require individual approval by the council. Two local real estate speculators stand to make millions from the transaction: They leased the site from the county, won its rezoning, and sold the lease to developer Abe Pollin for some cash and a large percentage of his profits. Pollin is also the owner of the Capital (formerly Baltimore) Bullets basketball team, and both the Bullets and a professional hockey team are to play in the arena, which Pollin has named the Capital Centre.

The county council, elected on promises to improve Prince George's, is proud of the arena, on which construction was completed near the end of 1973. The officials hope the complex will attract new businesses, including motels and restaurants, to the area and, in the words of one council member, "create for Prince George's a new image" that will attract to it "prestige companies" and the homes of the rich. Already, greedy speculators are fighting over farmland not far from the arena site, where the council has agreed to allow development of high-rise offices and apartments.

Even in a suburb where overly rapid growth has proved to be so obviously disastrous, the "growth is good" syndrome has not been defeated. Rather than stopping to patch the tears rent in its fabric of life by past development and then carefully making and sticking to workable plans for the county's future, the new government is rushing ahead to compete with Washington's other suburbs for still more development. The real estate speculators are still the real planners of what is left to become the Prince George's County of the future.

6

The Great Land Rush

On a sunny May afternoon in Rome an American man and woman were sitting alone on a worn, old stone bench inside the Colosseum. Suddenly, a young Italian man walked up, asked in English if they were from the United States, and invited them to join some other tourists the next day on a bus tour of the city. Drinks and dinner would follow at one of Rome's better-known hotels, and it would all be free. Their host, the young man explained, would be from an American company that wanted the tourists, in return, to see a film after dinner at the hotel.

It was raining the next day, so rather than walk around the city by themselves, the couple went to the address given them and, with a score of other couples, boarded the bus waiting outside. That evening they were introduced to their benefactor: the sales representative of a developer of vacation-home communities in the United States. The film showed what he said were some of his firm's completed developments in Florida and Arizona. Pictured were golf courses, tennis courts, clubhouses, swimming pools, boat docks, beaches, palm trees, and nice little houses. The narrator emphasized how much the lots in these developments had appreciated in value since those projects were begun several years ago.

The film ended with aerial views of arid, sparsely vegetated, vacant land in New Mexico—land that the salesman said was the site of the company's next project and the investment opportunity of a lifetime for the American tourists assembled in that hotel dining room in Rome. They were told that if they bought lots now, before development of vacation homes and recreation facilities began on this land 6,000 miles away in New Mexico, they would be paying the lowest possible prices for property to which the crowded masses of the cities of California and the Southwest would be flocking in the future. Buying immediately, the salesman said, would mean a shrewd investment of a few thousand dollars that would be quickly multiplied.

Each table in the hotel dining room was visited by an English-speaking Italian man or woman who handed out and explained glossy brochures and mimeographed fact sheets. Then, one by one, the couples were led to a small room where the sales representative made the climactic pitch, emphasizing again the property's unusual investment potential, the small required down payment of a few hundred dollars, and the easy 7-year payment plan with, of course, a reasonable finance charge. And buyers could even charge their down payments with a well-known American credit card.

A lot of questions about the land itself were never answered directly. Was it desolate desert? Where was the nearest water? How far was it really from Los Angeles, Phoenix, Albuquerque? Would recreation facilities like those shown in the film really be built on the New Mexico land? When? Instead, the salesman kept turning the conversation back to investment possibilities, as though he were selling stock, except, he said, land is always a safer investment.

Our couple bought nothing. They came away rather amused by the incident. But on the bus that took everyone back to their own hotels that night, they discovered that several other couples had bought lots, one with a check covering the entire purchase price.

These people became part of a swelling army of Americans who have bought land in vacation-home communities in every region and nearly every state of the United States. A surprising number of them were contacted by promoters working during the vacation seasons in European cities and Caribbean resorts or at conventions back home in places like the French Quarter in New Orleans, where college students hand out the free dinner invitations on nearly every street corner around the most popular restaurants, night clubs, and hotels. Many more lot buyers were first attracted by mailed circulars, telephone canvasses, door-to-door salesmen, and media advertising. Indeed, there are few middle-income citizens in the country who have not, in one way or another, been invited to invest. "Pick up any newspaper, turn on any radio or TV station," says George K. Bernstein, the U.S. Department of Housing and Urban Development (HUD) official who tries to police recreation land sales, "and you can hardly miss having the blue skies, clear waters and virgin woodlands of 'Lake Euphoria' extolled to you."

More than 3,500 recreation land developers seeking customers across state lines are now registered with Bernstein's office. Elsewhere in Washington the trade association for this suddenly large industry, the American Land Development Association, has enrolled 9,000 member developers who are busily buying up the country's remaining inexpensive open land. They are subdividing it all into lots averaging a quarter acre in size to be sold at big mark-ups, usually on credit, to city dwellers seeking vacation and retirement homes or just looking for a get-rich-quick investment in real estate.

Three million American families, according to the Census Bureau, already own and use second homes ranging from trailers and cheap A-frames to luxurious ski slope chalets and beachfront condominiums. Several times that many are making payments on vacant lots staked out in recreation land subdivisions along seashores, around lakes, in forests, on mountainsides, in what had been wilderness areas on the marshes of the East Coast, in the swamps of Florida, and all across the great deserts of the West. Some of these "vacation communities" are nothing more than miles and miles of barren land, much of it desert, where numbered stakes delineating individual lots are all that the lot buyers have, besides pieces of paper, to show for their investments.

Yet several hundred thousand more families contract to buy recreation land lots every year in what has certainly become the biggest American land rush since 50,000 settlers raced into the Oklahoma Territory after the stroke of noon on April 22, 1889, to stake out homesteads. In 1970 alone 650,000 recreation land lots were sold for $5.5 billion, according to the American Land Development Association, with the average quarter-acre lot selling for $7,300. This land rush is much less a necessity or a pioneer search for opportunity than it is a hedonistic impulse to escape today's cities and suburbs or a greedy desire to multiply extra money through individual real estate speculation. Mortgage interest, finance charges, and property taxes on these lots and second homes are deductible on federal income tax returns, just as expenses for a family's first home are.

The time has almost passed, however, when people with a little extra money are able to drive out into the countryside and pick up a little land themselves from some individual who wants to sell part or all of his property at a mutually agreeable price. Instead, available land everywhere is being assembled by professional real estate speculators who depend on their control of the market and high-pressure advertising and sales campaigns to sell subdivided sites at highly inflated prices and finance charges. Recreation land has become a big business, with the giants in the field selling hundreds of millions of dollars' worth of lots each year and starting their own finance companies to service customers who buy on credit. Just as suburban real estate speculation came of age in the 1950s, speculation in recreation land boomed during the 1960s.

Unlike the occasional promoter who sold desert lots to city slickers in years past, today's big recreation land speculators are threatening to monopolize and despoil all of the nation's remaining open land. In New Mexico, for instance, one hundred companies now control more than 1 million acres of open land and have subdivided it into enough lots to triple the state's population in the unlikely event that every buyer built on and moved to his property. The vast area around Albuquerque is ringed by staked-out subdivisions containing a total of more than 200,000 lots. To the south Horizon Corporation is marketing more than 160,000 acres—the equivalent of 250 square miles—parceled out in several subdivisions. Horizon, the largest landowner in New Mexico—$220 million worth—is a recreation land giant with 2,500 employees in 60 offices throughout the United States and abroad. Each year the company sells an estimated $80 million worth of lots in New Mexico, Arizona, Texas, and Florida, among other places. North of Albuquerque, another big firm, AMREP, owns the hundred-square-mile Rio Rancho subdivision, where many of the lots have been sold sight unseen to New Yorkers at Manhattan sales dinners. Near Rio Rancho are the smaller 7,500-acre Great Western Cities' subdivision of Cochiti Lake and the 12,000-acre Paradise Hills subdivision, a Horizon Corporation property.

Most of this New Mexico land is dried-out, overgrazed range

sold to the speculators by ranchers who could no longer use it. The land's condition is not helped much by the cutting of dirt subdivision roads, especially in hilly areas, where the removal of the bristly ground cover leaves the dusty ground vulnerable to flash floods in the brief rainy seasons and wind storms the rest of the year. Expensive reclamation of this land is not in any of the speculators' plans.

In a state like nearby California, which had been so much richer in soil, water, flora, and fauna, the damage done by recreation land speculators has been far more noticeable, extensive, and tragic. The speculators have attacked the state's long coastline, its grassy foothills and forested mountains, and its fragile but surprisingly abundant and varied desert life (including palm, Joshua and other trees, and hundreds of kinds of flowering plants).

Public access to California's Pacific coastline and inland lakes and streams has been lost; of the state's 290 miles of ocean beaches suitable for swimming, only 47 are now open to the general public. Trees have been felled by the thousands and hillsides bulldozed for roads to newly subdivided lots; the resulting erosion has filled streams with silt that smothers the spawning beds of fish, as well as the aquatic insects and plankton on which the fish feed. Most recreation land subdivisions in California lack sewers; vacation homes there use septic tanks or the alternative method of spraying sewage over open land, both of which pollute ground water, farm ponds, streams, rivers, lakes, and reservoirs. Feeding and breeding areas for wild animals have been destroyed, and their migration routes interrupted; in many places this could mean the extermination of deer, mountain lions, and sheep, just as the great California grizzly bear was killed off before them.

In the mountains popular with skiers in Colorado, Idaho, Utah, California, and New England, the mountainsides themselves and the valleys between them are being subdivided and developed. Tree-cutting and earth-moving are causing erosion of the steep slopes and filling once-clear mountain streams with silt. Polluted ground water is also seeping into those streams, and the once-clear mountain air is being darkened by auto fumes and soot.

Tourism, which includes recreation land development, has replaced ranching as Colorado's second largest industry (with manufacturing first). One of the state's most dramatically changed places is Vail, the crowded ski resort and second-home community crammed into the narrow, 11-mile-long Gore Creek Valley high in the Rockies. Before 1960 only a very few ranchers and their grazing cattle and sheep moved through the meadows along the creek, while elk, deer, and an occasional mountain lion inhabited the aspen, balsam, and pine woods on the mountainsides flanking the valley. Today, open land on the valley floor is so scarce that skiers' cottages built during the 1960s are already being torn down to make room for multistory condominiums. Automobile traffic has become so heavy and the smoke from fireplace chimneys so thick that smog frequently settles into the valley. And, of course, the water in Gore Creek is polluted now.

Those who are already there, and thus part of the problem themselves, have suddenly become worried about the state's environment—"Don't Californicate Colorado," warns one bumper sticker—but eager real estate speculators pay attention only to the spectacular increase in land prices. Gore Valley meadow land that sold for $50 an acre in the 1950s is now downtown Vail footage selling at the equivalent of more than $250,000 an acre for commercial and condominium use. Second-home subdividers looking for cheaper land with which to make the next killing are now buying up other valleys and mountainsides around Vail, in a process being repeated all over Colorado. Some speculators even sell lots from counters at Denver's Stapleton airport.

In New England, where vacationers go to ski in the winter and escape the hot, grimy cities of the East Coast in the summer, New Hampshire has counted at least 60,000 vacation homes inside its borders, with two more recreation land projects of 1,000 acres each now being developed. Three projects of 2,000 lots each are under way in Vermont, where at least 25,000 vacation homes already exist. Worried state officials and legislators, who want to keep Vermont the "state in a very natural state" described by Robert Frost, have responded by enacting and vigorously enforcing new laws setting strict guidelines for the preservation of the quality of the air, water, and soil in the area. Subdivision permits have become much harder to obtain under these laws, and many recreation land speculators have been discouraged from buying Vermont land by the prospect of huge expenditures for sewage treatment, site grading, and the like. Other speculators, however, are challenging the Vermont laws in court.

In upper New York State the forested Adirondacks have become another battleground. Speculators who have been buying up 3.7 million acres of private land in the Adirondack State Forest Preserve are pressing local officials to allow "rural residential" development of that land, meaning more subdivisions of vacation-home lots. In 1971 Horizon Corporation bought 25,000 acres in the Adirondacks on which it wants built 5,000 to 10,000 or more vacation homes, which could bring 40,000 seasonal residents to the area. Only the tiny town of Colton, population 1,200, now stands in the middle of the otherwise undisturbed woodlands. When its residents complained about paying for sewers and water lines for all those people, a Horizon executive told them at a public meeting that they had nothing to worry about. His firm's project would depend on wells for drinking water and septic tanks for sewage disposal—a one-two punch that would surely ruin the shallow soil and water table of the rocky Adirondacks.

While battles are still being fought over the nation's mountainsides, the war with speculators seem to have already been lost on its beaches. The Atlantic coastline is becoming one long strip city. Where there are not metropolises like New York, there are overgrown resort towns like Ocean City, Maryland, and back-to-back recreation land subdivisions, many of them tightly packed mobile home parks on the beach. "People come from many miles to the shore," one observer noted, "to live ten feet apart in metal boxes."

The Atlantic Coast is perhaps 1,500 miles long as the crow flies, but it has 17,864 miles of shore, counting the rims of all the bays and estuaries that reach inland from the ocean, according to the U.S. Army Corps of Engineers. Yet of all of that shoreline, only 8 per cent has been reserved for public use; much of the rest is being ravaged by real estate speculators. The public also is losing large chunks of its precious little shoreline in parks like Assateague National Seashore to the worsening erosion caused by nearby private development. As developers dredge and fill marshland, pushing the land line farther into the ocean to create more second-home lots, and thrust giant jetties out into the water to protect commercial beaches, as has been done at Ocean City, Maryland, they upset sand-bearing currents in the ocean and force changes in the contour of the coast. The southern tip of the Assateague National Seashore is disappearing at the rate of sixty feet a year. The Corps of Engineers has estimated that a total of 180 miles of beach on the meandering Atlantic coastline are presently being eaten away by erosion.

In Florida the land along the coastal beaches is nearly all being developed into giant subdivisions by huge corporations. International Telephone and Telegraph's ITT Community Development Corporation, for example, has mounted a nationwide campaign to sell lots at its 100,000-acre Palm Coast subdivision between St. Augustine and Daytona Beach. Other speculators have moved into the swamps of the interior and onto the slightly higher ground Floridians call the "ridge" in the center of the state. The swamps, of course, had been the last refuge for Florida's remaining exotic wildlife: alligators, otters, panthers, black bear, and deer among more than a hundred species of animals, and cypress trees, royal palms, and wild orchids among the tropical plants. The land on the ridge had been covered with forests, citrus groves, and rich pastures for cattle. All of this has now been threatened by the development of subdivisions of lots for vacation and retirement homes and trailers.

One of the most seriously threatened of Florida's irreplaceable swamps is Big Cypress in the Everglades near the southern tip of the state. The lifeline of Big Cypress is the Fakahatchee Strand, a 10-mile-wide, 2-foot-deep, river-like fresh-water channel lined with cypress trees that winds through the swamp, feeding its hidden lakes and sustaining its wildlife. The Fakahatchee Strand was first raped just after World War II by a New York lumber company that logged most of its 600-year-old cypress trees. That destruction was finally stopped in 1954, and new trees have miraculously sprouted from the huge stumps of those that were cut down and have already grown to heights of a hundred feet and more.

In 1966 the Gulf American Land Corporation, then Florida's largest land speculator, bought up 75,000 acres of swamp just west of the Fakahatchee Strand. Shortly thereafter Gulf American was taken over by new investors who created the GAC Corporation, which added to it a consumer credit company to collect finance charges on the notes signed by land buyers who make their purchases on credit. GAC has expanded its land holdings in Florida to more than 300,000 acres, in addition to other vast recreation land subdivisions it is promoting in Arizona. In 1970 GAC's reported sales volume, including the activities of its consumer credit company and a subsidiary insurance company, was $1.8 billion.

In order to drain the firm's swamp property so that it could be built on, GAC dug canals leading to the Gulf of Mexico in the Big Cypress Swamp. The canals also have drawn water from the nearby Fakahatchee Strand, however. The water level of that channel has been falling steadily, depriving the wildlife living in the area of the periodic fresh-water flooding necessary for life. Deadly salt water has begun to creep up into the strand to replace some of the lost fresh water, and the over-all lower water level of the swamp has exposed its peat, sawgrass, and trees to flash lightning fires that could completely destroy the strand area's vegetation in a few days' time.

Florida officials have been trying to force GAC to fill in those of its canals that are draining water from the strand. The state also is considering public purchase of 43,000 acres of swamp around the strand in order to gain undisputed control of its drainage. Unless the state acts, however, GAC is unlikely to do anything to protect the strand that might jeopardize the big profits it has already made on its own swamp land. Property that GAC bought for about $100 an acre was subdivided into lots sold at the rate of $3,000 to $5,000 an acre, even though much of the land was still under water.

GAC's oldest Florida development is Cape Coral, a combined suburban subdivision and vacation community for boatowners on the state's southern Gulf Coast, seven miles southwest of Fort Myers. Much of the Cape Coral land also was under water before GAC crisscrossed it with canals to drain the building lots and provide channels for pleasure boats and lot-front moorings. Sand and mud dredged from the canals were piled onto the drained soil to make it more substantial. In some places GAC extended the usable Cape Coral land out into the ocean by filling in marshes normally washed by the tides. In Florida this land belongs to the state, and officials and GAC executives have been haggling over what the firm will pay the state for this appropriation of public property.

What is even more significant about Cape Coral, however, is that the area had been "wetlands"—coastal land covered by shallow water. Wetlands are the nurseries of sea life and among the most naturally productive areas on earth. These marshes, swamps, and mud flats are highly efficient in converting the sun's energy into growing plants, which provide food for microorganisms. These, in turn, are food for larger water creatures, which, finally, are food for fish, oysters, crabs, and waterfowl. This chain of life is destroyed when developers dredge or cover over wetlands, as they are doing up and down the Atlantic Coast. In a July 1972 survey of various portions of the Atlantic shoreline adding up to about half the coast, the U.S. Bureau of Sport Fisheries and Wildlife found eighty-two places where the tidal marshlands, which are supposed to be under federal protection, were being illegally dredged and filled.

Little remains of the wetlands of Florida, where, for example, one entire shallow bay, Boca Ciega Bay, which contained thirty square miles of wetlands, has been dredged and filled by speculators on the Gulf Coast near St. Petersburg. Forty-five recreation land developments are presently being carved out of the coastline wetlands of the Carolinas; Virginia and Maryland also are fast losing much of their wetlands to filled-in lots for second-home trailers and condominiums. Even Delaware, which has what were considered to be model wetlands protection laws, is giving in to speculators who have begun dredging and filling Rehoboth and Assawoman bays. One man in North Carolina has turned the salt marshes of his shorefront land near New Bern into a vacation trailer park by filling the marsh with trash, including garbage, old tires, and bedsprings, and then covering it with topsoil.

A spirited battle is now being fought over what remains of the once plentiful coastal wetlands of adjoining Worcester County, Maryland, and Accomack County, Virginia. In the southern part of Worcester county, where the chicken farmers and shell fishermen had dominated life until recently, the real estate speculators are now moving in. Among them is none other than Jerry Wolman, who made a fortune strewing suburban Prince George's County, Maryland, with apartment developments and then lost much of his money when his paper empire of high-rise downtown buildings collapsed. Wolman is staking a comeback in real estate partly on a planned 3,200-acre recreation land subdivision projected for 40,000 people on what are now wetlands in Worcester County. Wolman had to weather a thus far unsuccessful legal challenge by fifty angry nearby residents before getting preliminary rezoning and dredging permission for his proposed "Harbour Towne."

Just across the state in Virginia is an object lesson in what happens when local citizens and government officials wait too long to act. There, on 1,000 acres of what had been farms and wetlands along the coast of Accomack County, is Captain's Cove—a recreation land subdivision of 3,754 lots, 600 of which are to front on winding canals being dredged out of the marshes. The project is be-

ing developed by the First Charter Land Corporation, formed by
three wealthy residents (including a municipal judge) of Fairfax
County, Virginia.

In 1970, without applying for the federal permit required for
dredging tidal wetlands, First Charter sent a huge hydraulic dredge
to the Captain's Cove marshes, where it began sucking up mud
teeming with sea life and throwing it up onto the land to be filled
for homesites. A shell fisherman eventually complained to Virginia
officials when he found that silt from the dredging was killing clams
in the open water of the bay in front of the project. The State Water Control Board ordered the dredging to be stopped—a year after
it began—and the U.S. Army Corps of Engineers finally cited First
Charter for dredging without a permit. Its officers pleaded guilty to
four of twenty-nine federal criminal charges of illegal dredging and
dumping of soil in navigable waters, and the corporation was fined
$4,000. Spokesmen for Captain's Cove later said that the owners
regarded their dredging violation as a "technicality" and their guilty
plea a "compromise" with federal authorities. Nevertheless, First
Charter was delayed from obtaining a dredging permit by opposition
from state officials.

Meanwhile, however, Captain's Cove salesmen—after luring prospective customers there with offers of free gifts, cash refunds of
their auto expenses, and a chance to win a free trip to Florida—were
still doing a brisk business selling lots, some at prices of more than
$20,000 each for just 150 feet of frontage on a drainage canal, al-
though many of the lots were still under water. The promised completion of the boat canals, a marina, and sewers was delayed by the
litigation over the dredging, and twenty-one lot buyers sued First
Charter for fraud. The corporation filed a countersuit charging that
these customers are out to defame it, and the case is still pending.

Too much damage already has been done at Captain's Cove,
however. A U.S. Bureau of Sport Fisheries and Wildlife report on
the project to the Corps of Engineers concluded that First Charter
"has destroyed a highly productive marine resource area" where
254 species of birds, including large herons and bald eagles, and 65
species of fish, including oysters, clams, and blue crabs, had thrived.
The report said the marshlands at Captain's Cove "that have been
altered are no longer a naturally functioning ecosystem, but a sterile
pile presently capable of furnishing only temporary feeding habitats
for shore birds and dabbling ducks." Biologists from the Virginia

Institute of Marine Sciences estimated that 240 acres of wetlands have been destroyed by dredging thus far at Captain's Cove. They found this advertised paradise to be a "large barren area" where "considerable erosion was evident," causing siltation that was continuing to harm a large area of the bay around the project.

An attorney for First Charter dismissed these reports as "bureaucratic harassment" of Captain's Cove. When asked about the threat to the bald eagle, the national symbol, he said, "Yes, well, what are we supposed to do about that? Maybe we could give him a waterfront lot."

Outrageous greed is what fuels the recreation land juggernaut. Money is the only consideration at every stage of a project like Lake of the Pines, marketed by Boise-Cascade in the Sierra Nevada mountains in northeastern California. The rugged, remote land for the project had been appraised by Nevada County tax assessors at $88 an acre, so the ranchers who owned it were grateful to receive $876 an acre from Boise-Cascade, which subdivided and sold it for the equivalent of $12,000 to $36,000 an acre. Of course, the lot buyers themselves hope eventually to make a profit reselling their parcels.

Several California recreation land subdivisions have sold lots at prices equal to nearly $50,000 an acre. Harold Berliner, district attorney of Nevada County, has estimated that an average project yields $50 million worth of lot sales in a few years' time. Berliner has been trying to police speculators who have already subdivided 58,000 acres of his mountainous county, whose population has never much exceeded 25,000 people. Berliner's investigations have shown that one-third of a project's income is spent on the cost of the land, subdividing it, laying out roads, and putting in a man-made lake or other sales attraction; another third pays for advertising and sales expenses; and the final third is profit.

That profit can be sizable for any investor with enough capital or borrowing capacity to make the initial outlay for the land, a minimum of improvements, and a promotional campaign, which is why recreation land sales have recently attracted so many big companies —from land specialists like GAC and Horizon to other corporations like Westinghouse (in Florida), Ralston-Purina (in Colorado), and Boise-Cascade. One Boise-Cascade executive called recreation land sales "the great earnings faucet in the sky." That was back in 1969 when that company sold $164 million worth of lots. At that time the firm was marketing land in twenty-nine recreation projects nationally. Eighteen of them, covering 71,000 acres, were in California.

To make big money, each project has to be large enough to justify an expensive promotion campaign and to give the speculator a monopoly on land in the area, so that the inflated lot prices he charges will not be undercut by smaller landowners nearby. The giant firms send out scouts to buy up land under a variety of names, so that no one else will know an assembly is under way. When possible, these agents pay only for options on the land, with final payment to be made after the assembly is complete, the land is rezoned and subdivided, and the lots are being sold; then the original seller of the land receives from the speculator a prorated portion of his payment as each lot is sold. The profit for the original landowner in the end usually exceeds even his most optimistic assessments of the land's worth.

To win zoning that allows subdivisions and lot sales, a big company like Boise-Cascade, Horizon, or GAC flies in lawyers and executives with glossy plans, color movies, and consultants' studies of the environmental impact of the proposed project. If local officials harbor doubts about the extravagant plans and grand assurances that the project will protect the natural environment, expand the locality's property tax base, and enrich its merchants, they are usually unable to afford expert studies of their own.

Officials are also often offered personal financial incentives to approve zoning changes, a practice that has been voluminously documented in the Ralph Nader task force study, *Land and Power in California.* In Riverside County, for instance, three county supervisors who had previously defeated rezoning for a 4,000-lot recreation land project, approved it after each received cash political campaign contributions of from $750 to $3,500 from the developer's attorney. The generosity of Boise-Cascade in particular was detailed in the Nader report:

> One local district attorney was hired by Boise-Cascade to handle a water problem in a neighboring county; a county planning director was hired off the county payroll by Boise-Cascade midway through a development project; the mayor of a North Coast city [was] also Boise-Cascade's public relations man for the area; the Boise-Cascade task force patronized the hotel and restaurant of one of the county supervisors, who also received free advertisements in the company

newspaper; in another county . . . another supervisor was awarded a sizable campaign contribution and yet another was graced by the project's purchase of three automobiles from his local dealership. In another county, a member of the planning commission is a licensed Boise-Cascade salesman . . . and Boise-Cascade made a plane available for one former county supervisor running for state-wide office.

In Maryland, where the dredging of boat canals and filling of land for Boise-Cascade's giant Ocean Pines seashore development is helping to destroy that state's Atlantic Coast wetlands, the firm has made campaign contributions to Maryland Governor Marvin Mandel, including one $2,000 contribution made at a Mandel fund-raising dinner in 1969.

The advertising and sales promotion of the projects are intended to convince prospective lot buyers that they, too, stand a good chance of making some fast money. Full-page newspaper advertisements artfully combine misleading impressions of the subdivision's recreational attractions with outlandish exaggerations of its investment potential. The ads for one California project were highlighted by a large picture of Yosemite Falls, which are located twenty-six miles away in a national park. A mountain lake encircled by trees and grassy banks is pictured in ads for Brooktrails, north of San Francisco, although the project's only lake is a small man-made reservoir surrounded by huge, sharp-edged rocks bulldozed from its bottom. Other ads feature full-color artist's conceptions of what country clubs, lodges, golf courses, and swimming pools are to look like when they are developed, although the fine print often points out that none of these has been started yet, so that smart investors will have a chance to buy lots at "low pre-development prices."

The point most often stressed in the advertisements is that available land is growing scarcer, especially where the advertised project is located, so it is certain to increase dramatically in price. For lots in what the speculators refer to as Antelope Valley, actually part of the hot, dry Mojave Desert northeast of Los Angeles, the scarcity of land elsewhere around the Los Angeles area is the primary selling point. "Looking for something just for the profit in it?" ask the advertisements of one Antelope Valley speculator. Another, Calindel Enterprises, presents this scenario:

We are talking about Orange County when most of it was still orange groves and a few sleepy towns. Just as Beverly Hills replaced bean fields and Anaheim shouldered aside orange groves, so is the Antelope Valley pushing aside alfalfa ranches to make way for the most courageous land boom in California's history.

The Antelope Valley's biggest subdivision is California City, where real estate speculator N. K. Mendelsohn bought 100,000 acres of desert land at $109 an acre and has been selling it at from $2,500 for a quarter-acre lot to $9,000 for a 2.5-acre lot. So far 32,000 buyers throughout the United States and in such faraway places as Germany and the Philippines have bought $100 million worth of lots in California City, even though most of them have never been there and do not know, for instance, that the temperature during the rainless summers goes up to 110 degrees during the day and down to 55 at night.

The manual for California City salesmen is wonderfully instructive in the ways of land promotion:

> 90 per cent of the people buy, because they lack the courage to continue saying "no." Thus, in our sales presentation at one point or another, we are certainly going to use both persistence and persuasion, knowing that if we persuaded our customer to save his money and invest it in a parcel of our land, we are doing him a favor, and that otherwise the money would probably be spent on some foolish or unessential thing. . . .
>
> Do NOT be trapped by the customer into describing the improvements [promised for the future].
>
> Never call the Mojave, the Mojave *Desert*. Call it the Antelope Valley.
>
> Special note:
>
> Referring again to the question of "Mojave," and "Mojave Desert." Because people get their idea of the kind of land represented by the words "Mojave" and "Desert" from their early school geography book, it is better to *never* use either word. Always refer to our part of Southwest California as "Antelope Valley."

The eventual discovery that Antelope Valley is really the Mojave Desert is only one of many disillusionments suffered by those who blindly and greedily sign to buy recreation land lots without investigating the project first. Promised country clubs are seldom built. A project's man-made lake turns out, like the one at Boise-Cascade's Lake of the Pines, to be accessible only to those families who pay, on top of the price of their lots, expensive dues to a swimming or country club owned by the developer. Buyers told by salesmen that they could use their lots for camping until they can build on them find out that state or local laws prohibit camping everywhere but in designated public campgrounds.

Advertisements for Shelter Cove, a project on the Pacific Coast north of San Francisco, promised that "all residents of Shelter Cove have free access to the beach," but it turned out that oceanfront lot owners could legally keep everyone else off. Salesmen for the Southwest Land Corporation, promoter of Santa California, in New Mexico, never told buyers of lots there that a previous mineral rights agreement allowed anyone to come onto any lot, no matter who had bought it, and dig it up to look for silver, coal, or gravel, or that the required land-offering report filed with HUD showed in Santa California "there are no provisions for street maintenance after 1975 [and] flash floods may destroy portions of the streets in certain units."

Then there are the financial pitfalls. In many projects the streets, sewers, water lines, wells, reservoirs, or man-made lakes were not put in at developer's expense at all; instead, the developer had local authorities sell public bonds to finance the improvements at the expense of the lot buyers, who will have to pay off those bonds in the future. The HUD report for the Brooktrails project in northern California states that each lot buyer there is liable for a $2,000 lien on his property and a special tax levy of up to ten cents per $100 of assessed valuation to pay off nearly $5 million worth of bonds for public improvements, mostly water and sewer lines required by state law. Another $4 million in improvement bonds can still be issued in the future without a vote of Brooktrails's lot owners. Owners of lots in many recreation subdivisions have been told, after putting their money down, that they may never be able to build on their property, because the local and state governments will not pay to put in public water and sewage lines, and local laws forbid the property owners to install septic tanks.

Even the actual purchase of a lot is not what it seems to be. Most recreation land lots are sold on credit: so much down and so much a month. At Rio Rancho, a relatively low-priced project on arid, unimproved New Mexico land, a quarter-acre lot generally has sold for $2,500—$260 down, $34 a month. When the monthly payments and down payment are all added up in most cases, however, the total comes to far more than $2,500, because the Rio Rancho developer, AMREP, Inc., collects a 7.5 per cent finance charge on top of the quoted lot price. Most other recreation land developers operate the same way. The finance charge is not mortgage interest because there is usually no mortgage. The lot buyer has no claim to title for the land until he has finished making payments in seven to ten years' time. Until then, if he misses a single payment, he could lose all rights to the land; meanwhile, the developer can keep the payments already made and resell the lot. In some places, buyers may never get a clear title to what they thought was their property. Many purchasers of lots in a mountain recreation land subdivision in the state of Washington have found their lots overlapped those of other buyers on the official local land records, and expensive court proceedings to straighten out the titles have resulted.

A few projects, including Rio Rancho in New Mexico, allow buyers up to six months to withdraw from the deal and get their money back if they are unsatisfied, provided they have visited the project. Thus, from New York, where Rio Rancho and other Southwestern recreation land projects (as well as those in Florida) draw a large share of their customers, lot buyers would have to pay to fly perhaps 2,000 miles to see their lots. And Rio Rancho, among others, generally requires that your visit be a "registered personal inspection" on an AMREP chartered tour with AMREP charging, in addition to the standard air fare, for meals, lodging at its motel, and transportation on its bus.

Recreation subdivisions can prove costly to the communities in which they are located. Local officials soon find that instead of the promised expanded property tax base, they are faced with a mounting debt for the public improvements and services needed at these projects, for which it is difficult to make either the developer or the lot buyers pay. Liens and taxes levied on the property itself mean little, when no one will pay them and no one else can be found to buy the property should the authorities want to confiscate and sell it to satisfy the debt. One rural county north of San Francisco found itself $2 million in debt after making necessary road, drainage, and sewage repairs in a recreation land subdivision where one-third of the property tax goes unpaid year after year.

Occasionally, the projects backfire for the greedy speculators. Boise-Cascade, for example, launched too many projects in too short a time, tying up so much money in land acquisition and sales promotion that the incoming flow of cash from the lot buyers' small down payments and monthly installments could not meet the over-extended conglomerate's needs after the first couple of years. "The great earnings faucet in the sky" eventually produced only a trickle, compared to what Boise-Cascade executives had expected.

Matters worsened when, beginning in 1970, consumer advocates like the Nader task force and governmental authorities like Nevada County attorney general Harold Berliner and the Maryland real estate commission began investigating sales practices at various Boise-Cascade projects. Court suits and judgments against the firm followed, and some of its sales offices were shut down. The conglomerate wound up $85 million in the red in 1971 and wrote off $200 million worth of real estate investments in 1972, when it began to ease out of the recreation land field.

Boise-Cascade's withdrawal did not come soon enough to save Maryland's coastal wetlands from dredging and filling at the Ocean Pines project, or the foothills of the Sierra Nevadas from erosion and water pollution at Lake of the Pines in Nevada County, California, or the landscape in other places from the gravel roads, bull-dozed lots, septic tanks, and other trappings of Boise-Cascade's two dozen recreation land ventures. And Boise-Cascade is pulling out of these projects too soon to correct the damage it has done or to finish the expensive improvements it promised those who bought lots. Like other speculators, the firm went into recreation land only for the money, and when it did not come fast enough Boise literally pulled up stakes and moved out in a hurry, leaving behind land that will never be the same again.

The way all recreation land speculators operate, and the effect they have on the landscape, can perhaps best be summarized by the ironic telegram that, according to Nader's California report, the sales manager at the Lake Wildwood project in Nevada County, California, sent to Boise-Cascade's headquarters in the days of the big profits after the last Lake Wildwood lot was sold: MISSION ACCOMPLISHED. WILDWOOD IS DEAD. WHERE DO YOU WANT US NEXT?

7

The New Town Hoax

On a Saturday afternoon in October 1971, in 100-degree Arizona desert heat, several hundred British and American public officials, journalists, entertainment personalities, and other celebrities—most of whom were flown in for the day from hotels in Los Angeles, Las Vegas, and Phoenix—sat down to a sumptuous black-tie dinner inside a huge, red-and-white striped circus tent on London Bridge. They ate New England lobster, caviar, English–style roast beef, Cornish pasties, champagne-glazed baby carrots, and French vanilla ice cream topped with liqueur. After the banquet the lord mayor of London and the governor of Arizona dedicated the reconstructed bridge, 700 people in medieval English costumes paraded across it, a water ski show and the First Annual London Bridge Channel Swim took place in the freshly dug waterway beneath it, and an authentic City of London–owned English pub was opened on a facsimile London street at its base.

Millionaire chain-saw manufacturer Robert McCulloch bought the 140-year-old stone bridge for $2.5 million from the British, who have replaced it with a new span across the Thames. McCulloch paid $8 million more to have it disassembled into 10,246 numbered pieces of granite and shipped by boat and truck to Arizona, where the 1,005-foot-long bridge was put back together under the direction of a British engineer with construction experience in the Sahara. McCulloch's site was in the Mojave Desert near the Arizona-California border, 250 miles east of Los Angeles and 200 miles northwest of Phoenix, on a small peninsula on the east bank of man-made Lake Havasu, a long forgotten reservoir created in 1938 by completion of the Parker Dam on the Colorado River.

Once the bridge was in place, with nothing but dry desert beneath it, McCulloch had a channel cut across the peninsula so that water would flow under the bridge and back into the lake, making part of the peninsula an island connected to the rest by the bridge. He then persuaded the City of London Corporation, the enterprising government of the autonomous mile-square financial district in the center of London, to build and operate a pub in what is to be a $1.5 million English village laid out at the mainland end of the bridge by Robert Wood, a designer of California's Disneyland. Palm trees and exotic plants also were transported to McCulloch's artificial desert oasis around the bridge and grouped in small, constantly watered tropical gardens that stand in bizarre juxtaposition with the gaslight-lined London street and the bridge itself. Normally, nothing grows in this desolate area but occasional squat scrub trees and sagebrush-like ground cover. McCulloch even brought sand to the desert to cover the otherwise rocky beach in front of his resort motel on the shore of Lake Havasu.

On the face of it all this adds up to no more than an outlandish promotional stunt in the grand American tradition of Buffalo Bill Cody and P. T. Barnum—or, as McCulloch and Wood hope, a unique tourist attraction that might in time rival Disneyland. But the absurdity and significance of what McCulloch is doing in the desert does not end there. Around London Bridge and Lake Havasu he also is building what he calls a "model city," Lake Havasu City, which has been widely and expensively promoted as a "prototype for the city of the future," based on a "master plan" drawn up by Wood. After nearly ten years of development, 8,000 people—a good number of them families of workers in McCulloch factories moved to Lake Havasu City from Los Angeles—have come to live in this hot, dry, remote wasteland of dust and rock, a landscape that except for the lake and McCulloch's trucked-in palm trees most resembles the surface of the moon.

It is disturbing, though perhaps revealing, that Lake Havasu City also has been cited by other developers, many urban experts, and journalists as one of America's important "new town" projects and a promising alternative to city decay and suburban sprawl. Gurney Breckenfeld, a Time, Inc., editor who writes about urban development for *Fortune* magazine, lavishly praised Lake Havasu

City in his recent book on U.S. new town projects. He called it a "diversified balance of industry and hedonism" that proves that private enterprise should be solely entrusted with American community building in the future. A long *New York Times* article seriously discussed Lake Havasu City as "an adolescent 'new town' " that could become, in an "unspoiled" natural area, a marked improvement on "the congestion in the nation's urban areas." The *Los Angeles Times* devoted almost two pages of one Sunday edition to Lake Havasu City and the rebuilding of London Bridge there. At the bridge dedication were correspondents from the *Los Angeles Times, New York Times, Washington Post,* many other American papers, and several London dailies, plus domestic and foreign television networks, almost all of whom dutifully reported that Lake Havasu City was an important and apparently successful new town experiment.

Except for its development in such an isolated location, however, Lake Havasu City is not really an experimental new town, model community, or the prototype for anything but another Los Angeles in miniature. The barren landscape has been scarred with a widely scattered confusion of cinderblock stores and factories, mobile-home colonies, and ranch-style houses with "lawns" of dyed pebbles from Las Vegas, 150 miles north.

Wood's master plan actually has planned for very little. Industry —which consists almost exclusively of McCulloch factories for the manufacture of chain saws, boat motors, and light airplanes—has been segregated behind a ridge on dusty land farthest from the lake. The house trailers in which many of the factory workers and their families live also have been banished to this least desirable part of town. The big motels, irrigated golf courses, and expensive golf course homesites have been allocated the choicest locations, and building heights have been limited so that the lake can be seen from more of the otherwise nonscenic site. The peninsula onto which London Bridge was moved has been reserved for other motels, marinas, beaches, and an airstrip for McCulloch's own airline, which is Lake Havasu City's only nonauto connection with the outside world.

The rest of the city has been allowed to just happen in whatever way has proved to be the most profitable for McCulloch. In order to sell lots to buyers wherever they want them, he has paved 373 miles of otherwise empty streets out to the most distant homesites, a practice that has so spread out the community that the cost of utilities and public services is likely to rise steeply in the future. So, too, will the property taxes, when it comes time for Lake Havasu City residents to repay the public bonds sold by McCulloch's own special irrigation district to finance the present roads, sewers, and water lines.

Despite glowing press and planning journal notices that blindly accept McCulloch's model community claims, not one innovation has been attempted in automobile traffic management, parking, public transportation (except for the single double-decker British bus that rolls across London Bridge), housing construction, shopping facilities, over-all land use, public services, trash disposal, pollution prevention, or social welfare. If it ever does grow to the 100,000 population figure predicted by McCulloch, Lake Havasu City can be expected to suffer from nearly every urban problem that its residents supposedly left behind when they moved to the new community. Some families, perhaps already looking to that day, have built their new homes in this escapist paradise with bars across all the windows.

What McCulloch really is engaged in, and what is sold hardest to prospective Lake Havasu City lot buyers, is real estate speculation. "Those with foresight to invest in this growth can look toward being richly rewarded," promises one sales brochure. Another points to the lake and London Bridge and adds: "Just as tourism and recreation are among Arizona's primary sources of income, Lake Havasu City landowners and businessmen benefit from an influx of profitable visitors." A quote from a Presidential message to Congress—"land [for residential use] is increasing in value almost ten per cent a year . . . the cost of land for recreation is spiraling at a considerably higher rate"—is followed by the admonition that "land at Lake Havasu City is the best of both . . . which can spiral in value for the benefit of all who invest in Lake Havasu City now." Rather than a bright, new, urban experiment, Lake Havasu City actually is just another old-fashioned desert land sales scheme.

McCulloch, a tall, slim, delicately featured man with snow-white hair, is no stranger to land speculation. Before beginning Lake Havasu City, whose 16,500 acres he bought from the state of Arizona at a public auction of surplus land, he added considerably to his manufacturing profits by making carefully timed sales of hundreds of acres he had accumulated over the years around his factories in suburban Los Angeles. And he recently announced plans to build another new community, to be called Fountain Hills, on 12,000 acres of desiccated Arizona range surrounded by mountains and federal Indian reservations thirty miles northeast of Phoenix.

McCulloch is shrewd to promote these projects as new towns because in the 1970s this is where real estate speculation action is. All manner of experts on urban problems have urged that future large-scale development in the United States be limited as much as possible to carefully planned new towns. In 1969 the National Committee on Urban Growth Policy—composed of the U.S. Conference of Mayors, National League of Cities, National Association of Counties, and Urban America, Inc.—recommended building 110 new towns in this country by the year 2000, a proposal that has received wide favorable notice. Each announcement of an individual new town project has, like Lake Havasu City, been well publicized by the media as a potential solution to city and suburban growth problems. The federal government, under legislation approved by Congress in 1968 and 1970, has encouraged new town development with hundreds of millions of dollars in public financial support and a variety of important bureaucratic favors. Local officials and planners, who have begun blocking new suburban subdivisions, have been more liberal in granting rezonings for projects presented as new towns. Lot and home buyers also have responded favorably to developments with new town images.

Dozens of projects that city planners and real estate professionals consider new towns have already been started with and without federal support—from the well-known Columbia, Maryland, and Reston, Virginia, projects to Westlake, Irvine, Valencia, Mission Viejo and Foster City in California, from Jonathan and Cedar-Riverside in Minnesota, Park Forest South in Illinois, and Stansbury Park in Utah to Lake Havasu City and Litchfield Park, Arizona, Clear Lake City, Texas, and New Orleans East, Louisiana.

Among the investors in these and other projects marketed as new towns are established suburban developers like Kaufman and Broad, Levitt and Sons, and James Rouse, the shopping center builder and developer of Columbia; recreation land lot sellers like McCulloch, Boise-Cascade, N. K. Mendelsohn of California City, and Del Webb of the Sun City retirement communities; and diverse corporations looking for extra profits in real estate, including Goodyear, Westinghouse, Philip Morris, Gulf Oil, Kaiser Aluminum, Aetna Life and Casualty, Humble Oil, Burlington, U.S. Gypsum, American-Hawaiian Steamship, Ford Motors, Sun Oil, Connecticut General Life, Occidental Petroleum, Stanley Marcus of Nieman-Marcus stores, and the huge Newhall and Irvine corporate ranches. At seminars held by James Rouse's Columbia development team for other businessmen interested in new town investment, there have been representatives from Owens-Corning Fiberglas, Chrysler Motors, Chemical Bank of New York, the Dillon, Read, & Company securities firm, and GAC Corporation, among others. "This is the kickoff period," said a Rouse Company vice-president, "of a decade during which I am sure we'll see an enormous growth in new communities."

"The new town movement is about to come of age in America," *Fortune* magazine announced to the business world in 1971. "The decade of the seventies will see scores if not hundreds of such new developments spring up, transforming not just the physical landscape, inside and outside of cities, but the human affairs of millions of Americans as well."

That is the promise attached to new towns in the United States: the making of a new, far different, and better urban America. The scattered city of suburbia would be pulled together into a livable and identifiable community. Some of the countryside that had once been the primary attraction of suburban living would be saved, and some of the concentration of varied activities that once made city living so convenient would be recreated without the pollution, social problems, and unmanageable scale of present cities. People of all races and incomes would be given an opportunity to share this new environment.

Hopes were high because of what the planners, academics, and journalists had reported about the many existing new towns in Europe. The first English "garden cities" of two generations ago pioneered new arrangements of buildings on the landscape to create more public green space. Since then European new town projects, with extensive government support, have been experimenting with everything from the creation of entirely separate circulation systems for pedestrians and autos and the integration of social classes and housing types to the incineration of residents' garbage in plants that use the resultant energy for the new town's utilities.

Privately developed American new towns, according to a frequently cited 1971 *Harvard Business Review* analysis, are "intended to serve the human desire to belong to a community having
a range of options for housing, employment and recreation." The
report added that new towns should have "adequate public facilities," protected environments, "diversity of housing and life styles,"
and enough economic self-sufficiency so that residents who do not
want to commute may work near their homes. Leaders of the
American new town movement have also promised bold experimentation with possible solutions to urban problems. Congress, for
its part, has required that federally assisted new town projects be
racially and economically integrated—an attempt to reduce some of
the residential stratification that the government's own housing programs have in the past helped foster in cities and suburbs. The
1970 new town incentive legislation, according to William Nicoson,
first director of the new communities office in the Department of
Housing and Urban Development, gave the United States "great
potential for organizing the growth of the country."

A *Reader's Digest* article summed up the popular expectations
for new towns as communities "designed to cut down the grind-
and-bore part of living, like commuting, traffic jams, parking problems, driving miles for a loaf of bread." Living in a new town, it
added, "should leave you more time and energy to be yourself and
do what you want to do." In contrast to past real estate development, the *Harvard Business Review* analysis promised, American
new towns could be expected to produce "an urban environment to
serve human needs."

This enthusiasm for new towns in the United States has been
easily exploited by much of the real estate industry to serve its own
need for new speculative profits. As a result, most of the projects
begun so far are largely unchanged large-scale speculative suburban housing developments repackaged as new towns to increase
sales, qualify for government financial help, and win local zoning
approval.

Their promotional material speaks rhapsodically of "a city in the
country—ecology in action" (Westlake, California), "living with
the land instead of on it" (Jonathan, Minnesota), "meeting civilization's challenge" (Laguna Niguel, California), "a city of tomorrow" (Litchfield Park, Arizona), "the next America" (Columbia,

Maryland), and "a community planned first for people" (Valencia, California). "When it comes to new towns," one of their few academic critics, Chester McGuire of the Institute of Urban and Regional Development at the University of California, Berkeley, has said, "the image is the message. This is why they hold such a profound fascination for planners, architects and interested laymen."

Behind the projected new town images are disappointingly familiar, sterile, primarily middle-class, predominantly white, 2-car suburbs of big, boxy single-family houses and strings of garden apartments. The streets may be slightly more curved; a little more green space (usually devoted to golf courses) may be evident; man-made lakes and swim clubs, drive-in shopping centers, and well-separated industrial parks to share the property tax burden may have been added. But these developments are perpetuating rather than solving the nagging problems of wasteful land use, traffic congestion, environmental pollution, inefficient and unequal distribution of public services, economic and racial segregation, and the shortage of decent, reasonably priced housing for lower- and even middle-income families. The worst projects, moreover, are crass land exploitation schemes designed to produce exorbitant profits at the expense of property buyers and the public. Nothing is *new* here.

Where the federal government requires it for federally assisted new towns, small token sections of subsidized housing for lower-income families have been tucked away in remote corners of the projects. At Jonathan, a federally assisted project well under way outside Minneapolis, where the emphasis is on low-density housing fitted carefully into a parklike setting of lakes, trees, and grass, the row houses containing ninety apartment units for lower-income families stand out like poor relations. They are isolated from and distinctly inferior in design to the rest of the development. In New Orleans East, a 32,000-acre suburban-looking development started by two Texas oil millionaires on marshy bayou land, the low-income units built to help win federal support for the project form the buffer zone between conventional middle-class neighborhoods of brick ramblers and a noisy freeway and smoky industrial area.

The rigid physical separation of housing subdivisions from recreation and school areas, drive-in shopping centers, and industrial parks combines with persistent economic stratification to destroy whatever over-all sense of community the developer tries to create with his image promotion. Even in Columbia, where a broader range of income groups and more black families can be found than in other projects, the development is cut up into homogeneous neighborhoods of $22,500 homes here, $28,500 homes there, $40,000 homes somewhere else, and subsidized apartments for low-income families and elderly couples segregated still elsewhere.

The residents of most of the new towns must still commute long distances to work. Many people who live in Irvine, an hour's drive south of Los Angeles, and in the Westlake and Valencia projects about the same distance to the west and north of the city, respectively, spend much of their morning and evening hours fighting freeway traffic. Each of the three projects has a large industrial park, but few employees of the businesses there can afford to live in the adjacent new town, where houses sell from $30,000 to $100,-000 (and higher for estates on an exclusive, guarded private island in the middle of Westlake's man-made lake).

Cars also are still essential for the simplest chores in most of the new towns because daily errands are so scattered, and most of the projects have no alternative form of transportation. None is connected directly to the nearest big city by dependable public transportation, although Park Forest, Illinois, is to have a station on the Illinois Central commuter line to Chicago, which is thirty-five miles away. Nor is there a regularly scheduled public transit system, not even buses, inside any of the projects. Separate pedestrian paths running behind the homes are put in by individual builders in several of the projects, but the paths seldom connect up to form a complete network through any new town. Auto roads remain the most direct routes from one place to another within each project. Even in Columbia and Reston, which have the most extensive pedestrian pathway systems, children can usually be seen walking in the main streets (where there are no sidewalks) because the pedestrian paths take too roundabout a way to the nearest school, playground, swimming pool, or shopping center. And their parents nearly always use cars to get to the store.

"The road needs of new towns are much like those of other metropolitan communities," *Highway User* magazine reassured its highway construction industry readers in a September 1972 report. It cited a survey made in Reston showing that walks taken on the pedestrian paths were in addition to, rather than instead of, trips made by car; as a result, members of the average Reston household still made between eleven and fifteen auto trips a day. "A Reston wife cannot be left without a car because she needs it for her necessary trips, like most other suburban wives," *Highway User* concluded.

So it is not surprising that car ownership in Reston now averages 1.8 automobiles per family and that more and more parking space has to be provided in its newer neighborhoods. Reston's experience has been repeated in most American new town projects, according to *Highway User*. "These towns," it noted,

> were begun with the idea that their superior design and emphasis on pedestrianism would substantially reduce the need for cars—or places to put them [but] again the suburban lifestyle replaces expectation with reality . . . auto ownership and parking needs within new communities differ little from those of other suburban developments. It remains high.

In addition to their internal dependence on cars, the new town projects also have depended for rapid growth and financial success on new freeways to the nearest big cities, *Highway User* added, so that "total road costs are about the same as those in ordinary suburban areas of similar size and population." More soil is paved over, more erosion-causing drainage problems are created, and more auto exhaust pollutants are added to the air. In this, as in so many other ways, U.S. new towns add up simply to larger-scale suburbia.

Why are American new towns such failures as urban experiments? Simply, unlike the European new towns on which they were supposedly to be modeled, the U.S. projects were not designed to be social, economic, architectural, or environmental experiments. Like all American real estate ventures, most U.S. new town projects were designed primarily for speculative profit.

The basic rules of the real estate game were not changed for new towns: A speculator still buys relatively inexpensive land, usually some distance from the nearest city, and devises a way to resell it at a substantial profit. The new town or planned community format just happens to be what speculators realized would sell best in the 1970s. Despite the innovative images they try to create, most new town developers are no more concerned than suburban subdivision builders were about the kind of housing and communities produced in the long run. These are still by-products of the land speculation process and need only to be made attractive enough, in comparison with what else the limited real estate market has to offer, to win local government approval and keep sales moving and money coming in.

Although the speculator is necessarily involved for a much longer period of time in a large-scale new town project than he would be in a small suburban subdivision, his involvement need not necessarily be much deeper. Most of the capital he works with is still borrowed money—and for federally assisted projects the loans are underwritten by the government. Developers of new towns also generally shift the responsibility for the actual homebuilding to smaller developers, to whom they sell parcels of a project's land. The speculator marks up the price of each parcel several hundred per cent above his cost, so that he will take in enough money to repay loans for projectwide "infrastructures"—roads, utilities, recreation facilities, landscaping, sales promotion, and the like—and still have a sizable profit left over in the end. Each homebuilder then inflates the land price still more to give himself a profit when he sells the completed house.

Some speculators have devised ingenious ways to lighten the burden of the huge infrastructure investment necessary for a new town project. At Lake Havasu City Robert McCulloch formed a special improvement district to pay for the installation of roads and utilities with money from the sale of bonds that Lake Havasu City property tax payers will have to repay later. A similar scheme proved even more profitable for T. Jack Foster, a speculative builder of suburban subdivisions and resort hotels in the Midwest and Hawaii, who began the new town of Foster City south of San Francisco on what had been a marshy point jutting from the San Francisco peninsula into the bay.

Although the Foster City site was ideally situated in an otherwise crowded suburban area not far from the San Francisco city limits, the marshy land had never been built on because it was several feet below sea level. Only an intricate system of dikes and large drainage ditches—the largest of which severed the 2,600-acre marsh from the rest of the peninsula and made it an artificial island—had allowed cattle to be grazed there, until Foster bought the site in 1963. He decided to build bigger dikes and dredge sand and mud from the bottom of the bay to fill in the marsh, making it suitable for development. The drainage ditches were enlarged, landscaped, and advertised as scenic "blue lagoons" for waterfront homesites and boat docks on what was promoted as the "island of blue lagoons" and a "New World Venice."

The master plan for Foster City included houses, apartment buildings, innovative schools, shopping areas, office buildings, industrial parks, recreation areas, and a lively town center. Distinctively different-looking street lamps, fire hydrants, and little bridges over the lagoons were specially designed and manufactured for Foster City. In addition, three renowned architects—Ludwig Mies van der Rohe, Edward Durrell Stone, and Le Corbusier—were commissioned to design buildings for what Foster called the "first actual new town in America." The San Francisco Museum of Art displayed the plans and some scale models of the Mies van der Rohe and Stone buildings in a month-long exhibition, "Design of a City: Foster City," that drew strongly favorable comment nationwide.

The real beauty of the project, however, lay in its financing. Instead of investing his own money or borrowing conventionally for the expensive job of filling in and preparing the land for development, Foster created a "special municipal improvement district" under a California law normally used for agricultural irrigation projects. The district, which had the power to float tax-exempt bonds, was controlled according to the law by the owners of a majority of the land within the district, for many years, Foster himself. During that time the special district sold more than $64 million worth of bonds to pay for the dredging and filling of the "island of blue lagoons," as well as the construction of roads, sewers, water lines, and other improvements. The bonds were to be repaid by future Foster City resident taxpayers.

Not only did Foster manage to have the Foster City infrastructure developed at someone else's expense, he also channeled some of the money for improvements into companies he owned or controlled. At least $900,000 from the bonds was paid to a Foster-controlled company that did some of the dredging. Another $113,000 reimbursed Foster for the expense of designing the master plan and conducting market research for Foster City. And the special district voted to pay $515,000 to Foster as landowner for rights-of-way needed for various public improvements.

As the improvements were gradually completed, Foster, who had bought the soggy site for less than $5,000 an acre, was able to sell parcels to builders at prices ranging from $30,000 to $50,000 per acre. He also made big profits on land he sold to the state at $23,-

000 an acre for highways through Foster City and to the local San Mateo County school district at $14,000 to $25,000 an acre for school sites.

Foster himself was doing well financially, but Foster City was being heavily mortgaged for the future. Its bonded indebtedness compared to assessed property value became the highest in the San Francisco area. Industrial and commercial investors, who saw through Foster's scheme and did not want to become liable for any of the future property tax bill, stayed out of Foster City. Only a handful of offices and industrial plants and a single, small shopping center were built. There was no town center, no Mies van der Rohe office towers, and the sprawling industrial park was left an expanse of barren, deathly gray dirt fill.

Only homebuilders, who could pass the tax responsibility along to the homebuyers, bought and developed large quantities of land in Foster City, and the community now has nearly 20,000 residents. Without much industry or commerce, however, these homeowners have had to shoulder most of the community's big tax bill, although unhappy residents of the rest of the San Mateo County school district have had to help pay for Foster City's expensive new schools. Foster City residents also were warned by geologists recently that a serious earthquake might rupture Foster City's dikes and wash the entire development into the bay. If the dikes held, the experts predicted, the vibrations might undermine the sandy fill and turn it into wet quicksand that would suck all the buildings under.

Some Foster City residents finally went to court and to the state legislature to stop the sale of any more bonds until they could take control of the special district, which they eventually did with the court's help. They then shifted a little more of the tax burden onto Foster, as the owner of large tracts of still undeveloped land. He died about that same time, however, and his sons sold off his remaining land to Boise-Cascade and Centex, a Dallas builder. These firms have promised to finish developing Foster City as a complete community with more businesses and stores, but Centex spokesmen admit it will not be the innovative new town that the exhibit in the San Francisco Museum of Art promised.

Increasingly, the entrepreneurs developing other big new town projects have turned out to be giant corporations. These firms have the necessary borrowing capability to finance a big project's infrastructure investment and are attracted by the prospect of extraordinary speculative profits in real estate. For these corporate speculators, however, a new town is just another subsidiary, one that must produce a profit or soon be written off as a tax loss. It cannot be carried for any length of time as an unprofitable social or technological experiment.

Westlake, California—12,000 acres of valley floor and surrounding foothills straddling the Los Angeles–Ventura county line about seventy Ventura freeway minutes west of downtown Los Angeles —is a joint venture of the American-Hawaiian Steamship Company and Prudential Insurance. American-Hawaiian Steamship, a conglomerate that owns the Princess lines, other shipping interests, and salt mines in Mexico, had the good fortune to buy the Westlake site in a single parcel from a single owner, a rancher, in 1965 for $32 million. That comes to about $2,700 per acre, a bargain price for so much land within distant commuting reach of Los Angeles. Prudential—like many other insurance companies an active real estate mortgage lender—made $50 million in loans to American-Hawaiian Steamship for the purchase of the land and initial infrastructure costs. When Westlake got off to a slow start, however, Prudential took over part of the management of the project as a full partner in 1969. Since then, Westlake sales officials say, the venture has begun to turn the corner financially and is certain to grow from its present 10,000 to 15,000 population to near the planned 70,000.

Westlake promotes itself as a new town, "a carefully planned city in the country," and an example of "ecology in action," whatever that may be. It appears near the top of any urban planner's list of American new towns and is a stop on periodic California new town tours conducted by the University of California's School of Architecture and Planning. Yet no attempts of any kind are being made in Westlake to experiment with possible solutions to urban growth problems; in fact, the development is helping make many of these more acute.

The least expensive home at Westlake sells for $30,000, the average is somewhere near $40,000, and a number of houses cost more than $80,000. The "country" that is being preserved at Westlake is available only at a price. To have access to the 150-acre lake, a family must buy an expensive homesite along its shore or pay to moor a boat at the marina; a private guard keeps everyone else away. Some individual builders have provided, and the Westlake hierarchy has promoted, narrow greenbelts of grass, some trees, and in some places paths between and behind the homes. But as the developer of one subdivision of homes at Westlake advertises prominently, the *"private* greenbelt and recreation area" (a small pool) is for the exclusive use of buyers of the homes in that subdivision. Some subdivisions have greenbelts and recreation areas; others do not, even though some homebuyers have complained that Westlake promotional literature and sales talks give the impression that the entire community has an interconnected greenbelt pathway system and all residents have equal access to the lake and recreation areas.

The huge tract of hilly land on which Westlake is being built happens to be located partly in Los Angeles County and partly in Ventura County. Because the developers were able to buy the entire parcel, they have tried to ignore the border that runs through Westlake, something that is easier for them than for Westlake's new residents. The two counties refuse to let the new town have a united government of its own, and local taxes, laws, and services vary considerably from one part of Westlake to the other. The telephone company also uses the county line to divide Westlake into two separate dialing areas, so that residents calling from one to the other, even if it is just across the street, must pay a toll charge.

In the one-third of Westlake that is situated in Los Angeles County, schools are being built almost as quickly as homes. In the two-thirds of the city inside more agricultural Ventura County, however, there are far too few schools, because other Ventura residents do not want their taxes increased to pay for facilities in Westlake. Some developers have put up temporary school buildings in quonset huts; children in other subdivisions of Westlake attend badly overcrowded schools.

The project also is bisected physically by the Ventura freeway, Westlake's only transportation link to the outside world. The light industry that has chosen to locate in Westlake—including IBM and Burrough plants and several new car dealers—naturally wanted to be near the freeway, and at a price Westlake's developers allowed them to do so. But as a result the project's roads are badly congested near the freeway, where its big shopping center, intended to draw customers from far outside Westlake, is also located.

According to Westlake's own marketing director, a very small percentage of the employees of the businesses and stores located there can afford to live in Westlake. Most of the others commute from lower-income Los Angeles suburbs up to sixty miles away, while the average Westlake resident, according to one survey, drives nearly an hour from his home to work. As might be expected, Westlake residents are not only nearly all middle and upper middle class, they also are nearly all white, even though there is a sizable proportion of black and Chicano families in both Los Angeles and Ventura counties.

As one perceptive participant on a University of California tour summed it up: "Westlake simply shows what new communities will look like when the goal is return on investment." The interest and taxes on its unrepaid mortgage loans and unresold land cost Westlake's developers $12,600 a day, so the lots must be priced high and sold quickly. Westlake's promotional materials and sales talks feature, for instance, the project's own Valley Oaks Memorial Park ("more than a cemetery . . . the scene of historical and cultural attention with statues, memorials and tributes") because, as one spokesman for the developers explained, "that's one of our big money makers."

Further west on the Ventura freeway is Amberton, a newer project being marketed by Kaiser-Aetna, a real estate speculation partnership of Kaiser Aluminum and Aetna Life and Casualty that began with the Hawaii-Kai housing development north of Honolulu on Oahu, Hawaii. Amberton consists of several unconnected parcels of land totaling 10,000 acres in Ventura County. Scattered between them are a number of existing housing subdivisions and farms that Kaiser-Aetna was unable to buy at a low price. The "master plan" promoted by the developers for Amberton consists primarily of locating a shopping center and apartments on a parcel adjacent to an existing shopping strip and putting a "college village" of single-family homes around a site bought by the state of California for a new university campus. Steep foothills that are obviously unsuitable for residential construction anyway have magnanimously been set aside for "multi-use recreation." The names of several other Kaiser-Aetna ventures—for example, Rancho California, with 95,000 acres of dry range located halfway between Los Angeles and San Diego in Riverside County—appear on many lists of American new town projects. These, however, are usually marketed more like retirement communities or recreation land subdivisions: Their lots are sold as speculative investments, even though they have "industrial parks" of a few warehouses and small shopping centers of convenience stores. In 1968 California Governor Ronald Reagan bought 771 acres of Rancho California land at the bargain price of less than $250 an acre. He has since received permission from the Riverside County planning council to subdivide the land and sell it off in parcels at a substantial profit.

Some new towns were started when corporations not normally involved in residential real estate found themselves holding large tracts of unused land. Ford Motors has begun development of a relatively small project called Fairlane on 2,360 acres adjacent to its headquarters in Dearborn, Michigan. Ford officials promise a rare new town technological experiment at Fairlane: use of Ford's "people mover" public conveyor belts, like those exhibited at world's fairs. Goodyear Tire and Rubber has undertaken a more ambitious project called Litchfield Park ("an extraordinary new kind of city . . . almost totally preplanned") west of Phoenix, Arizona, on 13,000 acres it had used as an irrigated farm for the production of long-staple cotton for truck tires until synthetic fibers made that unnecessary. Litchfield Park was designed by Victor Gruen, a well-known city planner, to be a giant suburb with a linear, city-like downtown of high-rise offices, apartments, and public buildings stretched out across the middle of the rectangular site. Only a few housing subdivisions have been built after six years of development, however; the lack of a freeway to Phoenix has kept most builders away.

When Humble Oil found itself with 13,000 otherwise unneeded acres, bought long ago for gas rights, it began building Clear Lake City, "a master-planned community" for up to 125,000 people on Galveston Bay in Texas. About 15,000 live there now in single-family houses strung out on conventional, suburban streets that feed into a few congested main traffic arteries lined with drive-in shopping strips. Master planning in Clear Lake City has meant underground utilities, sidewalks on the streets, and, most importantly, exclusivity for its white, middle-class residents, many of whom work in the nearby National Aeronautics and Space Administration complex or in petrochemical plants in Humble's adjacent Bayport industrial area. Acrid, multicolored smoke billows from the nearby plants but "blows away from Clear Lake City because we're upwind," according to a Clear Lake City sales executive. Sales materials for the development stress that Clear Lake City is "the area's prestige address," where "building covenants protect your investment," keeping out things like mobile homes and lower-income residents.

In California the Newhall Land and Farming Company, one of the Southwest's biggest commercial ranchers, decided to build a new town called Valencia on its 32,000-acre ranch forty miles northwest of Los Angeles. Victor Gruen also drew the Valencia plan and included in it an interconnected system of pedestrian pathways, which pseudo-Spanish Valencia promotional literature calls *paseos,* and a gigantic city center to serve the 170,000 people Valencia is eventually supposed to house. Like Westlake, however, Valencia is growing as a disjointed collection of subdivisions thrown up by a variety of builders to whom the Newhall firm is selling parcels of land at about $7,000 an acre. Builders of only nine of thirty-five subdivisions have put in *paseos,* and residents answering a 1970 survey complained about the long distances they had to drive to stores and their jobs.

Yet Valencia is being marketed as a good suburban property investment for young buyers of its $30,000 homes who can then move up to better houses and more convenient communities in the future. Its primary selling points are a large industrial park, where Lockheed, Texton, and Sperry Rand have plants; an already opened junior college and an art institute run by the Walt Disney conglomerate; and Newhall's own Disneyland-like Magic Mountain amusement park in the center of Valencia just off the Los Angeles freeway. The good-investment-value sales pitch to prospective homebuyers is best typified by this promotional message put out by a large Valencia homebuilder in his advertisements and sales brochures just before Magic Mountain and the Walt Disney California Institute for the Arts opened in 1970:

Valencia is coming on strong with dynamic growth potential. . . . Remember what Disneyland did for property values in Orange County? *Guess* how much values will go up when Valencia's Magic Mountain opens.

And now for the clincher. The Walt Disney California Institute for the Arts is due to open its door in the fall of 1970. This $36 million, 60 acre campus will make the city of Valencia an internationally known cultural center. Practically over night.

Remember what U.C.L.A. did for property and land values in

Westwood? *Imagine* what your home will be worth when the Institute is open. And in years to come.

There will never again be an opportunity like this for real value appreciation. Now is the time to get in on the ground floor.

Other big corporations that had been only the financial backers of new town projects have wound up in charge of them when their loans were not repaid on time. That is how Prudential Insurance became deeply involved in the development and marketing of Westlake. Perhaps the most unlikely of these reluctant new town developers is Philip Morris, which had to take control of its investment in Mission Viejo in Orange County, California, south of Los Angeles. Almost adjacent to Mission Viejo is Lake Forest, which wound up in the hands of Occidental Petroleum.

The best-known and most significant takeover of a new town by a corporate financial backer, however, is Gulf Oil's ouster of entrepreneur Robert E. Simon at Reston, Virginia. In its infancy Reston had been, along with Columbia, Maryland, one of America's most celebrated and widely studied new town experiments. Although the community offered nothing innovative in transportation or technology, Reston's land-use plan, architecture, and social goals excited urban experts and journalists all over the world.

The first section of Reston was a modern architect's gracefully coordinated version of a European village in an American country setting: Grouped around man-made Lake Anne with an open plaza at one end were a concentration of apartment buildings, townhouses, and small stores, backdropped by green hillsides with more townhouses scattered over them. Cars were kept hidden in a central parking lot behind the village center plaza and on loop roads running through the hillsides. Pedestrian walks were the most direct routes from one place to another.

"It was like a European city," remembered an economist who moved into Lake Anne Village in the new town's early days. "Sundays you could stroll down to the plaza and see your friends. Families would walk by with the baby. You'd buy a paper, get a sandwich, and sit around and watch the scene." On summer evenings, a lawyer recalled, "you could walk around the lake and meet some people you know and others you don't and there would be young people down by the water with flutes and guitars making music."

But Reston was still a speculative real estate venture, albeit a more altruistic one than most, started by Simon on 7,400 acres of wooded hills about thirty minutes from downtown Washington. He had borrowed $20 million from John Hancock Insurance, which took a mortgage on the land as security, and $15 million from Gulf, which was unsecured except for a share of the project itself. The lake, the plaza, the expensively designed townhouses, all the trees still standing, and open land left untouched had to be paid for by people buying homes in Reston. These amenities were included in the price of the land sold to each builder, and, in turn, in the price for each house, so that a little townhouse on Lake Anne cost as much as $50,000.

Simon could not sell homes quickly enough at those prices; nor could he interest enough other builders in buying big parcels of land from him for development. They were frightened away by the expense of Reston's public amenities and the strong hand Simon's lieutenants took in each home's design. The project's debt, which required an annual sales volume of $2.5 million merely to break even, fell into arrears. So Gulf stepped in to protect its unsecured investment. Another $12 million was immediately put into the project, and Simon was replaced by a suburban real estate consultant from Pittsburgh, Robert H. Ryan, who found many of Simon's planning innovations to be too utopian and economically unsound.

Under Ryan's direction detached single-family homes and garden apartments replaced townhouses in the new subdivisions. Higher-priced homes were given large private suburban lots, which Simon had eliminated around his townhouses in favor of larger public spaces. Automobiles were given more freedom in Gulf's Reston, as pedestrian pathways became narrower and less scenic and convenient, and even disappeared in some places. The second shopping area was a big drive-in center, in contrast to the Lake Anne village plaza. The mix of social classes promised by Simon (although it was always unclear how he would bring it about) was openly abandoned as a goal by Gulf. "The American ethic for 200 years has been for income levels to live with their own kind," Ryan said. And by the time there were 15,000 people living in Reston, only 200 resident families were black. Reston was becoming just another middle-class Washington suburb, but it was easily selling the 1,000 housing units a year that assured Gulf a good-sized profit.

When it approved legislation to authorize generous public incentives for some U.S. new towns, Congress hoped to prevent just this kind of slighting of innovation by speculators out for a fast buck and corporations intent primarily on realizing the biggest possible return on their investment. The landmark 1970 "new communities" bill, an expansion of the less bold new town provisions of the Housing Act of 1968, was pushed through Congress by Ohio Congressman Thomas L. Ashley, a Democrat, after a tour of government-aided experimental new towns in Europe. A new communities office was opened in the Department of Housing and Urban Development (HUD) to offer builders of qualifying new town projects an enticing smorgasbord of federal largesse: government guarantees for land and construction loans from private lenders (the treasury promises to repay the loan if the developer cannot, up to $50 million per project), direct, low-interest treasury loans to developers to help them pay the initially high interest on the land and construction loans, and grants from the treasury to help pay for innovative new town design. HUD-approved projects also were supposed to receive priority for other federal housing subsidies, including those for housing for low-income families, and for the grant programs of other federal agencies for transportation, sewage and water, and public health.

Although Congress actually has appropriated only $5 million of the $200 million requested for the direct grants and loans to new town builders, it has authorized the spending of up to $500 in federal guarantees for land and construction loans made by private lenders. And despite the Nixon Administration's temporary suspension of most HUD subsidies for housing for low-income families, federal aid to new town developers has been allowed to continue. Through late 1973 HUD had committed itself to a total of nearly $300 million in loan guarantees to the developers of fifteen federally approved projects, including one development, Cedar-Riverside, inside the city of Minneapolis; another, Soul City, to be developed by black entrepreneurs in the North Carolina countryside; and a number of satellite projects outside cities like Atlanta, Little Rock, Rochester, Chicago, Minneapolis, Dallas, and Houston.

The government guarantees are intended to reduce the new town developer's difficulty in finding financing for a truly innovative project and are expected to do for new town development what

Federal Housing Administration home mortgage loan guarantees did for the postwar growth of suburbia. They will also allow banks and other politically powerful financial institutions to enrich themselves by making no-risk loans to new town developers at prevailing high interest rates. Builders have been quick to accept this government help. Roy Nasher, a Texas real estate developer, planning, with Stanley Marcus of Nieman-Marcus, to build the HUD-approved new town of Flower Mound, has promised, "We'll be able to create truly new communities and not simply xerox what's been done in the past."

Unfortunately, however, most of the HUD-approved new towns are shaping up as just that: xerox copies of both the disappointing new town projects developed without government backing and the conventional large-scale suburban developments these mimic. Rather than encouraging innovation, the federal aid is helping developers cash in more quickly and potentially even more profitably on the development of suburban areas newly ripe for rapid growth.

The site for Flower Mound just happens to be in the vicinity of the huge new 16,000-acre, $500 million Dallas–Fort Worth International Airport, where the first of four mammoth terminals was scheduled to begin operation by early 1974. Construction of the airport, which is to be connected to the two cities by freeway, already has increased land prices tenfold, and speculators have rushed to buy up the fertile farm and ranch land there and begin building large new shopping centers, office buildings, motels, and housing subdivisions. Nasher and Marcus actually got to the area a few years ago, enlisted nineteen longtime landowners there as partners, and won formal HUD backing even before it was clear what they were going to build. HUD officials now say that the primary "innovation" they expect from the 6,500-acre development for a projected 70,000 residents is the soundproofing that will be required to keep the jets that take off and land at the nearby airport from making Flower Mound a noise pollution disaster.

The HUD land and construction loan guarantees, the only fully funded part of the federal new communities program, are merely continuing to underwrite an unchanged real estate financing system that always has made innovative or even responsible real estate development almost impossible to assure. Like all other real estate speculators, developers of HUD-assisted new towns must still pay for almost everything, including any innovations, from the proceeds of the sale of the project's land and housing. If home-builders and -buyers are not likely to pay higher land and home prices to cover the cost of an experiment, the new town developer is not likely to try it.

At Park Forest South, a HUD-approved new town south of Chicago, an experienced millionaire developer, Lewis Manilow, had promised to experiment with public transportation. His project may become the first with any kind of mass transit connection to the nearest big city, when one of Manilow's fellow investors, the Illinois Central Railroad, builds a promised station for commuters where its line to Chicago passes through the project. Manilow also planned to have an internal public transportation system in Park Forest South, but he said he could not afford to experiment with anything like a monorail or other nonbus system. There is no assurance that even the minibus system he was most recently considering will pay for itself and become a part of the project. Manilow also thought of reducing the waste of land normally paved over to provide car parking at the door of every house, but he concluded that homebuyers would be discouraged from buying there by any of the possible alternatives. "We can't just ban cars or put the parking 500 feet away or underground somewhere," he said. "People won't stand for that."

Near Minneapolis, at Jonathan, Minnesota, one of the furthest advanced of the HUD projects, the emphasis was to be on innovations in housing forms and preservation of the environment. The principal results so far have been some unusually good-looking houses and apartments hidden in the trees around man-made lakes in a kind of dreamland suburbia. Keeping the trees, creating the lakes, and improving home design have proved dangerously costly, however, and Jonathan has run into the same trouble that ruined Robert Simon at Reston: Its home prices had to be set too high to pay for its architecture and landscaping, and sales came too slowly. So Jonathan turned to the federal government for help.

After getting their HUD loan guarantee, Jonathan's developers, mostly local investors, tried producing some other experimental housing with space-saving design and fairly modest prices. This seemed to sell, even though it appeared a bit structurally flimsy in places. But the experiment still ran up what the developers considered an unacceptable loss, and they failed to interest homebuilders in trying to construct the same housing more economically on a larger scale. Instead, most of the new homes now being sold in Jonathan are big, standard suburban boxes being marketed by Kaufman and Broad at $35,000 to $50,000 and up. A 1972 survey showed that the average sales price of a new single-family home in the Minneapolis–St. Paul area had reached $38,000, a price that 85 per cent of the families of that area could not afford; thus, Jonathan, a federally supported new town, no longer offers anything for that huge low- and middle-income majority.

In some cases desperate developers have been able to turn to the federal government for new town loan guarantees even when it was perfectly obvious to others that they had no serious plans for innovation. This appears to be the case with a $24 million loan guarantee approved by HUD for St. Charles, thirty miles south of Washington, D.C., in Charles County, Maryland, where the present 40,000 population would be tripled by the addition of the 80,000 people projected for the development. About a thousand houses and an elementary school are the only improvements on the 8,000-acre site, despite fifteen years of efforts by various ambitious developers to cash in on the Washington area's rapidly spreading growth.

The first developers bought the property in 1967 for only $100,-000 down and a mortgage for nearly $6 million. On this speculative shoestring they set about to build what they called Linda City, but they could not persuade the rural county to lay sewers to the site or allow houses on 60-foot-wide lots. So, after four years and only a few hundred houses, the project folded, and the land was sold for nonpayment of the mortgage. The property changed hands several times, before it was bought by a New Englander, Frances J. Finnerman, who changed the project's name to St. Charles and eventually brought in a quite successful developer and financier, James J. Wilson. Development again slowed after a few hundred more homes and the one school were built.

It was Wilson who thought to draw up a fancy new master plan for St. Charles and obtain HUD financial backing for a new city. He succeeded, despite the strong objections of Maryland state officials, who feared that St. Charles would never attract the industry and commerce necessary to repay in taxes the estimated $100 million that the state was obligated by law to spend there for schools, sewers, roads, and parks. One Maryland official called the project "sloppily planned" and "just more suburban spillover from Washington—bedrooms that don't pay." And a Charles County commissioner protested that "we don't want to become another Prince George's County."

A 1971 HUD memorandum, made public during the controversy, characterized the developer's staff at St. Charles as "relatively inexperienced in the land development business. . . . Some question exists as to their ability to successfully implement the development plans agreed to with HUD." Nevertheless, the St. Charles project was approved by HUD a few months before Charles E. Stuart, husband of Mrs. Nixon's press secretary, Connie Stuart, left his own White House job to become vice-president of James J. Wilson's real estate firm in charge of the St. Charles development.

HUD listed as "innovations" to be provided by St. Charles the usual grouping of neighborhoods around elementary schools, scattered neighborhood health clinics for which there is as yet no financial support of any kind, and federal subsidies to help low-income families buy 80 per cent of the housing. (This last is a most unlikely eventuality politically and hardly the way to build an economically balanced community, but the developers fear that nothing but very low-priced housing can sell in big volume in a still so remote location.) HUD also pointed to the preservation of open space in St. Charles as one of the project's important assets, but in fact only 18 per cent of the now mostly wooded tract is set aside in the master plan as open space, and much of that will be taken up by private golf courses.

HUD is seriously considering the applications of several other rather uninspiring projects seeking federal loan guarantees. One of the most audacious proposals made was that of a group of Pennsylvania real estate speculators to put up apartments for 39,000 people in what is now a giant gravel pit just west of Washington near Franconia in Fairfax County, Virginia. The promoters of New Franconia had promised, with much fanfare, an "ecologically harmonious" community built around a monorail system. But they were unable to explain how, even with federal help, they could finance the monorail or avoid further overcrowding the roads and polluting the air and water of an already congested suburban area by cramming so many people into a new development of high-rise buildings.

The local newspapers nevertheless gave the announcement of the New Franconia plans large display; local officials praised them; and the influential architectural critic of the *Washington Post,* Wolf Von

Eckardt, an articulate, well-meaning booster of new towns, called on "the bureaucrats and politicians" to show that they "really believe in the promise of new towns" by throwing their full support immediately behind this "splendid opportunity to advance American community design." The fact that no detailed design for New Franconia was yet available beyond the grand promises and vague drawings first presented by the developers betrays the blind faith of Von Eckardt and many Americans like him in the new town mystique.

But when both HUD and Fairfax County, despite Von Eckardt's urging, failed to approve the New Franconia proposal without normal deliberation, the would-be developers became impatient. It turned out that they had several other real estate deals tying up their money elsewhere and that they had been hoping for a quick infusion of federally guaranteed mortgage money through New Franconia, money that they soon realized they would not get without a long wait. So in 1973, a year after their momentous announcement of plans for a new city of the future, New Franconia's promoters quietly issued a second announcement, this time saying that "plans for the new town of New Franconia have been abandoned." It was now finally clear exactly how determined this group of developers had been in the first place to "advance American community design."

One *Washington Post* reader who was not fooled from the start, however, sent this letter to the editor shortly after the plans for New Franconia were announced:

> If I were not a Fairfax County taxpayer and a resident of the Franconia area, I would be laughing uproariously at the grandiose plans for the proposed "New Franconia."
>
> The blithe and effortless way the planners would solve the attendant problems of this teeming city in suburbia would do credit to a science fiction writer.
>
> I don't wonder that the developers have plenty of private backers. After HUD has poured its untold millions of taxpayers' money into the project, the private sector stands to make a bundle.
>
> The developers' busy public relations people are promising a new Utopia, but I can foresee a high-rise, high-density ghetto with all the problems those conditions so often create.
>
> In view of the Disneyesque quality of this proposed "New City," I suggest it be renamed "Fantasia."
>
> —GEORGIA A. MARTIN
> *Alexandria, Va.*

8

Super Suburbs: Irvine, California, and Columbia, Maryland

Around the turn of the century, when Theodore Roosevelt was becoming a popular American hero, another rugged autocratic individualist and outdoorsman, James Irvine, began building a multi-million-dollar agricultural empire on the enormous Southern California ranch he inherited from his father. Irvine made extensive use of irrigation and added bean fields and orange, grapefruit, and lemon orchards to the barley and livestock his father had raised on the 130 square miles of plateau, stream valleys, and foothills stretched across the middle of Orange County from the Pacific Ocean to the Santa Ana mountains. He bought an expensive home in San Francisco, where he often went to enjoy the finer things that a cosmopolitan city offered a man of means, but Irvine's few surviving friends have said he was happiest when working outdoors on his ranch or hunting in its hills.

In 1937, a decade before he died at the age of eighty, Irvine created a charitable foundation to keep control of the ranch and prevent its being split up by heirs or threatened by inheritance taxes. The foundation was to continue anonymously giving money to worthy California causes as Irvine had done, though he had angrily refused direct solicitations for contributions or investments of the wealth he gained from his ranch. Irvine's feelings about the ranch were made clear in the document he wrote establishing the Irvine Foundation charitable trust:

Inasmuch as the development and operation of said property [the Irvine ranch] has constituted the life work of the trustor [Irvine], it is the purpose . . . by the creation of this trust and by vesting in the trustee [the Irvine Foundation], through its holding of stock, the exercise of a controlling voice in the operation thereof and thus insure an adequate foundation for the charitable purposes provided.

It is the trustor's firm conviction that no other security could afford the James Irvine Foundation a more safe and stable investment than the capital stock of the Irvine [ranch] Company, if this land holding is preserved and sustained at its present rate of development, with such improvements, if any, as may be justified in the future.

Today the tax-exempt Irvine Foundation still holds a majority of the stock of the Irvine Company, which is the corporate owner of James Irvine's 83,000-acre ranch (along with nearly 10,000 acres of farmland in the Imperial Valley and a 100,000-acre cattle ranch in Montana), and gives more than a million dollars to charity each year. The company still farms much of the Orange County ranch profitably and now also raises asparagus and strawberries as cash crops there. But on thousands of acres of the ranch's flattest, most productive land, citrus trees are being uprooted and farm and pasture land bulldozed and built on as the giant ranch succumbs to "development" of a kind that James Irvine probably did not have in mind when he wrote his trust document. His ranch, now located on the edge of greater Los Angeles, is being rapidly turned into the single largest real estate development in this country, if not the world: the new city of Irvine, which has become internationally known, along with Columbia, Maryland, as one of America's most significant, privately developed new town projects.

Although a campus of the University of California, some housing subdivisions, and a mile-square "downtown" of office towers and a giant regional shopping center all were under construction on the Irvine ranch land during the 1960s, it was not until 1970 that the mammoth project was announced publicly as a new town venture. It was first explained in detail to the people of Orange County in a 40-page, full-color supplement published by the Irvine Company in local newspapers. The September 1970 publication put the project in perspective this way:

> In 1955, Disneyland put Orange County on the map. In 1969, national attention was focused on this area when President Nixon located his western White House in San Clemente [on the ocean on the southern tip of Orange County]. Then in March, 1970, Orange County made nationwide headlines again . . . the Irvine Company revealed its plans to build a new city in Orange County . . . the largest master planned city on the North American continent . . . the city of Irvine.

There can be no doubting the significance of the size of the undertaking. The 53,000 acres of the Irvine ranch suitable for development (the rest is too mountainous) constitute a city site twice as big as San Francisco and three times as large as Manhattan. The Irvine Company expects that as many as 500,000 people will eventually live there—which compares to the 400,000 target population for Brasilia, the 37,000-acre new capital city of Brazil; the 110,000 planned for 14,000 acres at Columbia; and the 75,000 expected to live on 7,000 acres at Reston, Virginia.

The question is whether Irvine will really be a *new* city or just an extension of metropolitan Los Angeles suburban sprawl, which already covers all of Orange County to the northwest. A large chunk of the site located near the ocean and containing the new "downtown" offices and shopping center has already been annexed by the coastline city of Newport Beach, and much of the rest of the ranch is coveted by other adjoining municipalities. Even the part of the project around the University of California Irvine campus that was recently incorporated as the city of Irvine by vote of its 30,000 residents encompasses only 18,000 acres of campus, housing subdivisions, and small shopping centers. In reality, the "largest master planned city" in America is evolving as a very loose collection of large California-style suburban subdivisions of big, expensive houses and walled-in yards built around private swimming clubs. Connecting each subdivision to the others and to the campus, the "downtown," the other shopping centers, and a huge industrial park are wide boulevards feeding in and out of the three freeways that run through the old ranch.

The people of Irvine are almost all white and upper middle class, except for some university students and workers in the industrial park (most of whom cannot afford Irvine homes). Few black or Chicano families or families making less than $15,000 a year are expected to be living there any time soon. Irvine is fast becoming a replica of existing "exclusive" suburbs and neighborhoods of Los Angeles—with which Irvine homebuilders compare their subdivisions in advertisements—but so greatly enlarged that its damaging effect on the environment, unchecked by innovations in transportation, water supply, sewage, or land use, will likely be more comparable to an Anaheim or Los Angeles itself.

Before this development began, the Irvine ranch had long been a formidable barrier against the spread of suburban sprawl from Los Angeles farther into Orange County. West of the ranch is a densely developed jumble of suburbs incorporated as cities: Anaheim, Santa Ana, Orange, Fullerton, Buena Park, Costa Mesa, Huntington Beach, Westminster, Newport Beach, and a dozen others. They are so intertwined by annexation wars, just as the suburban cities of Santa Clara County south of San Francisco are, that despite political divisions they blend into one undifferentiated blur as a driver passes through them on the freeway.

Here "there are only homes, a sea of roofs without provisions for the needs of a community such as parks, schools, churches and shopping areas," according to Forest Dickason, the county's planning director. Actually, there are schools (many of them overcrowded), a few churches, some overloaded shopping centers, and a surprising abundance of factories and offices. But everything is so inconvenient to get to that residents are always driving from one suburb to another. And, of course, there are also Disneyland and its surrounding forest of hotels, seas of parking lots, and wide concrete rivers choked with cars. Half of what had been the most scenic, climatically appealing, and richest county in Southern California was turned into a treeless, smog-filled wasteland of urban clutter and is now faced with embryonic slum, social, and health problems with which it has not even begun to come to grips.

The sprawl had always stopped abruptly at the Irvine ranch border, however, because, except for the small coastal resort towns of Laguna Beach, San Juan Capistrano, and San Clemente, the land east and south of that line consisted mostly of large, individually held ranches and farms. The large land holdings were originally land grants from the Spanish monarchy to adventurers in Spanish California. After a brief period of Mexican control, the Americans came, and they bought or simply took the huge land-grant ranches. For more than a century these large holdings, some of which remained in the ownership of single families for generations, were devoted almost entirely to increasingly productive agricultural uses, and they remained resistant to mounting development pressures.

"The half of Orange County in large land grants had always been different from the other half," said county planning director Dickason. Long after the western half had been swallowed up by the suburban expansion of Los Angeles, the eastern half, one of the most important citrus-growing areas in the country, kept alive the Orange County depicted in its official orange-and-green circular seal as furrowed farmland with a line of mountains in the background and ripe oranges in the foreground. In 1960 the population of the eastern half of the county was only about 30,000, and most of those people lived in the three coastal resort towns.

When it became evident during the 1960s that several of the ranches were finally going to be built on, like the old ranches on which Valencia and Westlake were being developed, Dickason still believed that the eastern half of the county would be saved from suburban sprawl. He thought the ranches could be developed carefully as planned, innovative new towns, because each consisted of "good, clean flat farmland with no buildings or other obstacles to complicate its development." Moreover, their single ownership could facilitate planning, control of development, and experimentation.

So Dickason persuaded Orange County officials to do just what the nation's new town boosters had been advocating: release the developers of large land holdings from traditional lot-by-lot and subdivision-by-subdivision zoning restrictions and allow them the freedom to design and build each individual segment of a project as they saw fit, as long as they worked from an approved over-all, new town master plan that promised marked improvement on piecemeal suburban development. This farsighted work by its planners and the availability of suitably large sites already under single ownership gave Orange County a unique opportunity to build innovative projects that would minimize environmental and social damage and perhaps change urban growth from an unmanageable negative force to a controlled positive one.

Despite the adoption by Orange County's officials of Dickason's new town zoning law, however, the master plans submitted by the corporate developers of most of the giant ranches were not for new towns at all. The builders instead promised conventional, if fancy, suburbs with such country club amenities as golf courses, lakes, swimming clubs, private beaches, walled lots, and, in one project, street lights in the shape of old California mission bells. There were no plans for public transportation inside these sprawling developments, no mixing of income groups, almost no housing at all for low- or even middle-income families, no experiments in community health care, no advanced water or air pollution safeguards, no significant innovations in housing design or land use, and far too little preservation of public open spaces.

One ranch east of Irvine is being developed by Occidental Petroleum—an oil, chemical, coal, and metal-finishing conglomerate —as Lake Forest, "a multi-million dollar master-planned community." In reality the project is a confusion of badly laid-out streets and subdivisions of $30,000 to $60,000 houses with a small man-made lake accessible to swimming or boating club members only, a riding stable, a few tennis courts, and little more. The Avco Corporation—operator of finance companies, aviation engine factories, broadcast stations, and recreation land subdivisions—is developing the larger ranch tract of Laguna Niguel, 8,000 acres of gentle hills sloping down to the ocean, as a recreation-oriented upper-income enclave ("planned evolution of an unlimited new town") where the highest-priced homes, up to $80,000 in subdivisions and $275,000 custom built on large lots, line the fairways of a country club golf course, surround private swimming clubs, and front on an "exclusive, guarded" private ocean beach. Philip Morris, the diversifying cigarette-maker, is trying to finish Mission Viejo, begun by an independent developer on 11,000 acres of the 53,000-acre Mission Viejo ranch; before Philip Morris stepped in to bring the project out of the red, Mission Viejo ("America's most outstanding new town") was one of the more progressive of eastern Orange County's new developments, with generally lower-priced housing, a solitary isolated group of garden apartments for low-income families, and neighborhood recreation centers with swimming pools open to any Mission Viejo resident for a monthly communitywide recreation fee. It is uncertain whether Philip Morris will be able to maintain these features of the project and unlikely that it will institute other innovations, as it seeks to make the venture much more profitable as quickly as possible.

County planner Dickason found that he and his staff could do little about the abundant shortcomings in these developers' plans because of what he called "a politically supercharged atmosphere." The big corporate developers were able to strongly pressure the county supervisors, who made the final zoning decisions, and the independent water and sewer districts, whose pipelines followed wherever the user fees paid by the developers led them. While the planners fought against the unacceptable new town master plans, the county supervisors and the water and sewer agencies allowed the developers to begin building where and how they wanted. The results are new towns in name only. As a 1971 consultant's report to the county described it, the huge ranches are being allowed to develop haphazardly, "gradually producing patterns of land use, streets, jurisdictional boundaries and public facilities (or rather the lack of them) comparable to what exists west" of the Irvine ranch. The rush of development has made Orange County in the 1970s the equivalent of Prince George's County in the 1960s and Santa Clara County in the 1950s.

No single eastern Orange County new town project has been more disappointing in its false promise than Irvine itself. It had the size (the ranch covered one-sixth of the land area of the entire county), the money (the Irvine Foundation was valued "conservatively" at $1 billion in 1967 in a 1,130-page congressional report), some freedom from normal real estate economic limitations (the foundation is tax-exempt, and the land cost it nothing because it had been in the Irvine family for decades), the cooperation of local officials (the county planners wanted to encourage true new town development, and the rest of the county government had long been dominated both economically and politically by the ranch and the foundation), and the time (nothing had to be rushed because the undeveloped land could still be profitably farmed) that no other proposed new town venture in the United States has ever had. Unfortunately, however, the project also presented an unprecedented potential for speculative profit. This last incentive, unchecked by effective government supervision, has precluded development in the public interest.

Although the Irvine Foundation is tax-exempt and supposedly nonprofit, the millions of dollars it handles each year, thanks to its ownership of just half of the Irvine Company's stock, provides considerable remuneration in fees and contracts for such services as legal work for its officers and staff. The Irvine Company's other stockholders, many of them Irvine's descendants who have not inherited his emotional attachment to the ranch, stand to profit even more from its rapid development. In fact, some of them, led by James Irvine's granddaughter, Joan Irvine Smith, wish the Irvine Company would sell off land faster to housing developers and increase their dividends immediately. They do not understand that the large initial investment necessary for the project's physical infrastructure and sales promotion means the biggest profits will come in the future. These future returns are likely to be especially generous because the Irvine Company is keeping ownership, at considerable initial expense, of the shopping centers, some office buildings, a marina, and other facilities that will continue to be big money-makers long after the development of Irvine is completed. In fact, the flow of cash and profits to the company, its stockholders, and homebuilders at Irvine already have been unusually good for the early stages of so large a real estate project.

At every turn, as one steps behind the new town image marketed by the Irvine Company, one finds that profit was the one yardstick used throughout its planning. In the initial newspaper supplement advertisement Raymond L. Watson, executive vice-president of the Irvine Company, was quoted as saying, "As other major developers have done, we could have subdivided the land, sold it and run. The easy way. Instead, we chose to remain and build phase-by-phase in accordance with a long-range master plan of land use." However, in a speech he made at about the same time to a group of real estate professionals, Watson explained that the Irvine Company "was motivated to enter the city-building business upon realizing that the phased development of large new communities would produce more profits through master planning than any other alternative available."

Clearly, the most profitable master planning was designed to provide an expensive single-family house on a large lot in an "exclusive neighborhood" for upper-income Irvine homebuyers. The homes would be near a private swimming club in a community convenient for driving, with shopping centers, offices, and factories to help pay taxes (but kept away from the houses to protect property values). There would also be a university campus to give Irvine class and the potential for increasing property values that supposedly resulted from locating the UCLA campus in the upper-income Westwood section of Los Angeles. This carefully planned sales appeal was best summed up by a full-page advertisement paid for by the Irvine Company and the builder for the Turtle Rock Hills subdivision of large $55,000 to $75,000 houses in Irvine:

A better home . . . big customized homes on big lots to match the big views and the big scene. These are exciting luxury homes from every angle. . . .

A better environment . . . right in the center of the network of sweeping tree-lined and landscaped avenues of the great new master plan for the new city of Irvine is Turtle Rock Hills. San Joaquin Golf Course is close by. Turtle Rock Hills' own five-acre swim and tennis club is across the street. Fashion Island shopping in Newport Center is a few minutes away, as are Newport Beach, Corona del Mar, Pacific Ocean beaches and marinas. . . .

A better investment potential . . . Turtle Rock Hills has been described by writers and editors as "the future Westwood of Orange County." They have reported that Turtle Rock Hills has the potential for increases in the value of homes that the community of Westwood near the UCLA campus had (and has). Higher priced homes in Westwood have doubled, tripled and quadrupled in value in the past 20 years. Turtle Rock Hills has everything going for it to assure this potential, bolstered by the Irvine master plan in which open spaces, parks, boulevards and landscaping will never be diminished.

For the benefit of Orange County planners, the Irvine master plan also included references to several proposed "innovations": drainage canals running down toward the ocean to reduce erosion, "environmental corridors" or narrow greenbelts along these drainage channels, an undefined kind of public transportation that also could utilize these corridors, a vaguely described communitywide health insurance and treatment program, an experimental 2-level local government that would include a citywide Irvine government and smaller councils for each of several "towns" within the project, and a cable television system using cable laid underground with the infrastructure utilities before home construction began. On later versions of the plan the Santiago foothills of the Santa Ana mountains in the northern part of the area were reserved for agricultural use and open space. However, that was only after Forest Dickason and his planning staff convinced the county supervisors to refuse to allow homes on those foothills, where they were indicated in earlier master plan drafts. There have also been frequent promises to build some low-income housing in Irvine, but this has been consistently omitted on every version of the master plan.

According to an Irvine Company spokesman, construction of low-income housing would require federal subsidies, and so far there has been too much red tape. But this "innovation" is not the only one that has failed to materialize. No experimental local government system has been tried, because the Irvine Company allowed the city of Newport Beach to annex part of the new town site. (In exchange the company received permission to build high-rise office buildings in Irvine's commercial downtown, which is now located in and pays taxes to Newport Beach.)

No public transportation system has been started in the Irvine master plan area, and Irvine Company officials now say that any such system would have to be built by the county or by a Los Angeles area transit authority because of the expense. The county claims the master plan's "environmental corridors" would not be suitable for a transit system. And, in fact, the environmental corridors—in reality barely strips of grass and trees along drainage canals—will be too narrow to be much use even as parks. They also are too far apart to serve as pedestrian paths.

The only new feature in the Irvine master plan to become a reality thus far, besides the lush landscaped boulevards constantly referred to in subdivision advertisements, is the cable television system which has proved to be a highly profitable innovation. The Irvine master plan forbids outdoor home television antennas, so the only way a resident can get decent reception is to a pay a monthly fee to hook onto the cable. And the only cable television company in Irvine—the Community Cablevision Company—just happens to be a wholly owned subsidiary of the Irvine Company.

How has the Irvine Company gotten away with it all? Its financial and political power has helped. The men who sit on the boards of the Irvine Company and Foundation are also directors of many of California's biggest corporations and utilities. They are the campaign contributors to candidates running for office in Orange County and nationally. When Irvine Company officials decided that a large university would increase the prestige and sales potential of the Irvine project, they easily convinced the University of California's regents—one of whom was an attorney being paid for part-time work by the Irvine Foundation—to locate a full-sized campus there. The Irvine Company donated some of the necessary land to the university and later sold it the rest for more than $3 million ($6,500 an acre).

When the Irvine plan was being sold to Orange County officials, just before the project's big promotional push began, President Nixon sent his entire Cabinet—including then Attorney General John Mitchell, Housing and Urban Development Secretary George Romney, Health, Education, and Welfare Secretary Robert Finch, Interior Secretary Walter Hickel, Transportation Secretary John Volpe, and Agriculture Secretary Clifford M. Hardin—to tour the Irvine site by car and helicopter in August 1969. "The President told us several weeks ago we should take a tour of the Irvine property while we are out here" at the San Clemente White House, reporters were told by Lee A. Dubridge, the President's science adviser at the time. The Cabinet officers praised the project's plans highly, and Hickel, at that time the outspoken conservationist of the group, declared that he was impressed by "the great imagination of the long-range planning." No Presidential parties have been to Irvine since, however, to see how that planning has been carried out.

The project's upper-income residents are happy with the way Irvine has evolved, however. They don't want low-income housing in their community nor families with wide-ranging incomes in their neighborhood. Public transportation does not interest them because they have two or three cars per family, and they think of air pollution as something left behind in Los Angeles. The homeowners don't necessarily want to walk anywhere either. And they certainly do not want a corner grocery store or someone's place of business just down the street because they fear it would hurt their property values. (In reality, contrary to the beliefs of most suburbanites, property values are highest in many in-town commercial and mixed commercial-resident neighborhoods in most cities.) These homebuyers are looking for a profitable real estate investment in a status-symbol home and neighborhood. This, as the Turtle Rocks Hills advertisement made clear, is precisely what Irvine is designed to offer and what the Irvine Company *really* means by new town and master-planned community.

"A planned community is nothing more in some people's minds than glorified subdivisions with a few more amenities," explained county planner Forest Dickason. "They want to live in a planned community that is single-family homes and parks. 'That's what we left L.A. for,' they say."

Most homebuyers see master planning as a way to keep out apartments, corner stores, cheap housing, and undesirable neighbors. In their minds, it is a sort of insurance that property values will go up. To residents of California new town projects and planned community suburbs surveyed by the Institute of Urban and Regional Development of the University of California:

> . . . "planning" is thus generally defined as the process of minimizing the financial risk [of buying a new home] while maximizing the social status and profit potential of a community. . . . Since developers have full control over land use policies in [these] communities, the risk of suffering social contamination and financial hardship at the hands of outside market forces is felt to be significantly diminished.

"We don't have to worry that some time in the future the area will be changed," a homeowner in one planned community told the California researchers. "You can't have a neighbor painting a purple and pink house next door," said another. When asked what the concept of planned new town meant to him, a telephone company executive said, "I picture a planned community as a place where they have recreational areas planned, community centers, shopping areas, industrial and research areas—all these areas zoned off," away from the residential neighborhoods. A clothing store manager living in a project promoted as a planned community said he moved there because he knew it would "be exclusive to some extent." Another homeowner felt that the developer would have to keep the project attractive and profitable to upper-income homebuyers in order to protect so large an investment. "He's not going to bring in any dingbats [in cheaper houses] 'cause he'd lose money doing that now."

The homebuyers in Irvine and the other new town projects of Orange County are trying both to buy escape and to share with the new town developers in the profits from what they all know is basically real estate speculation. None of them is interested in experiments or truly improved urban communities for all citizens; that would be too risky all around. And Orange County officials, elected with large campaign contributions from builders and businessmen profiting from rapid, still essentially unmanaged development, are generally content, in the words of one report by the county planners, "to equate progress with growth and expect that the problems already being experienced by other metropolitan areas will somehow pass us by. But they won't."

The once remarkably clean air, still a selling point used by salesmen for Irvine and the other eastern county projects, is already being fouled. In recent years the incidence of respiratory disease, which seems to be causally related to air pollution, has risen at a much faster rate in Orange County than in California as a whole. "Spinach, which was a common crop in the county [and particularly on the Irvine ranch] five years ago, can no longer be grown here due to the smog," a 1972 county planners' study noted. "Various lettuce varieties, barley and tomatoes have been damaged. . . . Together, all of these factors indicate the seriousness of the air pollution situation, and little real improvement is expected in the 1970–80 decade."

Others of Orange County's once-prolific crops also are dwindling, simply because the most fertile and productive agricultural land is being lost to development, particularly on the Irvine ranch. In

1950 Valencia orange groves covered 56,000 acres, the majority of them inside the Irvine ranch, but by 1970 less than 15,000 acres of orange groves remained. Little land is being kept for public open space either, so that the county as a whole now has only 4,000 acres of public park land—less than 1 per cent of its total land area and much less per capita than in the crowded cities of San Francisco, Detroit, Philadelphia, Chicago, or Minneapolis. Miles of Pacific Ocean access also have been lost by the public to Orange County's beachfront developments; some of the most beautiful beaches within the boundaries of the Irvine ranch are now barred to everyone but Irvine beachfront homeowners by high walls and guards at checkpoint gates.

And the water is being polluted. Partially treated sewage from Irvine is being dumped directly into the ocean through a long underwater pipe, and federal clean-water grants—which were badly needed to curb longtime pollution of the Santa Ana River in the already built-up western part of the county—have had to be diverted to the construction of sewage treatment facilities for Irvine and the other supposedly self-sufficient new town projects. Siltation from construction-caused soil erosion is threatening dozens of small canyon streams that cut through the foothills in Irvine and run down to the ocean. A large wetlands marsh in a 3-mile-long estuary on Irvine's oceanfront, which had been nurturing a wide variety of small wildlife, also is threatened by the Irvine Company's development of a large commercial marina in the estuary.

"The quality of the environment in the county," Forest Dickason said late in 1971, "is now in serious jeopardy." Rather than experimenting with ways to reduce or even prevent environmental damage, the developers of Irvine and the other Orange County new town projects are causing still more.

They are having the same effect on the county's social and financial health. The developers have failed, for instance, to provide any new housing for the western county's thousands of presently ill-housed, low- and middle-income factory workers, many of them Chicanos. Yet they continue to draw on those same people as employees of the large, new industrial plants that broaden the tax bases of Irvine and the other projects and lower the property tax bills of their upper-income residents. As a result, "the present housing situation could soon reach crisis proportions as the county continues to grow," a consultant's report warned in 1971.

Low and moderate-income families will be drawn to work opportunities in industry, and will want to reside close to their jobs. Unless adequate housing is provided, these families may be forced to move into existing ghettos [in the western half of the county] where lack of transportation opportunities, language barriers and inadequate school facilities limit their earning potential.

At the same time, public money that should be spent to improve schools, public facilities, and social services for these families in western Orange County has instead been paying for new schools, community centers, fire stations, and the like in Irvine and the other new town projects, where these facilities help to sell houses. Ironically, in Irvine schools still cannot be built as quickly as new homes are sold, and children there have been attending half-day double sessions for years. These schools likely will remain overcrowded for some time to come. Moreover, the need to provide enough other facilities for the million new residents of eastern Orange County will prove quite expensive, since much of what will be needed has not been properly planned for in advance.

The "better environment" and "investment potential" so highly touted in the ads for Irvine's Turtle Rocks Hills already are being jeopardized by the certainty of much higher taxes, social discord, persistent smog, poisoned water, and the disappearance of most of

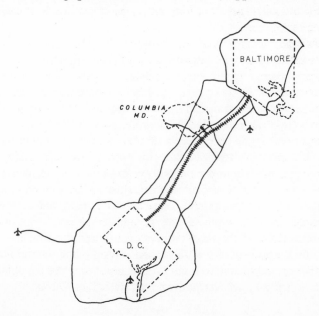

the once seemingly endless open space. A golden opportunity to model a new and better kind of urban growth in eastern Orange County has been lost. Instead, the developers of Irvine and its neighboring projects are perpetuating and even aggravating all the old suburban development problems with their 1970-style new town sprawl.

"Ask me anything you want about new communities," William Atkinson, a veteran homebuilder from Oklahoma, declared at a conference of real estate professionals in the new town of Columbia, Maryland, late in 1972. "I've gone all over the country to see them. Went up and down the coast of California three times in a rented car. And I tell you, Columbia is the place."

During the first five years of its development Columbia has been visited by more than a million people from every state and sixty foreign nations. It has been studied closely by scores of U.S. developers, planners, and financiers at six Columbia Process conferences, and it has been written about glowingly in nearly every major American newspaper and magazine, plus many others abroad. Columbia is the place *Life* magazine called, in an enthusiastic 8-page color layout, "a city made to human measure." It is the place that inspired George Romney to say: "The establishment of Columbia shows the entire nation and the world an important viable step toward solving the crushing problems of our wildly expanding and exploding cities."

Columbia, located halfway between Washington, D.C., and Baltimore, is America's best-known and most admired new town. For many people, in the words of its own 5-year progress report, it has become a symbol "generating hope that the urban dilemma can be solved—that man can build on the face of the earth cities worthy of his aspiration." Columbia definitely is not just another suburban real estate speculator's new town hoax—although its developer, James W. Rouse, made his fortune building giant, enclosed suburban shopping malls (twenty since 1958) that have contributed to what Rouse himself describes as "anti-human suburban sprawl . . . the bits and pieces of a city splattered across the landscape . . . by whim of the private developer," part of an "irrational process" by which "non-communities are born."

In 1963 Rouse set out with unique sincerity and determination to do better. He wanted to build "a new city . . . that would constitute in fact a better alternative to sprawl." It was to be, again in

Rouse's words, "a real city, not just a better suburb, but a complete new city" with

> business and industry to establish a sound economic base . . . and houses and apartments at rents and prices to match the income of all who work there, from company janitor to company executive [and] schools, and churches, libraries, college, hospital, concert hall, theaters, restaurants, hotels, offices and department stores.

It would "respect the land" and protect the environment. Socially, Columbia would be planned "from the needs and yearnings of people to be the kind of community that will best serve and nourish their growth."

To help his architects, land planners, engineers, and financiers realize this, Rouse convened a novel think tank planning group of fourteen well-known and widely respected consultants, including Christopher Jencks, education specialist; Herbert Gans, urban planner, sociologist, and writer; Alan M. Voorhees, transportation expert; Robert W. Crawford, Philadelphia city recreation department commissioner; Antonia H. Chayes, member of the President's Commission on the Status of Women; Wayne E. Thompson, city manager of Oakland, California; Robert M. Gladstone, economist; Stephen B. Withey, social researcher; Donald N. Michael, psychologist; and Henry M. Bain, Jr., political scientist. The group met every two weeks for two days and a night over a 6-month period, and from their discussions, suggestions, and cautions, Rouse and his planners evolved the new town goals and innovations to be incorporated in Columbia.

Each neighborhood was to be built around its own elementary school, playground and small park, swimming pool, and convenience grocery–drug store, all reachable by pedestrian paths routed safely over and under auto streets on bridges and through tunnels. A cluster of neighborhoods forming a village would encircle a village center containing a supermarket, several specialty shops and services, secondary schools, a nondenominational worship facility, a library, a community center for use primarily by teenagers, and a "major" recreation facility, such as a large indoor swimming pool or skating rink. The villages would be arrayed around what Rouse envisioned as a "beautiful, lively, efficient downtown" with department stores, many more specialty shops, restaurants, hotels, theater, movie houses, a main library, offices, a concert hall, a park, and a lake. Downtown Columbia, a Rouse planner promised, was not to be a mere shopping center but rather "the central symbol of the community, a second-hand bookshop or a sidewalk cafe, a bench and a fountain, people working, shopping, visiting, meeting." Industry would be located in industrial parks on the edge of town.

Six thousand acres of the 14,000-acre site would be preserved as open space, including several man-made lakes, parks, and existing forests. To minimize domination of the town by automobiles and prevent the isolation of housewives and children during weekdays, a transportation system of minibuses running at 5-minute intervals was planned. Half of Columbia's working residents were to be able to work inside Columbia, so they could be nearer their families and even go home for lunch; conversely, anyone who worked in Columbia was to have the opportunity to live there if he or she wished. At least 10 per cent of the residents were to be low-income residents, and black families of all income levels were to be integrated throughout the community. A prepaid community medical plan was to provide complete medical care for all Columbia residents right in the town at an extraordinarily low individual family cost. The schools were to be innovative in physical design and educational techniques and remain open at night, on weekends, and even during the summer for adult education and community activities.

Rouse—a balding man of nearly sixty with a round open face—had labored for years in real estate finance for the Federal Housing Administration, a commercial bank, and his own mortgage banking firm. Naturally, he strongly stressed that Columbia should make a profit, a good profit that would be the envy of the developers of suburban sprawl. "This was no residual goal, not something just to be hoped for as a possibility," he said. "It was and is a prime objective." This was important for two reasons.

Rouse believed, first, that the project's profitability, and thus its salability, would be the best measure of whether the community truly pleased people: homebuyers, merchants, and company executives. "A continuing examination of profitability," he said, "is simply a responsible attempt to perceive the market place votes and respond to them. It resists the pull toward sentimentality, sophistication and arrogance. It hauls dreams into focus with reality and leads to bone and muscle solution."

Secondly, "by producing an outstanding profit" in the development of Columbia, Rouse said,

> we speak loud and clear to the city-building industry. It will induce attention to a good environment as the right product in city building. It will warn against the unmarketability of sprawl. . . . Failure or even moderate success [at Columbia] would be a blow to better hopes for urban growth. It would support the myth that it is not economic to produce a good environment.

It was, typically for Rouse, a fresh, honest argument that seemed to make remarkably good sense when first heard. Unfortunately, its flaws can be seen by examining the actual development of Columbia. The one goal the project has clearly already achieved is profitability and market acceptance. By 1973 Columbia's population was nearly 25,000, and enough lots had already been sold to home and apartment builders to insure that 46,000 people would live there (out of a target population of 110,000). Columbia also has, in place and operating, 68 industries (including a giant General Electric appliance plant already employing 2,700 people in its second year of operation), 138 retail businesses (many of them in one of Maryland's largest indoor shopping malls located in Columbia's downtown), 6 banks, 9 restaurants, 6 office buildings, a hotel, library, outdoor concert pavilion, hospital, clinic, 2 colleges, 2 other college extensions, 8 elementary schools, 3 middle schools (junior highs), 2 high schools, numerous nursery schools and day-care centers, several small neighborhood swimming pools, a large indoor pool, a skating rink, and 2 golf courses.

Columbia houses nearly a third of the people living in the otherwise predominantly rural Howard County. The new town also accounts for nearly half the assessable property tax base for the county. In fact, for the past several years Columbia has contributed more tax money to Howard County than the county has had to spend in the new town for schools, police and fire protection, road maintenance, and other services. This helped enable the county to lower its property tax rate by 10 cents per $100 assessed valuation in 1971, a very rare occurrence in a locality with a rapidly increasing population.

More importantly, after experiencing the expected early deficits —covered by $80 million in loans from Connecticut General Life (a full partner with Rouse in the Howard Research and Development Company, the actual corporate developer of Columbia), Chase Manhattan Bank, and Teachers Insurance and Annuity Association—Columbia began paying its investors a profit in its sixth year and is expected to yield what one of Rouse's financial advisers calls "a really sizable profit" by the end of the 1970s. Columbia's homebuyers also stand to profit richly: Houses that sold for $15,-000 to $20,000 when home sales began in Columbia in the late 1960s were already worth $25,000 to $35,000 by late 1972, and higher-priced houses had appreciated proportionately more.

Real estate speculation is still the primary source of these profits at Columbia, however. The entire project and all of the goals Rouse set for it have been dependent on old-fashioned speculation in land values. And in that very significant way Columbia is no different from any other American real estate project.

Like any other developer, Rouse first had to find a way to buy up a lot of land as cheaply as possible. Several lawyers and other Rouse associates began accumulating farms in central Howard County in their own names and those of fictitious land-holding companies. They served as what real estate professionals call "straw parties" for Rouse himself, enabling him to buy the land at low prices. If the farmers and other sellers had known that a developer was out to assemble a site for a project the size of Columbia, the cost of the land would have skyrocketed.

"It was a top secret, cloak and dagger operation," remembered attorney Albert Keidel, Jr., now a director of Rouse's development company. Over a period of nearly a year Rouse's agents bought 140 different parcels of land, adding up to 14,000 acres, for a total of $23.5 million—all in cash borrowed from Connecticut General Life. The offer of immediate cash also helped encourage farmers to sell at a lower price. "If you had a reluctant farmer on your hands," Keidel said, "you'd just ask him if he had ever seen $300,000—or whatever it was you were offering him—and then you'd just put the money down on his kitchen table." Keidel said he and Rouse's other agents "used every device you could think of" to convince farmers to sell. "It was an extraordinary process," said Morton Hoppenfeld, a Rouse Company vice-president, "that may be very, very difficult to repeat."

To help pay for the project's infrastructure, the open space that was to be preserved, and other amenities—as well as to pay Rouse and the project's investors a good profit—parcels of the land were sold to builders of houses, apartments, offices, and factories at greatly inflated prices. Land that had been worth $700 an acre for farming and had been bought for $1,500 an acre by Rouse's agents was then sold to builders at from $7,000 an acre (for some single-family-home neighborhoods) to $47,000 an acre (for office and apartment sites near Columbia's downtown shopping mall). And the price of land sold to builders at Columbia has continued to rise since.

"Inflation is working for us," Albert Keidel said. Much of Columbia's infrastructure was put in and paid for at mid-1960s prices with money borrowed at interest rates that seem quite low compared to what was being charged in the early 1970s. Many of the best located parcels—around the shopping mall, the village centers, the lakes, and elsewhere—have purposely been held back by Rouse until they can be sold at the absolutely highest prices at the last possible minute. Moreover, Rouse has built the mall, the village center stores, and some office and industrial park factory buildings himself and kept ownership of them. Thus, he can use them for depreciation deductions on his firm's taxes and collect ever-increasing rents from their commercial tenants until the best time to sell.

"We depend on the cash flow from creating urban land values out of rural land values," explained Morton Hoppenfeld. "That's what this business is all about." Or, as Columbia's marketing director, Robert Shulman, said more directly: "The name of the game still is to sell land"—even in the new town of Columbia.

The builders who buy parcels of land from Rouse also primarily make their profit by further inflating the value of the land, which is reflected in a higher price for finished homes or larger rents for completed apartments and offices. "After the developer has taken his land profit," Shulman said, "the builder tries to profit from price inflation, too." In Columbia, as elsewhere in suburbia, "10 or 20 per cent of the sales price of a home amounts to an inflation of the price of the land under it," Shulman explained.

As time passes the inflation increases even more. The price to the homebuyer of an average quarter-acre lot in Columbia, which was about $4,500 when the project opened, according to Keidel, had increased to about $9,000 by 1972. "Maximizing land values is the tendency in the business," Keidel said.

Fast-rising land values and high-volume sales—the keys to profit in Columbia and in all real estate speculation—have, however, undermined many of James Rouse's goals. "There really is little innovation in Columbia," Shulman admitted. Radically different housing forms or land uses, he explained, might not sell fast enough to bring the Columbia population to the "critical mass" needed to create a sufficient market for commerce and industry. And these are what ultimately will provide Rouse and his investors with their biggest profits. Offering a residential product that will sell quickly, Shulman said, "means going for the good, easy middle market and giving people what you know they want," namely, a traditional "good" suburb.

By 1972 the average selling price of a home in Columbia had jumped to $34,000, and the median family income in the project was up to $17,000 a year. Columbia was well on its way to becoming another upper-middle-class, country club suburb, rather than a heterogeneous new city. When the $15,000 to $20,000 homes disappeared into much higher price brackets, middle-income residents also vanished from Columbia. Left with the affluent are pockets of lower-income families—mostly black and making up a little less than 10 per cent of Columbia's population in 1972—who live in government-subsidized housing built by Interfaith, a Rouse-organized consortium of local churches. The big income and social gap between Interfaith residents, who are grouped in clusters of rather cheap-looking townhouse apartments, and the upper-middle-class homeowning majority in Columbia has unfortunately helped create the kind of polarization that Rouse wanted to do away with.

"The Interfaith apartments were stigmatized as low-income places before they were even built," a black mother said. "They're dispersed around, but you can tell 'em, all right. All the American prejudices about low-rent housing are being preserved intact here. If something is stolen, everyone looks at the Interfaith kids."

Many middle-class black homeowners speak favorably of life in Columbia and of contacts with their white neighbors, one of whom pointed out that "the Negroes here are well educated, have good positions, and many live in the better homes." Yet in some ways the high- and low-income polarization carries over into all black-white relations at Columbia. Teenagers have segregated themselves into one all-black village recreation center and another that is all white. Shopkeepers complain that loitering black youngsters outside their doors frighten away white patrons. There have been tense black-white teen gang confrontations on the shore of Columbia's downtown lake at night. And a growing and disturbing incidence of drug use among Columbia youth is blamed by many residents on the blacks, although Howard County police say it is a community-wide problem.

"The problems of the cities have not been left behind when people come to Columbia," said Rouse's director of security, Mel Blenheim, "the people bring their prejudices and fears here." Blenheim is a black law school graduate hired by Rouse to run the small force of security policemen who patrol his shopping mall and village centers and help county police with Columbia problems. "I'm always getting calls from merchants saying, 'there are eight black kids hanging around,' and it turns out they aren't doing anything," Blenheim said. "The same thing with the kids they call 'hippies.' No street corner life is being allowed here.

"Young blacks from the inner city are not interested in dog obedience, swimming, or exercise classes," which are among the many white, middle-class-oriented activities provided in Columbia. "There is nothing in the health club, for instance," Blenheim went on, "for the real athlete—no track or weight lifting or boxing." Similarly, he noticed when he came to Columbia that the drugstores had "no black magazines or football magazines or Afro hair treatments—so black people look around and say, 'Columbia is not for me. It may be planned, but it is not planned for me.'"

Both black and white upper-income Columbia residents on a local citizens' equal rights council have complained that there are very few blacks among Columbia's schoolteachers, nonmenial employees of Columbia businesses, or Rouse's own development cadre in the new town. "Columbia is not becoming the dream we had hoped," complained Leonard Simmons, a black professor of social work at the University of Maryland, twenty miles south of Columbia. "It seems to be a place where we all can live, but there is serious question whether it's a place where we all can work."

Indeed, only 18 per cent of Columbia's working residents, black and white, hold jobs in Columbia. Most of the big firms in Columbia's industrial park, including General Electric, brought employees with them from elsewhere, employees who cannot afford most homes in Columbia and yet earn too much to qualify for its limited government-subsidized Interfaith housing. To cope with this problem General Electric is planning to build its own small, barracks-like community of mobile homes or inexpensive row houses just outside the Columbia boundary.

Meanwhile, most Columbia residents commute by car to jobs outside the new town. Many travel twenty to forty miles to work in Washington and Baltimore and their suburbs. And because the regularly scheduled public minibus proved a financial failure that could not be subsidized by Rouse without endangering profits, housewives need and use second cars. Driving is still such a suburban habit in Columbia that, according to a survey, 90 per cent of the adult shoppers at the neighborhood convenience stores drove to them, even though they could have walked the distance in five to ten minutes on scenic pedestrian paths without crossing streets. Downtown Columbia, encircled by a broad boulevard, is essentially a giant parking lot. The shopping mall is surrounded by parking space for thousands of cars, and each of several nearby office buildings also has a huge concrete lot.

More land seems to have been paved over for parking lots and streets in Columbia than has been preserved as open space. To make the project work financially, Rouse was forced to sell more land than he expected to builders, leaving only 3,000 acres—rather than the 6,000 he promised—for public use. Only half of those 3,000 acres is actually park, forest, or other open space available for public use. The rest is taken up by the median strips and shoulders of boulevards, the surface area of the man-made lakes, and the ground used by private golf courses. Some residents have fought and lost battles with Rouse over woodlands they thought were to be protected but that builders leveled for development after buying the land.

Although Rouse did a universally admired job of protecting stream valleys and providing for proper grading and drainage, so that soil erosion has thus far been kept to a minimum at Columbia, serious air pollution has been detected by scientists studying the development of the new town. The air pollution comes, of course, from the automobiles, which already are causing traffic jams during rush hours and on busy shopping days at the downtown mall. Similarly, waste and sewage disposal in Columbia suffer from a lack of innovative solutions, because such experimentation was not financially feasible. Howard County must dispose of Columbia's garbage and sewage the same way it must everywhere else, which adds to sewage treatment plant, incinerator, and landfill problems. If its real estate economics had only permitted, Columbia could have been the first American project to use the incineration of the town's garbage to produce its electricity—a system since installed in some French new town projects. Or Columbia's underground utilities could have been put in easy-to-work-in, man-sized lighted tunnels, as has been done in new developments in several European countries.

What most sets Columbia apart from the average suburb, in addition to its specially designed, Howard County–built schools, are the Columbia Medical Plan and the Columbia Association. The medical plan utilizes a modern new clinic and hospital in Columbia staffed by doctors from Baltimore's Johns Hopkins Hospital and Medical School. For a monthly prepayment of $51 for a family with children or $15 for a single person, plus a charge of $2 per visit, a member of the plan has access to the hospital and clinic for any ailment, emergency care, shots, eye examinations, and an annual health review. Maternity care costs $100 extra. Medicine required during hospitalization is free; prescription drugs are $2 a prescription. The monthly prepayment fee actually goes to a consortium of insurance companies that reimburses Johns Hopkins for the expense incurred in running the program. The plan is truly innovative and has just one drawback—its price. Only 45 per cent of Columbia's first 25,000 residents paid to join the plan. Some of the rest undoubtedly belong to cheaper, although less convenient, group insurance plans at jobs outside Columbia. And some of Columbia's lower-income, subsidized-housing families cannot afford any kind of care at all.

The other special feature is the Columbia Association, a nonprofit organization of all of Columbia's landowners—both its homeowners and Rouse—that owns and operates all the special facilities that make Columbia so undeniably attractive to many middle-class families: neighborhood swimming pools and parks, tennis courts, recreation centers, community buildings, golf courses, the man-made lakes, child-care facilities, and the pedestrian pathways and other open space areas. Its capital comes from an annual tax (75 cents per $100 assessed valuation) on all Columbia property, and the tax has the same legal standing as the county property tax. If it is not paid, the Columbia Association has a first lien on the property, even before the home's mortgage holder.

That money—$15 million in 1972—enabled the Columbia Association to buy and build all those recreation facilities. The open spaces it maintains are for use by the public, and free after-school child care and a wide variety of social activities for children and adults also are provided by the association. For access to the swimming pools, ice-skating rink, tennis courts, golf courses, health club, and certain other facilities and activities, the Columbia Association charges an annual $200 per family user fee, in addition to the property tax. That fee also allows Columbia Association members to ride to association facilities on half-hourly minibuses from the fleet that Columbia tried unsuccessfully to use for public transportation.

The Columbia Association—controlled by Rouse representatives as long as he owns a certain percentage of the property in Columbia —also acts as a quasi-governmental body for a city that really has no local government and probably never will have, because Maryland gives most local powers to its counties. The Columbia Association's architectural review committee approves all builders' plans and has given the project an almost uniform appearance of soft white and beige, broken up by red brick and green grass. Covenants on all the property deeds authorize the Columbia Association to force any Columbia resident to cut his grass and curb his dog and can stop him from putting up the wrong kind of fence or painting his house the wrong color.

However, the lien-enforced property-taxing power that finances the Columbia Association is likely to remain unique to that development. The Federal Housing Administration (FHA), which allowed the prior lien on the mortgages it insured in Columbia, has decreed it will not make that exception again. Instead, the agency prefers that its own liens on FHA-financed homes take precedence. Yet it is the Columbia Association that provides Rouse's project with many of the new town amenities that he wanted. In fact, Columbia's recreation facilities—which help immeasurably in selling land and houses—could not be financed with proceeds from land sales without at least doubling the development's already high real estate prices.

The Columbia Association facilities and maintenance of open space are among the primary reasons why the majority of Columbia's middle-class residents are so happy there. (Sixty per cent registered complete satisfaction with Columbia in a recent University of Michigan study.) These amenities are, after all, the attributes of ideal suburbia: plentiful recreation and some green space in a community of mostly single-family homes with single-income neighborhoods, enforced home and yard care standards, good schools, convenient drive-in shopping, and steadily rising property values. Columbia, which must be judged a failure as a new city, despite Rouse's good intentions, is clearly a qualified success as the dream suburb—a *super suburb*—that is becoming the capital of the growing, affluent, predominantly white suburban corridor stretching from the northern outskirts of Washington, D.C., to the southwestern suburbs of Baltimore. This is the market area for Columbia's downtown shopping mall, and Rouse Company surveys show that the median family income for this area of nearly 500,000 people is a startling $16,500—almost exactly the same as that for families in Columbia itself.

What is wrong with a super suburb? A majority of its residents love Columbia. And although many old problems of suburbia are being perpetuated, some advances (many of which, however, probably cannot be duplicated elsewhere) have been made. No other project calling itself a new town in this country has nearly so high a percentage of black residents—between 15 and 20 per cent—as does Columbia. And Rouse, as well as many residents of Columbia, insists that the suburb will improve greatly as it continues to grow and prosper: that some workable kind of public transportation will be found, that its outdoor concert stage and its several colleges will make it a cultural center, that its downtown night life, virtually nonexistent now, will be greatly improved by a coming commercial theater and movie-house complex, and that, in salesman Robert Shulman's words, "Anything else you don't find in Columbia today will probably be here tomorrow"—as long as it pays.

Until—and unless—its developing pollution, transportation, and social problems become massive, Columbia is fine for those who can afford its idealized, isolated, recreation-oriented, suburban atmosphere. But it is not in any true sense an experimental prototype for American cities of the future; it has had to be, first and foremost, a profitable real estate venture based on unchanged land speculation methods. It is this fact that will always separate Columbia and all other well-meant attempts at building new towns in the United States from the truly innovative European projects that were supposed to have inspired them. In the meantime the utopian promotion of Columbia only lulls us into a belief that we are really coping with our pressing urban problems. Thus, even the best of the American new town projects merely diverts our attention from a more determined search for something other than deceivingly escapist super suburbs.

Epilogue

Building the Next America

Between now and the year 2000 urban America will expand by at least half its present size. The number of new households being formed is actually increasing even faster than the population and, because families are smaller, fewer people are living in each housing unit. "From now until 1985," predicts the federal Task Force on Land Use and Urban Growth in its 1973 report to the Presidential Council on Environmental Quality, "more than 27,000 new households are anticipated every week—equal to a city the size of Kalamazoo, Michigan." More households means, of course, more homes and urban growth. In addition, as the task force points out, steadily increasing income levels mean growth with a greater impact, because of increased "automobile ownership, recreation, travel, the purchase of bigger homes and even second homes, with the result that people spread out farther over the land."

The next America is already taking shape all around us: Cities are building higher, suburbs are spreading farther, towns are growing into cities, and once-undisturbed remote landscapes are being subdivided into recreation land lots. Even where no new development is taking place, existing neighborhoods are changing hands and undergoing dramatic alteration. Increasing numbers of Americans are becoming concerned about how this continuing urban growth and change will affect their own lives, the kinds of homes they will be able to live in, the communities in which they will be located, the air they will breathe, the water they will drink, and the condition of the little land that will be left around them.

This concern has produced what another report to the Presidential Council on Environmental Quality calls a "quiet revolution in land control": Policy-makers at local and national levels are finally trying to slow the uncontrolled sprawl of American cities and suburbs. "A new mood in American attitudes has emerged that questions traditional assumptions about the desirability of urban development," adds the Task Force on Land Use and Urban Growth. Some localities, many of them middle-class suburbs hoping to shut out urban problems, have abruptly limited further growth with exclusionary zoning and sewer hookup moratoriums. The federal government—through the Environmental Protection Agency, the Presidential Council on Environmental Quality, and new land control legislation in Congress—is trying to impose strict limits on air and water pollution and land despoliation, which would necessarily lead to similarly arbitrary curtailment of growth.

"We have been the most prodigal of people with land, and for years we wasted it with impunity," William H. Whyte wrote in 1968 in *The Last Landscape*. But the "good side to the mess" of previously rapid, untrammeled growth, Whyte argued, is the backlash that is now "disciplining us to do out of necessity what we have refused to do by choice."

Yet as long as our population continues to expand and millions of Americans remain ill-housed, a policy of no growth would be just as shortsighted and socially undesirable as uncontrolled growth has proven to be. "No growth is simply not a viable option for the country in the remainder of this century," concludes the Task Force on Land Use and Urban Growth.

> The case for more development does not come simply to demography —to the fact that we must house the people who are already around or whose birth is foreseeable--nor even to any inevitability of economic growth. There is also an ideal involved, of respecting the free choice of Americans to move in search of a better job or a better life. Mobility has been a traditional road to opportunity in American life. Wholesale growth restrictions, imposed by many communities, could block that road for many who still want most to travel it.

The necessary alternative, then, is a policy of controlling growth without limiting it absolutely and of somehow shaping a better urban environment. And an important part of any such policy would have to be the elimination of most forms of real estate speculation—or at least sufficient control of speculation to eliminate its most destructive effects. Many of the planners, social scientists, journalists, and others who have recently begun to examine the problem closely have nevertheless ignored the realities of real estate speculation in giving the American public confusing, conflicting, and frequently naïve advice about what basic form the next America should take.

Those who favor city living urge that old, mixed inner-city neighborhoods of low-scale dwellings and neighborhood stores and services be preserved and helped to prosper in the European tradition. They insist that attractive central cities, by retaining residents and drawing back some of the middle class, would slow down suburban sprawl. Because these cosmopolites have easy access to and frequently work in the mass media, they have succeeded in widely broadcasting their message that first priority should be given to revitalizing our central cities.

But it may be too late to save much of what had been most attractive about in-town living in many U.S. cities. Real estate speculators already have turned countless varied old neighborhoods into slums or torn them down altogether and replaced them with lifeless high-rise office and apartment enclaves. A few neighborhoods have been saved from blight and the bulldozer and have been resurrected through restoration and repopulation. But these are primarily inhabited by a social and economic elite, the only ones who can afford the speculation-inflated cost of renovation and the expensive alternatives, like private schools, to the bankrupt public institutions of central-city areas. Except for transient young people, almost everyone else living in many U.S. cities wants to get out; large numbers of the poor, blacks, and Spanish-speaking have simply been unable to join middle-class whites in their flight to the suburbs.

Public-opinion surveys show that many Americans do not take naturally to city living anyway. A frequently cited 1968 Gallup Poll found that only 18 per cent of a random sample of Americans preferred to live in big cities. Another 25 per cent preferred the suburbs. And 56 per cent, a startling majority, wanted most to live in small towns or on farms—well away from the huge metropolitan areas where so many of them are now forced to live in order to work. With this poll in mind, Irving Kristol, outspoken New York University Professor of Urban Values, suggests that what we constantly refer to as the American "urban crisis" might better be viewed as an "agrarian crisis."

A return to our agrarian past obviously is unrealistic, however. So it should not be surprising that a growing number of American city planners and social scientists are now arguing, like Kristol, that our present pattern of middle-class suburbanization should be accepted and developed as the only alternative to entrapment in unfriendly central cities. Kristol says we are today witnessing the growth of "an urban civilization without cities." Sociologist Don Martindale concludes that "the age of the city seems to be at an end." Planner Melvin Webber at the University of California, Berkeley, agrees, adding that the news comes, ironically, just "when policy makers and the press are discovering the city."

Yet these social scientists are themselves just discovering and ascribing new virtues to the suburbs at a time when many suburban residents are becoming increasingly disillusioned. Trees, grass, and the old feeling of having moved out into the country are disappearing. The air and water are no longer clean. And the same social problems from which cities suffer, plus some unique to the suburbs, are becoming epidemic. Crime—including the antisocial acts of alienated youth—is increasing much more rapidly per capita in the suburbs than in the cities. Traffic congestion and gasoline rationing threaten to curtail severely the freedom to move quickly by car to and from widely dispersed activities in the suburbs—a freedom persistently touted by social scientists as one of the big advantages of suburban living. The dissatisfaction of many American housewives with their lot in society today can doubtless also be traced to their frequent isolation with other women and their children in the suburbs. The same public opinion polls that have been used to prove the relative unpopularity of U.S. big cities also show that Americans are scarcely more eager to live in the suburbs when offered a full range of alternatives. But what real choices have middle-class families had in recent years?

The answer to this dilemma has been the attempted synthesis of the best of city, suburban, and small-town living in a semirural setting in American new towns modeled on those of Europe. "We have lived so long with grim, congested, worn-out inner cities and sprawling, cluttered outer cities that we have come, subconsciously, to accept them as inevitable and unavoidable," argues James Rouse, the developer of Columbia. What we need, he says, are "good new communities."

Nevertheless, U.S. new town projects, including Columbia, are turning out to be neither very new in concept nor very good examples of complete communities. Nor are they innovative in the ways that experimental new towns of Europe are. Instead, by most resembling large-scale suburbs and perpetuating many of their mistakes, they are wasting more land and further polluting the environment. In addition, as a "social concept," sociologist and urban planner Edward Eichler concludes, U.S. new town projects "commit what is to America's activist youth the worst sin of all: they are irrelevant."

Most arguments over what urban forms we should be planning for the next America also are largely irrelevant, however, as long as they continue to ignore the real estate development realities that actually shape urban growth—both here and abroad. Look, for example, at London and Paris, the usually cited models for attractive central-city living. Both cities have strong metropolitan planning agencies of the kind frequently advocated for the control of urban growth in this country. But they are now under virtual siege by real estate speculators who have been biting away at old neighborhoods and substituting massive new glass and concrete towers of offices for businessmen and luxury apartments for the rich. Displaced working-class families are being banished to isolated, high-rise public housing ghettos in the least desirable sections of the two cities. The colorful mix of varied activities and life-styles, distinctive neighborhoods, and sidewalk life so characteristic of both London and Paris have largely disappeared in areas invaded by the speculators.

In London, where office rents and building prices are now among the highest in the world and are still rising at a rapid rate, speculators are rushing to buy old buildings, tear them down, and put up cheaply built new high-rises. Some speculators have advertised that they will pay up to 25 per cent of a project's profit to anyone offering them well-located property for redevelopment. "More millionaires have been thrown up by the property business in Britain since the war than by any other industry," according to the British financial journal, *The Economist*.

Stark new office, apartment, and hotel towers now hem in old landmarks like St. Paul's Cathedral and tower over the old, low, red-brick buildings, many with white stone and plaster Georgian facades in favored West End neighborhoods. Still more demolition and construction of gigantic multibuilding office and apartment complexes have been proposed by speculators, and given preliminary approval by local planners, for some of London's remaining best-known and most popular areas: the neon-lit Piccadilly Circus entertainment district; the little streets of restaurants, night spots, musty shops, flats, and pushcart markets of nearby Soho; the historic Covent Garden central produce market, and the cluttered, old East End Jewish neighborhood (now the home of many recent Asian immigrants) where the hundreds of stalls of the Petticoat Lane outdoor market attract tens of thousands of shoppers each Sunday. These most recent plans have turned the once-sporadic controversy over new development in London into a loud, sustained, public clamor that regularly makes big headlines in the British press.

A Sunday newspaper supplement entirely devoted to the issue characterized the speculators' activities in the city as "the Second Blitz of London." A BBC radio commentator complained that "the heart is being torn out of London." And a *Sunday Times* columnist wrote in the spring of 1972:

> To come back to London after even a brief absence is to realize all over again that in our infinitely abused capital city, almost all change is for the worse. . . . So much money is to be made from the dehumanization of London that it may be naive to suppose that it will ever be arrested. Perhaps it is inevitable, with things as they now are, that posterity will say, "By the end of the 1970's, London was unliveable."

It is indeed disillusioning to read this about London, which most Americans have believed to be, in the words of a *U.S. News & World Report* article of a few years back, "the one city that is solving its problems." Its strong metropolitan planning agency, the Greater London Council, has succeeded, for example, in eliminating the city's once-notorious smoke pollution. It has managed to stop the flow of industrial waste into the Thames, which is no longer foul-smelling and to which fish are returning. The planners also prevented new development from encroaching on a 90,000-acre greenbelt of legally protected forests, farmland, open space, and tiny, old, rural villages that rings London. They succeeded instead in channeling much of the London area's post–World War II growth beyond the greenbelt into planned new towns of homes, commerce, and industry and into older towns chosen for carefully staged expansion.

Yet London's planners have at the same time allowed real estate speculators to do almost anything they please inside the central city and its suburbs, and for the same reasons that much less powerful American planners have allowed developers so much freedom here: Many officials of the Greater London Council and its subsidiary borough councils are themselves large investors in real estate, whose long-run financial interests are similar to those of the speculators they are supposed to control. In just one case that has come to light, it was widely reported in 1972 that the top officer of the Greater London Council, Sir Desmond Plummer, had more than $50,000 invested in the three big real estate firms that were seeking council approval for their controversial plan to completely redevelop Piccadilly Circus.

The Greater London and borough councils also have official policies favoring increased office development inside London in order to expand the property tax base that supports an impressive variety of still dependable municipal services. Thus, the planners have sometimes been proudest of what appear to be the most disturbing projects socially—those that have replaced old blocks of residences and small commercial buildings with huge, monolithic office complexes that are lifeless at night and on weekends—because they have given the biggest financial boost to the city.

London's powerful planners often have also been misled by their own good intentions. In order to achieve economies of scale that should make possible such desirable ends as safely separating pedestrians from automobile traffic, the planners have allowed and even encouraged developers to tackle gigantic projects of many buildings around central pedestrian precincts. Unfortunately, however, developers attempting to maximize their profits have used this freedom to put up collections of monstrous, bland new buildings, with little or no housing in them, surrounding uninteresting, bare pedestrian malls. In this manner, the human warmth of once-crowded, narrow, inner-London streets is being replaced by cold concrete slabs. Among the most noticeable of these disasters are the St. Paul's and Paternoster Square blocks of offices, shops, and sterile open spaces now surrounding St. Paul's Cathedral.

In their zeal to provide more safe and sanitary housing for residents of the city's East End slums, London's planners are allowing everything to be razed and replaced by public housing towers, like those that have spawned serious social problems in the United States. As part of a citizens' campaign to save some of the old neighborhoods, East End residents in 1972 opened an exhibit of photographs of what had been recently demolished. The pictures showed run-down buildings and undistinguished little streets that were clearly expendable in the eyes of upper-class planning officials. But they also depicted the little shops and familiar nooks that held meaning and provided social opportunities for the lower-income residents of those streets, something sadly lacking in the new public housing towers.

Finally, land values in London are escalating at such a dizzy pace that even officials with the best of intentions are hard-pressed to withstand the pressures of potential windfall profits. The Piccadilly Circus redevelopment plan, for instance, has been blocked and delayed several times during the past several years through the efforts of protesting citizens, but developers and their lawyers keep coming up with new versions of the proposal, new legal avenues to force the plan on the government, and official allies for its approval. It seems increasingly unlikely that the Piccadilly Circus redevelopment can be stalled much longer.

The effect of recent real estate speculation is even more noticeable in Paris. The once uniformly low Paris skyline of elegant domes, church spires, and gray tile roofs of Haussmann-era brownstones—a familiar view from the high slope of Montmartre just below the Sacre Coeur cathedral—has been broken by scores of new office and apartment towers of twenty to thirty and more floors. The tallest, the new 60-story Maine-Montparnasse Tower, stands two-thirds as high as the nearby Eiffel Tower and looms menacingly over the treetops of the Tuileries and Luxembourg gardens. Clumps of concrete and glass high-rises have risen on the very banks of the Seine, in one place right next to the Eiffel Tower, and huge complexes of giant buildings have been set down in the hearts of several once—distinctly individual neighborhoods, such as Montparnasse.

"This will be the last season before the destruction of the banks of the Seine, the site of Notre Dame and the 2,000-year-old heart of the city," darkly warned an advertisement placed in *Le Monde,* a leading French newspaper, in the spring of 1972 by Les Bateaux

Mouches, operator of sightseeing boats on the river. The Paris city council spent the greater part of that year ineffectually debating whether the many new development projects, almost all of them approved and partly subsidized by the city and national governments, were ruining the scale of the city and providing far too few public services, commercial establishments, and green spaces for the increasing office and residential populations of these new buildings. The Socialist Party charged that the Gaullist government and French banks and developers had conspired to push working-class residents out of the central city to make room for the higher-income tenants of new luxury apartments and offices. A group of architecture students warned that the sterile new developments were destroying the vital tissue of the city's traditional mixed neighborhoods of homes, shops, cafes, and parks.

In a Paris theater actors impersonating greedy real estate speculators manipulated models of 1900-style buildings and the boxy new skyscrapers in a kind of giant Monopoly game to dramatize a playwright's contention that devious means were being used to buy up the old houses of workers at low prices and replace them with high-profit high-rises. One French newspaper reviewer went beyond an appraisal of the play itself to warn his readers that "unless something is done . . . Paris will be indistinguishable from Queens or Long Island." And another columnist, noting this and other signs of growing concern, conjured up a vision of the city in 2072 in which "what was once Paris will have become the roof of an immense underground garage, pierced by the Eiffel Tower, the Arc de Triomphe and Notre Dame [and supporting] a limited number of drugstores, pubs, pizza joints, supermarkets and apartment skyscrapers."

Much of Paris, largely untouched since its rebuilding (and the purposeful destruction of many of its medieval neighborhoods) by Haussmann under Napoleon III, had undisputably worn out; too much of its housing was without sufficient sanitary facilities or heat. But in helping to underwrite the renewal, the government—which exercises considerable control over urban development through local planning councils, a national interdepartmental planning team, heavy government investment in housing construction, and summary condemnation powers—has appeared to do more to help speculators maximize profits than to improve the city. Speculators with inside knowledge have quietly bought up renewal project land as cheaply as possible and then cashed in on the tremendous increase in property values created by government-subsidized redevelopment. The developers also have been allowed to forget their promises to provide a minimum of social service facilities and housing for lower-income families in many projects.

The key to the failure of government supervision of the speculators in Paris is, as might be expected, money. The profits in redevelopment are large, mostly due to rising land values and a steady demand for high-interest mortgage money to finance the construction. The major part of these profits goes to a few big developers, banks, and insurance companies who control most of the new development. Many of these giant firms are, in turn, partly owned by the local and national governments and also have private financial ties to important government officials. It was no surprise to Parisians, for example, that when the former prefect of Paris (the city's combination mayor and chief city planner) left public life, he went to work for a real estate subsidiary of the Banque de Paris et des Pays-Bas, a bank that is the largest investor in and developer of Parisian renewal projects. In the suburbs of Paris, meanwhile, where other planning bodies theoretically hold sway, rampant speculation, encouraged by competition for tax-producing new development, has produced American-style sprawl.

If the problems caused by development in London and Paris sound surprisingly familiar to American ears, it is because real estate speculation is basically the same everywhere. Inflation of property values produces big profits and other financial gains that can lead to the corruption of any government's mechanisms for controlling growth, if those mechanisms do not get at the speculative roots.

Government in the United States, and, theoretically, the American people operating through government, can control real estate sales and development here in dozens of ways—from zoning decisions, sewer and highway location and construction, and building inspection to tax policy-making and enforcement of antidiscrimination laws. These levers have seldom been used against real estate speculation, however. Most zoning decisions, for example, actually encourage developers to buy land zoned for one use at a low price and to reap a windfall profit by having the property rezoned for a more lucrative purpose; it is instructive to note that Houston,

Texas, which has no zoning laws, has developed in no more wasteful or illogical a fashion than any other American city.

Zoning could be more profitably used if it were changed from the present variable classification of permitted development for individual parcels of land to the permanent allocation of vast areas of a state or region for a certain general use. For example, a proposal by a nonprofit conservation group, California Tomorrow, suggests dividing that state's 100 million acres of land into four principal zones: agricultural, conservation, urban, and regional reserve. All land in the agricultural zone—which, like the others, would actually comprise several unconnected regions of the state—would be forever limited to agricultural and some rural residential use. The conservation zones of mountains, foothills, forests, river and stream valleys, seashore, and other natural areas deemed worthy of permanent protection—a majority of the state's acreage altogether—would similarly be placed forever off limits to development, except for strictly controlled recreational and perhaps some vacation-home use. Urban zones, comprising currently urbanized areas, some of their environs, and other selected suitable sites, would be open to urban development within guidelines laid down by newly created regional authorities throughout the state. These regional authorities also would be responsible for land set aside in the fourth category, regional reserve zones, which they could designate for more urban development, public facilities, recreation areas, or additional protected open space.

Although no part of the California Tomorrow plan has been enacted into law, California voters did recently approve a state referendum designed to save what is left of their Pacific coastline. This strategy, partly based on, but not as restrictive as, California Tomorrow's conservation zoning, provides for an immediate moratorium on new shoreline development, a state study of what should be done with the coastal land in the future, and implementation of the study's recommendations, if the voters go along with them, by regional coastal land councils. Several other states—from Vermont to Florida and from Massachusetts to Washington—already have enacted more limited laws aimed at protecting specified natural areas such as coastlines and forests, usually by requiring that developers demonstrate how they will minimize water pollution, soil erosion, and tree-cutting before they are given permission to build. Unlike the solution advocated in the California Tomorrow plan, however, no state has designated large areas to be ruled entirely off limits to large-scale development.

Property tax reform—which has been proposed again and again in this country but never tried in any large local jurisdiction—could be another effective weapon against real estate speculation. Tax laws could be changed so that they would no longer encourage land speculation and discourage housing improvement. At present any improvement that increases a building's value also proportionately increases the owner's tax bill. If, however, local property taxes were based more on the worth of the land under a building and much less, if at all, on the building itself, the tax could confiscate some of the profit gained from the inflation of land values and would no longer penalize landlords who improve housing they own.

Individual states also could impose confiscatory taxes to take the profit out of obviously exploitive speculation. Vermont recently did just that, in an attempt to stop speculators, many of them from outside the state, from buying up Vermont farms and forests for quick, profitable resale to recreation land subdividers and mountain resort developers. The new levy, a stiff capital gains tax, takes up to 45 per cent of the profits made on the resale of previously undeveloped land held for just one year; the rate decreases to 7.5 per cent on land held five years before resale. Speculators who are fighting the tax in local courts contend that it unconstitutionally discriminates against one group of taxpayers, but the state government is vigorously arguing that the tax is both constitutional and necessary to protect the state's environment. "We want to put Vermont in a holding pattern while we work out better environmental controls," said an aide to Governor Thomas Salmon, a Democrat elected in 1972 on his promise, later fulfilled, to push the tax bill through the Republican-controlled legislature.

On the federal level speculators' profits also could be taxed at higher capital gains rates or even as ordinary income at still steeper graduated personal income tax rates. Depreciation deductions also could be greatly reduced or eliminated to help discourage disinterested ownership of rental housing primarily for its value as a tax shelter. These proposals also have been argued over for years, with the real estate industry claiming that no one would continue to invest in housing without today's tax incentives. It should be possible, however, to substitute for these tax loopholes—which have helped make housing a neglected by-product of investment in tax shelters—other government incentives, such as direct low-interest construction loans that could be more dependably expected to help produce more livable housing.

Better decisions could be made by local governments about where to put new roads and water and sewer lines, amenities that now attract new urban growth to wherever the pavers and sanitary engineers want them to go. Physical and social planners, government officials, and citizens could carefully decide where, if anywhere, growth would be best and then order the engineers to provide roads and pipes for those areas and only when development should begin. The independent power now enjoyed by most state road commissions and local water and sewer agencies would have to be sharply curtailed to make such planning decisions possible.

New development is now seldom served by public transportation because most government money earmarked for this use can be used only to build roads. But funds have been piling up since several localities have blocked further federal freeway construction within their borders, and some of this money could be diverted to the development of public transportation systems that could improve life in existing urban areas and make possible quite different development of new communities. Congress recently took a first timid step in this direction by voting to spend a tiny fraction of the federal Highway Trust Fund money for public transportation.

A benefit of better transportation, water, and sewer decisions would be the opportunity to eventually decrease air and water pollution. In the short run the most effective step to protect the environment, now being taken by several states and localities, as well as by the federal Environmental Protection Agency, is the enforcement of maximum air and water pollution and soil erosion limits. This action, in turn, has had the effect of limiting urban growth in some places—notably as a result of moratoriums on new sewer connections—but in an indirect, arbitrary way that is much less preferable to well-reasoned planning of urban growth.

Officials of the Presidential Council on Environmental Quality believe that there are many ways in which federal, state, and local governments could legislate absolute statutory protection of large land areas from encroachment by developers and speculators. Representatives of the council have been meeting with state and local officials to draw up and lobby for model laws. Legislators, however, demur; they fear, in addition to pressure from local landowners, past court decisions that appear to make such legislation an unconstitutional limitation of private property rights under the Fifth Amendment: "nor shall private property be taken for public use, without just compensation."

The federal Task Force on Land Use and Urban Growth has answered that more recent court rulings in scattered environmental cases show that judges are likely to take a different view of the Fifth Amendment these days if test cases are undertaken. The task force also pointed out that "just compensation" could be made to property owners—whether they owned agricultural land ruled off limits to future development, or low-destiny, inner-city buildings to be saved by legal prohibitions against redevelopment—in some form, such as lower property taxes. The task force has gone on to recommend that Congress offer the states legal and financial aid for land-use control and that the federal government withhold highway and other federal funds from those that do not make some start toward land conservation.

What effect would all this have? Exploitive speculation probably would disappear from areas absolutely protected from further large-scale development. But what would happen inside the newly protected California coastline regions or inside the urban and regional reserve zones designated by the California Tomorrow proposals? Would controlled development without exploitive speculation be possible? What is to stop real estate speculators and their powerful financiers from manipulating the proposed regional authorities just as they have subverted most other local governments and zoning and planning agencies? And what if state legislatures and the Congress fail to enact legislation protecting from further development even those natural areas that nearly everyone agrees should be preserved?

The newest studies, including the California Tomorrow plan, suggest an old answer to these questions: public land reform. Wherever the public can in no other way stop or control harmful speculation or repair the damage already done—from the burnt-out, central-city areas where the speculators already have come and gone, to the countryside where the developers of suburban sprawl are about to strike, to the forested mountainsides and the wetlands and beaches where the recreation land hucksters have arrived—government and public corporations could simply buy the land themselves to keep it in its natural state or, where development is deemed necessary, develop it more responsibly.

The federal government could buy threatened natural areas of great importance, such as coastal beaches and wetlands, and add them to a strengthened system of national parks and public lands. Few people realize the government already owns one-third of the nation's land. But even that land has been too open to exploitation by lumbermen, miners, the military, and unlimited tourists. And too little of those holdings include the country's most valuable and critically threatened land resources; the government owns more desolate deserts than beaches or wetlands, more mountaintops than precious green areas around cities. The Task Force on Land Use and Urban Growth has proposed creation of a National Lands Trust "within the Interior Department or by national charter with federal funding of $200 million annually to be made available on a matching basis with a 75 per cent federal share to assist public bodies, particularly state land-use agencies, in the conservation of extensive greenspaces in and around major urbanizing areas."

Municipal, state, or regional governments—or public corporations set up by those governments, perhaps with financial aid from the federal treasury or some new kind of public development bank —could buy up inner-city land for redevelopment and suburban land for more carefully staged future development free from the pressures and compromises of private speculation. These public landowners, or "land banks" as city planners call them, could themselves build on the land or lease it to private developers, who would have to work within plans and restrictions laid down by the public corporation or government landowning body. As the new development increased the value of this land, the "profits" gained from proportionately higher lease rates charged the private developers could help finance continued land-buying, among other things.

Private land speculation would be impossible, and those entrepreneurs investing in the development of buildings on government land would, for the first time, have to look to the buildings themselves as their real investment. The salability of those buildings, based in large part on their competitive quality, would then be the primary determinant of their profitability. To increase the profitability of building, owning, and maintaining housing under this system, the property tax on buildings could be abolished entirely in land-bank areas, with the local government making up the lost tax revenues with its land-lease income in those areas.

Another new report, "A Strategy for Building a Better America," issued in 1972 by a national policy task force of the American Institute of Architects (AIA), urges that government or public corporations "as a matter of highest national priority" immediately spend $5 billion to buy up 1 million acres inside fifty-eight of the nation's largest cities and begin massive public redevelopment of central-city areas. The AIA strategy also calls for the development by the government, or public-private land corporations, of entirely new communities on suburban land bought and then leased out by government. In theory, if this strategy were followed, the money made from the increase in land values and the leasing of high-priced shopping center and office space—money that now constitutes the profits of successful private new community developers—could pay for experimental solutions to technological problems like transportation, housing construction costs, and waste disposal, and social problems like the workable integration of housing for lower-income families into new communities. It is this kind of experimentation that has been missing from private American new town projects.

Several Western European nations have had long and varied experiences with government land ownership and development within basically capitalist economic systems. They have operated public land banks, undertaken massive renewal projects that dwarf any in this country, and built scores of government-developed new towns. Out of these programs have come lessons, both good and bad, from which the United States could benefit.

In Sweden, for example, more land is owned by government, and urban development of all kinds is more tightly controlled, than in any other Western nation. To begin with, all of Sweden, including rural areas, has been placed for planning purposes into one local municipality or another. Each of these has much broader legal and fiscal powers than the typical U.S. city and can almost completely control development within its boundaries. Since 1947 private landowners and developers have been absolutely forbidden to make their own subdivisions or build anything larger than a single family's home until the municipality has decided that a specific area can be developed and has drawn up its own detailed plan for that development.

Moreover, the city of Stockholm usually buys the land itself before allowing development. Stockholm began to acquire farms on its fringes in 1904 and now owns 80 per cent of the land within its sprawling municipal limits, plus other land beyond its borders. When Stockholm city officials decide to redevelop a central-city area (its entire downtown is undergoing renewal now) or build a new suburb, they buy the land if it is not already city-owned, then plan the project meticulously, down to the use of each square foot of land and floor space. Population densities; the basic location of different kinds of buildings and all roads, footpaths, and open spaces; and the provision of recreation facilities, schools, day-care centers, and social services are all decided in advance. Developers then rent the land from the city and design and build each individual building and facility within the over-all specifications. The city government can easily enforce its standards because it owns the land and can revoke the lease if its contracts with developers are breached.

This strong municipal control of growth gives Stockholm and its suburbs, which are functionally and politically integral parts of the city, an unusually orderly appearance and strong working relationships with each other. Although the density of each developed area is purposely high, with no real suburban sprawl, more of Stockholm than any other major European city has been set aside as public parks. These reach out from downtown in all directions, like giant fingers, separating the developed areas from each other. At the same time, the built-up areas, including the newest large suburban communities, are all connected to each other and to downtown Stockholm by a modern subway that speeds the residents boarding at the most distant stops to the downtown central station in thirty minutes.

Each new suburban area around Stockholm is built around a string of stops along the far end of each subway line emanating from downtown in a giant web. One of the four or five subway-stop neighborhoods that make up each new suburban community serves as the local downtown for that community, with a center of high-density and often high-rise office and apartment buildings, a large shopping mall, and an industrial center all built closely around this key subway stop. Mixed in are the police, fire, and social service centers for the community, as well as recreation facilities, libraries, theaters, meeting halls, and the like. The focal point of this intensive development is usually a large pedestrian plaza, from which pedestrian and bicycle paths take one in any direction through the compact developed area to the park land surrounding it.

Each of the other subway stops along each new suburban community spine is encircled by a smaller commercial and civic center, a ring of low-rise apartment developments, a second ring of single-family homes, and, finally, park land. Thus, each of the neighborhoods making up an entire new suburban community is separated from the others by park, and yet is also closely connected to them by the subway. Each has a complete network of footpaths putting nearly all residents within walking distance of the subway stops and commercial and social centers. And yet these same residents also have easy access to modern highways connecting them with distant country cottages now owned by half of Sweden's city dwellers.

These suburban communities, Sweden's new towns, are usually known in the United States by the name given to the downtown center of each community: Vällingby west of downtown Stockholm, Farsta to the southeast, Skärholmen to the southwest, and so on. They resemble bustling miniature cities in the country, with tall pines, huge gray boulders, and green grass always only a short walk away from the center of each community, rather than the jumble of separate, spread-out shopping centers, government complexes, industrial parks, and residential subdivisions that make up American suburbs.

The traditional willingness of Swedes to limit individual rights of private property and enterprise for the protection of land and the environment is, of course, an important ingredient in their strict city planning and government ownership and development of land. For many years there also was little public participation in the planning by experts of new communities in Sweden, one condition that has recently caused controversy.

There was no problem during the early 1950s. Then the money lavished on a community like Vällingby, the first postwar Stockholm new town, allowed the planners plenty of leeway to soften their creations with lush landscaping and to fill the community with the helpful social services for which the Swedes pay such high taxes. But as the Swedish economy weakened in recent years and the cost of construction materials and labor soared, planners were pressed to provide more housing for low-income families with less government funds. In the process, the various and expensive amenities of

Vällingby were replaced by stark government-housing high-rises and by cost-cutting in landscaping and social services.

In Skärholmen, one of the newest Stockholm satellites, the biggest investment was made in the huge commercial center, which was intended to produce much of the revenue to help finance the rest of the project. The result has been widespread disappointment with the way Skärholmen looks, unhappiness among its residents with the quality of its buildings and services, a disturbingly high vacancy rate in the housing for the poorest families, and shocking juvenile vandalism throughout the project. The problems of Skärholmen have caused the Stockholm city government to open up the planning and development of the next new suburban community to public competition; entries have been put on display for general comment and submitted to panels of experts in various social, technical, medical, and other disciplines for their detailed advice.

The question of planning for people rather than for artificial order or government budget-balancing has also arisen in Great Britain, which has undertaken more new town projects—twenty-eight throughout England, Scotland, and Wales since the end of World War II—than any other Western European country. Most of these new towns are satellite communities located twenty to forty miles from the nearest big city, although each has its own commerce, industry, schools, recreation facilities, and social and local government services. London is encircled by nine of these new towns.

Each project is developed by a separate public corporation created and financed by the British Government under postwar new town legislation. The corporation has the full authority and sufficient capital—lent by the government—to buy the needed land and develop all public and private facilities for a complete town of 50,000 to 250,000 people. Local government funds and other national grants help pay for roads and public utilities, while private developers, directly supervised by and under contract to the public corporation, build much of the housing, stores, and factories. The public corporation, which retains ownership of some land and buildings, uses the income from home sales, rentals, and commercial leases to pay back the government loans, so that national funds can be channeled to other projects. No new town corporation has yet failed to fulfill its obligations, and several, after having paid for themselves and realized a surplus, have been dissolved. These projects are then taken over by the British Government New Towns Commission, which manages them and uses continuing rental income to maintain and improve public facilities. The British new town program has been a surprisingly dependable financial success for the government, unlike American programs in which the federal treasury never recoups subsidies for urban renewal and private new town financing.

Moreover, British new towns have succeeded in providing inexpensive new homes for working-class families, many of which moved to them directly from industrial slums in London, Glasgow, Manchester, Newcastle, and other cities. The right kinds of jobs also were made available for wage earners in these families, so that those who chose to work where they lived were spared the long, expensive daily commutes so familiar to American suburbanites and new town residents alike.

British new town planners arranged for the combined transfer of willing businesses and their employees from inner-city slums like London's East End to new towns like Harlow and Stevenage, north of London, and from central Liverpool across the Mersey River to Runcorn. In some places the move was so well coordinated that as many as 85 per cent of a new town's working residents (as is the case with Harlow) have jobs inside their own community and continue to enjoy many of the interests and friendships of the old big-city neighborhoods from which they came. Workers out of a job in economically depressed Glasgow and Newcastle have been matched with, and trained for, jobs in new plants, including those of IBM, Timex, RCA, and Proctor & Gamble, attracted to the new towns being developed outside those two cities. And, just as important, those workers have found homes they can afford in the new towns.

More homes for working-class families are available in British new towns because the price or rental of each home does not include excessive inflation of the land value to help return a sufficient profit to a private developer. In addition, instead of detached homes on wastefully large suburban lots, a majority of the homes in each new town are attached—both in familiar British brick rows and in experimental clusters around walled-in patios—with small yards, but located near large public commons, gardens, and recreation areas. Only in recent years have these concepts begun to be copied in so-called planned suburban subdivisions and new towns in the United States.

The British new towns have been carefully located where they would relieve badly overcrowded cities but would do the least violence to the British countryside. Rather than deprive the Newcastle area of the few open spaces left unspoiled by mining, for example, its two new town satellites have been located on played-out coal fields. Northwest of Birmingham, in the heavily industrial Midlands of England, a new town is to replace rusting ghost towns near abandoned ironworks.

Despite all these obvious advances, however, the new towns of Great Britain can be something of a disappointment to an American visitor. Despite their generous, green open spaces and gardens, which give them a natural vitality, they appear somewhat dull and uninteresting. Dynamically, they have improved little on their own immediately postwar prototypes, because of their essentially conservative bureaucratic operation. The retired military officers and civil servants who run the new town corporations have seen themselves as responsible primarily for providing decent, reasonably priced homes in an era of housing shortage, and for making certain the projects break even financially and repay their government loans. They have not been much interested in really radical, expensive experimentation in transportation or development technology. Consequently, the widespread postwar use of the automobile found them totally unprepared. The narrow lanes of the earliest garden cities have been overrun by cars, a problem that made such an impression on British planners that recently they overcompensated by designing their "third generation" new towns around American-style internal freeway networks, huge parking lots, and drive-in shopping centers.

When the French began building new towns, they tried to learn from the shortcomings of the British program by marrying government goal-oriented planning with the practical experience of private developers. The nine projects—five of them around Paris—recently begun by the French Government are not really free-standing new towns. They are, instead, huge composites of existing suburbs and open land on which the French new town corporations plan to put the new housing for all income groups, integrated shopping and industry, and public recreational, cultural, and other facilities lacking in French suburban subdivisions and old outlying towns. In essence, the French are trying to reorganize their suburbs into more nearly complete, working, urban communities.

A strong French national new town law authorizes the creation of a new local entity for each new town site—an organization that swallows up existing suburban political bodies and territories whether they like it or not. Land prices are immediately frozen within the project area until the public new town corporation buys what it wants. The corporation, which is similar in many ways to its British counterpart, buys only the land it needs for new building and leaves acceptable existing development alone. It builds public facilities itself and sells land to private developers for everything else, at a sizable mark-up. Each project is supported by this land-sale revenue and by taxes levied on the existing development.

The strength of this approach is its potential flexibility. Government and private developers are theoretically free to do what each can do best, and, as a result, experimentation has been encouraged. A new, high-speed, experimental rail transit system is to connect two new developments west of Paris, for instance, and all five Parisian new towns are also to be served by extensions of the Paris subway system. One new town, Evry, held an international competition to choose the design and developer of a town quarter for 7,000 people. In that quadrant new ways of dealing with pedestrian-vehicular separation, local public transportation, and the integration of housing with commerce and social services will be tested. Another competition is being held to design an entire new town, Le Vaudreuil, as an experiment in environmental protection. The community is somehow to be built in a beautiful, unspoiled part of the Seine River Valley outside Rouen in northern France without polluting the water or air or destroying the landscape.

Some prototypes for this kind of experimentation already exist in a new quarter for 250,000 people now under construction on vast former estate grounds inside the city of Toulouse, in southern France. This project, Le Mirail, is being developed by a regional public corporation funded both by the area's local governments and by private investors. Much of the housing in Le Mirail consists of interconnected apartment buildings arranged in novel patterns around interspersed parks, recreation facilities, social service agencies, community buildings, shops, schools, and a college, plus a château and other artifacts preserved from the original estate. The emerging new community is pedestrian-oriented, with a continuous system of walks and plazas extending throughout. In addition, a separate auto-roadway system feeds into freeways that will cross the Garonne River to downtown Toulouse and other parts of France. Le Mirail's technological innovations should attract world-wide interest. A trash-incineration system uses combustion energy to generate heat and electric power, and a system of large, lighted underground galleries houses all of the project's pipes and utility lines, so that workmen can walk or ride to where repairs or improvements must be made without ever digging up a foot of Le Mirail's ground.

The weakness of the French Government's new town building partnership with private enterprise is that developers and speculators still have too much leeway to pursue maximum profit at the expense of the public goals. In some projects the government has cut back on promised educational, recreational, transportation, social, and cultural improvement grants, forcing the new town corporations to finance these out of land sales and tax revenues. To keep the projects solvent, the corporations have become more dependent on—and compromised by—private developers and businesses willing to move to the area. And the developers have too frequently responded by simply producing traditional suburban subdivisions without social or technological advances.

Some of the French projects, however, notably Cergy-Pontoise, just northwest of Paris, and Evry, to the south, near Orly airport, are doing much better financially, because of their locations in the paths of strong natural suburban expansion. Thus far, their public corporations have been able to stick to their guns; the planning and early stages of development promise important innovations in income integration, community variety, transportation, and environmental preservation that may well make them significant models for other nations, including the United States.

All in all, Americans can learn much from both the encouraging successes and the conspicuous failures of European land control and new community experiments. To do so, they must ignore the carping of real estate industry spokesmen who use the shortcomings of foreign experimentation to justify inaction here. And to give real innovation an honest chance to succeed, Americans must break away from the business-as-usual real estate industry economics that has shackled meager experiments to date. The HUD new town program, for example, can only be considered an acute embarrassment for a nation with the wealth, daring, technological ability, and political determination to put men on the moon.

Without settling on the final details that would require closer study and enlightened public discussion, one can say that an American strategy to experiment imaginatively in new development and reduce destructive real estate speculation should include:

• Outright purchase by the federal and state governments of much more of the nation's most important and direly threatened natural areas—including ocean beaches and wetlands, inland lakes and mountainsides, and remaining significant wild areas—to be held for reasonably controlled public use by strengthened national and state park and public land authorities

• State and local legal prohibitions (conservation zoning) against further development of areas to be kept in agricultural or open-space use, but under private ownership, with necessary compensation paid to the landowners

• Similar prohibitions against the razing and redevelopment of healthy, old city neighborhoods and historic buildings, again linked to a program of compensation for financially injured property owners

• Tax reforms to take the windfall profit out of real estate speculation in areas left open to private development, coupled with new incentives to make responsible development and rental profitable

• Public land-banking and development of new neighborhoods, new towns, and new cities by local, state, and regional public corporations with some financial aid from the federal government—and in competition with continued private development to increase innovation and prevent the sterility and unresponsiveness to public needs noticeable in some public new town projects in Great Britain and Sweden

• Creative zoning or other government planning of both private and public urban development to ensure more imaginative construction; greater integration of housing, commerce, and community activities; increased environmental protection; and better planning for the social as well as the physical community

Public land control and increased public participation in community building do not have to mean the end of private real estate enterprise. Executed properly, they could improve and strengthen private *development,* as opposed to speculation. What must end, however, is exploitative real estate speculation that chews up the land, fouls the atmosphere, and destroys community life.

Defenders of unfettered real estate operations point to an American tradition of dependence on the land for national wealth and family security. They talk about a constitutional right to unrestricted private ownership and development of land. But at the rate we are going what land will be left in the future? What wealth will be derived from the ruins of America's cities?

In fighting real estate speculation we are doing more than trying to save trees from bulldozers, we also are trying to save people and restore what once were their communities. We are trying to save the equality of opportunity, pride of community, and enjoyment of the land that have been part of the true American way of life. Unless we take steps to do this now, the speculators who hold the mortgage on America will foreclose—Americans will lose that way of life —and the next America will not be a fit place for anyone to live.

Suggested Reading

The following quite selective, annotated bibliography contains no examination of the evils of real estate speculation. This is not a purposeful omission; rather, none could be found, which is one of the reasons why *Mortgage on America* was written. Here, however, are assorted books, reports, and pamphlets on the real estate industry, city planning, and urban sociology that might interest readers of this book, if only, in some cases, as interesting presentations of the other side of the question:

Books

ABRAMS, CHARLES. *The City Is the Frontier.* New York: Harper & Row, 1965.
A classic essay on the decay of American cities and an eloquent plea for strong federal intervention that, unfortunately, does not examine the role of real estate speculators in the cities.

BELLUSH, JEWEL, and MURRAY HAUSKNECHT, eds. *Urban Renewal: People, Politics, and Planning.* Garden City, N.Y.: Anchor Books, 1967.
An exhaustive collection of more than fifty essays by planners and officials on federal urban renewal programs, highlighted by Herbert Gans's insightful first-hand description of the destruction of Boston's vibrant lower-class West End neighborhood by upper-middle-class urban renewal bureaucrats.

BROADY, MAURICE. *Planning for People: Essays on the Social Context of Planning.* London: Bedford Square Press, 1968.
An uncritical survey of social planning for Britain's new towns.

CANTY, DONALD, ed. *The New City*. New York: Praeger, 1969.
The report of the National Committee on Urban Growth Policy, which advocates building 110 new towns in the United States, plus essays by several real estate industry spokesmen that give an overly rosy outlook for privately developed new towns here.

DOBRINER, WILLIAM M. *Class in Suburbia*. Englewood Cliffs, N.J.: Prentice-Hall, 1963.
A sober, detailed study of the social promise and problems of suburbia that avoids stereotypes.

FRIED, JOSEPH P. *Housing Crisis U.S.A.* New York: Praeger, 1971.
A properly outraged account of the governmental inaction and bungling that allows shocking slums to grow in our central cities. The author, the housing reporter for the *New York Times,* never really penetrates real estate speculation in the slums, however.

FRIEDEN, BERNARD J., and WILLIAM W. NASH, JR., eds. *Shaping an Urban Future*. Cambridge, Mass.: MIT Press, 1969.
A collection of city planning essays, highlighted by Edward P. Eichler's sharp critique of private new town development in the United States.

GANS, HERBERT J. *The Levittowners: Ways of Life and Politics in a New Suburban Community*. New York: Random House, 1967.
The sociologist–city planner's classic account of what he observed while living in a new Levitt community in New Jersey. To some extent, unfortunately, he substitutes for the stereotyped middle-class suburbia an equally misleading working-class utopia.

————. *Peoples and Plans: Essays on Urban Problems and Solutions*. New York: Basic Books, 1968.
The best of Gans. The essays clearly delineate the limits of the effectiveness and legitimacy of city planning.

GORDON, MITCHELL. *Sick Cities: Psychology and Pathology of American Urban Life*. New York: Macmillan, 1963.
A news magazine journalist's strong description of what is wrong with our cities and his weak explanation of why.

GREBLER, LEO. *Urban Renewal in European Countries: Its Emergence and Potentials*. Philadelphia: University of Pennsylvania Press, 1964.
In an account that glosses over shortcomings, the author describes bold, European, central-city renovation of the kind that has never worked here.

HALL, PETER. *London 2000*. New York: Praeger, 1969.
The Ralph Nader of Britain's city planners describes and critiques, in richly illustrated detail, the efforts to keep London livable as it grows.

HERTZEN, HEIKKI VON, and PAUL D. SPREIREGEN. *Building a New Town: Finland's New Garden City, Tapiola*. Cambridge, Mass.: MIT Press, 1971.
An admittedly biased but fascinatingly detailed description of the development of Tapiola by its chief developer, von Hertzen, with a wealth of photographs, maps, and planners' diagrams.

HOLLAND, LAURENCE B., ed. *Who Designs America? The American Civilization Conference at Princeton.* Garden City, N.Y.: Anchor Books, 1966.
A symposium of essays exploding many American city planning myths and documenting the lack of public control over development here.

HOSKEN, FRAN P. *The Function of Cities.* Cambridge, Mass.: Schenkman, 1973.
An architectural expert and free-lance critic's interviews with generally optimistic city planners and officials. The interviewer inadvertently shows how little in touch with reality so many of the latter are.

HOWARD, EBENEZER. *Garden Cities of To-morrow.* Cambridge, Mass.: MIT Press, 1965.
Reprint of the turn-of-the-century historic essay proposing new towns for England.

JACOBS, JANE. *The Death and Life of Great American Cities.* New York: Random House, 1961.
The architectural critic's love poem to traditional American cities and her plea for their salvation from ruin and urban renewal.
———. *The Economy of Cities.* New York: Random House, 1969.
A brilliant discussion of most economic factors affecting the health of cities except, unfortunately, real estate speculation.

LOWE, JEANNE R. *Cities in a Race with Time: Progress and Poverty in America's Renewing Cities.* New York: Random House, 1967.
Urban renewal case histories in extensively documented detail but seen through badly distorting rose-colored glasses.

MUMFORD, LEWIS. *The Culture of Cities.* New York: Harcourt Brace Jovanovich, 1966.
The revised edition of the best collection of Mumford's thoughts on cities.

OSBORN, FREDERIC J., and ARNOLD WHITTICK. *The New Towns: The Answer to Megalopolis.* Cambridge, Mass.: MIT Press, 1969.
Despite its title, a hard-headed and very meticulously researched and documented study of Great Britain's extensive new town program.

REILLY, WILLIAM K., ed. *The Use of Land: A Citizen's Policy Guide to Urban Growth.* New York: T. Y. Crowell, 1973.
The report to the Presidential Council on Environmental Quality by the Rockefeller Brothers Fund–supported Task Force on Urban Growth. An unusually readable and hard-hitting government report that accurately describes the land-use crisis in this country and, buttressed by some understanding of the role of real estate speculation, makes some good suggestions for change.

RODWIN, LLOYD. *Nations and Cities: A Comparison of Strategies for Urban Growth.* Boston: Houghton Mifflin, 1970.
A good comparative study that might be a bit too esoteric for laymen.

STEIN, C. S. *Toward New Towns for America.* Cambridge, Mass.: MIT Press, 1966.
A reprint of another early new towns advocacy tract by a follower of Ebenezer Howard, with a supportive introduction by Lewis Mumford.

STERNLIEB, GEORGE. *The Tenement Landlord.* New Brunswick: Rutgers University Press, 1969.
Sternlieb's defense of private real estate enterprise and a well-documented study of slum housing ownership that clearly suggests harsher interpretations of the problem than he gives.

WILSON, JAMES O. *Urban Renewal: The Record and the Controversy.* Cambridge, Mass.: MIT Press, 1966.
More well-detailed case histories, again lacking an explanation of how real estate speculation has undermined renewal efforts.

Reports and Pamphlets

ALONSO, WILLIAM. *What Are New Towns For?* Berkeley: Institute of Urban and Regional Development, University of California, 1970.
America's most advanced thinking on new town development, with strong warnings about expecting too much of the present privately developed projects or the HUD new communities program.

American City Corporation. *City Building: Experience, Trends & New Directions.* Columbia: The Rouse Co., 1971.
A lot of revealing false promises from private new town developers at a seminar sponsored and published by the propaganda arm of the developer of Columbia, Maryland.

———. *The Greater Hartford Process.* Hartford and Columbia: The Rouse Co., 1972.
A more realistic and solid proposal for coordinated development and social planning for the Hartford metropolitan region that, however, still does not come to grips with the real estate exploitation that could easily undermine it all.

British Information Services Central Office of Information. *The New Towns of Britain.* London: Her Majesty's Stationery Office, 1972.
A flat, uncritical, but well-detailed survey of Britain's new towns.

Commerce Clearing House. *How To Save Taxes on Real Estate Transactions.* New York: Commerce Clearing House, 1968.
A law report publisher's revealing primer on the tax loopholes available to real estate speculators.

KAMM, SYLVAN. *Land Banking: Public Policy Alternatives and Dilemmas.* Washington, D.C.: The Urban Institute, 1970.
A complete, scholarly survey of public land-banking in Europe that timidly concludes that Americans probably would never stand for such a break from their tradition of private land ownership and development. The author takes no pains, however, to suggest ways to tailor the European experiments to make them more palatable here.

McCLEAN, R. A. *California Property Pyramid*. Torrance, Cal.: Universal Heritage Research Corporation, 1967.
A real estate speculator's unwittingly shocking and sometimes outrageously funny tract on how to pyramid real estate investments into a financial empire in booming California.

MIELDS, HUGH, JR. *Federally Assisted New Communities: New Dimensions in Urban Development*. Washington, D.C.: The Urban Land Institute, 1973.
Although published by a private, nonprofit group, this flat and uncritical description of the HUD new communities program reads like a badly done government handout. It nevertheless contains a wealth of statistics and objectives that reveal, on close reading, how meager this new town innovation effort really is.

National Commission on Urban Problems. *Building the American City*. Washington: U.S. Government Printing Office, 1968.
The report of the Douglas Commission, chaired by former Senator Paul Douglas of Illinois. Despite its consensus conclusions and watered-down recommendations, the report is still the best encyclopedic look at the housing mess in the United States.

Ralph Nader Task Force. *Power and Land in California*. Washington, D.C.: Center for the Study of Responsive Law, 1971.
The Nader report on land use and real estate speculation in California — uneven, overly long, but valuable as a research tool.

SLITOR, RICHARD E. *The Federal Income Tax in Relation to Housing*. Washington, D.C.: U.S. Government Printing Office, 1968.
In a report to the Douglas Commission, a tax expert shows clearly how tax loopholes discourage responsible housing development and ownership but offers no bold reforms.

Stanford Environmental Law Society. *San Jose: Sprawling City; A Report on Land Use Policies and Practices in San Jose, California*. Palo Alto: Stanford University, 1971.
A surprisingly thorough and mature examination by Stanford law students of the rape of the Santa Clara Valley.

STANSBURY, JEFFREY. *Suburban Growth: A Case Study*. Washington, D.C.: Population Reference Bureau, 1972.
The February 1972 issue of the Population Research Bulletin examining in revealing detail the relationship between decisions on sewer development and suburban growth in Fairfax County, Virginia.

WEBBER, MELVIN M. *The Post-City Age*. Berkeley: Institute of Urban and Regional Development, University of California, 1968.
Reprint of a fall 1968 *Daedalus* article arguing that urban growth needs to be viewed from new perspectives.

WERTHAM, CARL, et al. *Planning and the Purchase Decision: Why People Buy in Planned Communities*. Berkeley: Institute of Urban and Regional Development, University of California, 1965.
Voluminous survey, conducted under Edward P. Eichler, of homebuyers in California documenting their primary role as individual real estate speculators.

Index

Abrams, Charles, 52
American-Hawaiian Steamship Co., 158, 166
American Institute of Architects, 222
American Land Development Association, 137
AMREP, Inc., 138, 151
Antonelli, Dominic, 78–80
Architectural Forum, 57
Ashley, Thomas L., 173
Atlanta, Ga., 54–55
Avco Corp., 184

Baggett, Jesse S., 119–20, 123–24, 128–32
Baker, Charles, 27–28
Baltimore, Md.: Activists, Inc., 19–26; Bel Air Road area, 19–20; Bolton Hill, 8; contract buying in, 20–22; Edmondson Village, 19–22, 40; Real Estate Board, 21
Banks, 5, 16–18, 22, 76, 93, 216; Bronx Savings (New York City), 93; Chase Manhattan, 46, 70, 198; District of Columbia National, 34; Equitable Trust (Baltimore, Md.), 23; Maryland National Bank (Baltimore), 23; Southern Maryland Bank and Trust, 131
Banks, Henrietta, 27–28
Banks, Saul, 27–28
Bartell, H. Robert, Jr., 29–30
Basiliko, George, 34

Bazelon, David L., 78–79
Beecher, Henry Ward, 4
Belser, Karl, 106–7, 111–12
Bennett, John Gordon, 126, 129–30
Berliner, Harold, 146, 152
Bernstein, Leo, 34–35
Bernstein, Stuart, 34
Boise-Cascade, 83, 146–49, 151–52, 157, 165
Bosselman, Fred, 89–90
Boston, Mass.: Beacon Hill, 40; urban renewal agency, 61; West End urban renewal, 63–64, 80
Boston, Richard, 29–31
Branden, A. L., 116
Breckenfeld, Gurney, 102–3, 154–55
Bresler, Charles S., 49
Brown, Sidney J., 35–37

California, 88, 95–96, 139, 147–52, 217–18, 220
California City, Calif., 148–49, 157
California Tomorrow plan, 217–18, 220
Callies, David, 89–90
Cape Coral, Fla., 143–44
Carnegie, Andrew, 4
Cedar-Riverside, Minn., 157, 173
Centex Corp., 165
Chicago, Ill.: contract buying in, 27–31; John Hancock Center, 72–73; Lawndale, 27–31, 40; zoning in

75
76
77
79
81
83
85
88